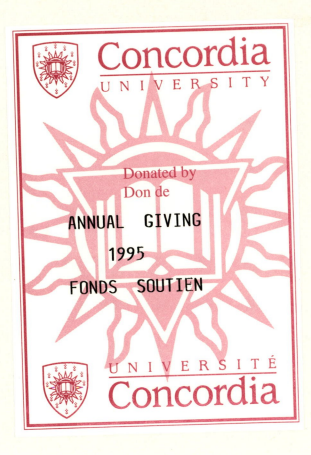

Pluralism, Politics and the Marketplace

Communication and Society
General Editor: James Curran

Pluralism, Politics and the Marketplace

The Regulation of German Broadcasting

Vincent Porter and
Suzanne Hasselbach

London and New York

First published 1991
by Routledge
11 New Fetter Lane, London EC4P 4EE

Simultaneously published in the USA and Canada
by Routledge
a division of Routledge, Chapman and Hall Inc.
29 West 35th Street, New York, NY 10001

Typeset in 10/12pt Times by
Selectmove Ltd, London
Printed in Great Britain by
TJ Press (Padstow) Ltd, Padstow, Cornwall

British Library Cataloguing in Publication Data
Porter, Vincent
  Pluralism, politics and the marketplace: the regulation of German
  broadcasting.
  1. Germany (Federal Republic). Broadcasting
  I. Title II. Hasselbach, Suzanne
  791.450943

Library of Congress Cataloging in Publication Data
Porter, Vincent
    Pluralism, politics, and the marketplace : the regulation of
  German broadcasting / Vincent Porter and Suzanne Hasselbach.
       p.   cm. – (Communication and society)
    Includes bibliographical references and index.
    1. Broadcasting–Government policy–Germany (West)
  I. Hasselbach, Suzanne, 1957–   . II. Title. III. Series:
  Communication and society (Routledge (Firm))
  HE8689.9.G4P67   1991
384.54'3–dc20   91–14012

    ISBN 0–415–05394–3

Contents

Preface

The regulation of broadcasting in the Federal Republic of Germany has been undergoing profound change. New technological developments, such as cable and satellite broadcasting, have opened up new opportunities which have called into question the post-war regulatory arrangements that were settled by the early 1960s.

This study examines the changes which took place from the late 1970s up to December 1990 – a decade during which the new German broadcasting system emerged and in which the fundamental philosophy of pluralism, which underpins broadcasting regulation in the Federal Republic, experienced a number of widely varying interpretations.

The new broadcasting order has evolved from the interplay of a number of regulatory actors in the FRG. The Federal Constitutional Court, the federal government and the policies of the Deutsche Bundespost, the media policies of the major political parties, the CDU and the SPD, and their influence on the politics of the eleven West German *Länder*, and, last but not least, the expansionist policies of the private media groups, such as the German publishing and film industries and foreign private broadcasters. This has led to the establishment in each of the *Länder* of a new regulatory authority for private broadcasting, with its own rules and regulations and political accountability.

The emergence of a private broadcasting sector has led in turn to changes in public broadcasting, notably in the field of competition, which has allowed a further regulatory actor, the Federal Cartel Office, to enter the fray.

Increasingly, however, broadcasting is also an international business, and the Competition Directorate of the Commission of the European Communities, and the directive on transfrontier television of the European Council of Ministers have also influenced broadcasting regulation in the FRG.

Finally, in recent months, the unification of East and West Germany has meant a further upheaval for broadcasting regulation as efforts are made to convert the centralised broadcasting system of the GDR to the *Länder*-regulated dual broadcasting order established in the West.

Vincent Porter
Suzanne Hasselbach

Acknowledgements

We should like to thank the many individual politicians and officials who so generously gave their time to talk to us about many diverse aspects of broadcasting regulation in the FRG. In particular, we should like to thank Dr Sabine Astheimer, Landesanstalt für Rundfunk, Düsseldorf; Professor Dr Klaus Berg, legal adviser, NDR; Dr Reinhard Bestgen, Hessen state chancellery, Wiesbaden; Dr Wolf Bierbach, WDR Radio, Cologne; Dieter Bopp, Northrhine-Westfalia state chancellery, Düsseldorf; Clara Burckner, Basis Filmverleih, West Berlin; Jürgen C. Busch, cultural department, senate of West Berlin; Dr Michael Busse, media research department, Südwestfunk, Stuttgart; Peter Dehn, SPD member, Lower Saxony *Land* parliament, Hanover; Dr Helmut Drück, Director of Television, WDR, Cologne; Dr Rolf Dünnwald, Gesellschaft zur Verwertung von Leistungsrechten, Hamburg; Helmut Elfring, CDU, member of the Northrhine-Westfalia *Land* parliament, Düsseldorf; Dr Hans-Geert Falkenberg, CIRCOM/ INPUT, Cologne; Wolfgang Fischer, Managing Director, Tele 5, Munich; Paul Leo Giani, SPD, Hessen; Gerhard Gizler, FDP, member of the supervisory board, Lower Saxony Landesrundfunkausschuss, Hanover; Professor Dr Wolfgang Hoffmann-Riem, Director, Hans-Bredow-Institut, University of Hamburg; Professor Dieter Huhn, Rundfunkrat, SFB, West Berlin; Hans Janke, member supervisory board, Landesanstalt für Rundfunk, Düsseldorf; Ilse Klingner, member supervisory board, Lower Saxony Landesrundfunkausschuss, Hanover; Dr Gerhard Mahler, Landesanstalt für Kommunikation, Stuttgart; Rudolf Mühlfenzl, President, Bayerische Landeszentrale für Neue Medien, Munich; Dr Burkhard Nowotny, director Bundesverband Kabel und Satellit, Bonn; Dr Jürgen Oehlerking, Lower

Saxony state chancellery, Hanover; Jürgen Plagemann, Wissenschaftliches Institut für Kommunikationsdienste der Deutschen Bundespost, Bad Honnef; Manfred Purzer, Director, Anstalt für Kabelkommunikation, Munich; Professor Dr Christian Starck, Professor of Public Law, University of Göttingen; Wolfgang Thaenert, director, Lower Saxony Landesrundfunkausschuss, Hanover; Dr Peter v. Tiling, member supervisory board, Lower Saxony Landesrundfunkausschuss, Hanover; Jürgen Trittin, the Greens, member of the Lower Saxony *Land* parliament, Hanover; and the many other individuals in the following institutions who supplied us with information: Antenne Bayern, Munich; Anstalt für Kabelkommunikation, West Berlin; Bundesministerium für Post und Telekommunikation, Bonn; CDU, CSU, FDP, Greens and SPD party organisations; CEC, Audiovisual Directorate, Brussels; Degeto-Film GmbH, Frankfurt; Hamburgische Anstalt für Neue Medien, Hamburg; Landesanstalt für privaten Rundfunk, Kassel; Landesanstalt für das Rundfunkwesen, Saarland; Landeszentrale für private Rundfunkveranstalter, Ludwigshafen; Presse-und Informationsamt der Bundesregierung, Bonn; Radio 100, West Berlin; Radio Freies Dreyeckland, Freiburg; Radio Z, Nuremberg; Unabhängige Landesanstalt für das Rundfunkwesen, Kiel; and many others.

We should also like to thank the Economic and Social Research Council for supporting this research as part of its Programme on Information and Communication Technology.

The conclusions are our own.

Glossary of terms and abbreviations

App.:   Appendix

ARD: Arbeitsgemeinschaft der Rundfunkanstalten Deutschlands – association of the *Länder* public broadcasting corporations founded in 1950

Astra: Medium-power satellite operated by Société Européenne de Satellites in Luxembourg, carrying European TV programmes

BBC: British Broadcasting Corporation

BDZV: Bundesverband Deutscher Zeitungsverleger – federal association of newspaper publishers

BR: Bayerischer Rundfunk – public broadcasting station

CDU: Christlich Demokratische Union – German conservative party; leader of the federal government coalition

CEC: Commission of the European Communities

CLT: Compagnie Luxembourgeoise de Télédiffusion – Luxembourg's broadcast holding

CSU: Christlich Soziale Union – Bavarian conservative party; federal government coalition partner

D2-MAC: Digital television satellite transmission standard

DBP: Deutsche Bundespost – West German state posts and telecommunications authority; DBP Telekom – public telecommunications operator

DBS: Direct Broadcast Satellite – a high-power satellite for direct-to-home broadcasting as opposed to low- or medium-power telecommunications satellites which are primarily intended for satellite-to-cable distribution

DCTP:	Entwicklungsgesellschaft für TV-Programm mbH: Alexander Kluge/DENTSU advertising agency – Northrhine-Westfalian private TV broadcasting station
DFF:	Deutscher Fernsehfunk – public TV station in East Germany
DLF:	Deutschlandfunk – radio station broadcasting under *Bund* jurisdiction for Germany (East and West) and Europe, affiliated to ARD
DLM:	Direktorenkonferenz der Landesmedienanstalten – standing conference of the directors of the private broadcasting regulatory authorities
DT 64:	East German youth radio station
DW:	Deutsche Welle – West German external service under *Bund* jurisdiction, affiliated to ARD
EBU:	European Broadcasting Union – association of European public broadcasting stations
EC:	European Communities
EEC Treaty:	Treaty establishing the European Economic Community
Eins plus:	ARD's satellite TV channel
Eutelsat:	European Telecommunications Satellite Organisation – operates fixed and mobile communication satellites for its members, i.e. public and private telecommunications organisations in twenty-eight European countries
FDP:	Freie Demokratische Partei – West German liberal party; federal government coalition partner
FRG:	Federal Republic of Germany, West Germany
GDR:	German Democratic Republic, East Germany
HR:	Hessischer Rundfunk – public broadcasting station
Intelsat:	International satellite organisation with headquarters in Washington, DC
ITU:	International Telecommunications Union – association of the world's telecommunications operators; determines the allocation of the frequency spectrum and orbit
ITV:	Independent Television – commercial television system in the UK
KEF:	Kommission der Ministerpräsidenten zur Ermittlung des Finanzbedarfs der Rundfunkanstalten –

	commission set up by the Minister-Presidents of the *Länder* to assess the level of the licence fee of the public broadcasting stations
KtK:	Kommission für den Ausbau des technischen Kommunikationssystems – a federal government commission
La Sept:	Société d'édition de programmes de télévision – French state-owned cultural television channel
MATV:	Master Antenna Television – an aerial for community reception, serving a block of flats, or a housing estate
MGM/UA:	Metro-Goldwyn-Mayer/United Artists Entertainment Co.
MHz:	Mega Hertz – unit of measurement for frequencies in the electromagnetic spectrum
NDR:	Norddeutscher Rundfunk – public broadcasting station
NWDR:	Nordwestdeutscher Rundfunk – public broadcasting station in the British occupation zone in northern Germany; later separated into NDR and WDR
PAL:	Conventional analogue television transmission standard, used in most Western European countries
Pro 7:	Pro 7 Television GmbH – private television station
R&D:	Research and development
Radio NRW:	Joint venture of WDR, Bertelsmann and newspaper publishers in Northrhine-Westfalia
RB:	Radio Bremen – public broadcasting station
RIAS:	Radio in the American Sector – US Information Service station broadcasting in German, affiliated to ARD
RTL:	Radio Télé Luxembourg – name for CLT's broadcasting activities; RTL plus Deutschland Fernsehen GmbH & Co. KG – German private television station
SAT 1:	SatellitenFernsehen GmbH – private television station
SDR:	Süddeutscher Rundfunk – public broadcasting station

SECAM:	Analogue television transmission standard used in France, Eastern Europe, and in the former GDR
SFB:	Sender Freies Berlin – public broadcasting station
SMATV:	Satellite Master Antenna Television – a satellite reception dish serving a block of flats or a housing estate
SPD:	Sozialdemokratische Partei Deutschlands – German social democratic party
SR:	Saarländischer Rundfunk – public broadcasting station
SWF:	Südwestfunk – public broadcasting station
3Sat:	ZDF's satellite TV channel produced together with Austrian and Swiss public broadcasting stations
TEC:	Subsidiary of Turner-Broadcasting Co.
Tele 5:	Kabel Media Programmgesellschaft mbH – private television station
TV:	Television
TV-Sat:	Name of the German direct broadcast satellite
UHF:	Ultra high frequency part of the electromagnetic spectrum – the UHF spectrum from 470 to 790 MHz is used for TV broadcasts in the FRG
UK:	United Kingdom
VHF:	Very high frequency part of the electromagnetic spectrum – the VHF spectrum from 87.5 to 108 MHz is used for sound broadcasts in the FRG
WDR:	Westdeutscher Rundfunk – public broadcasting station
ZDF:	Zweites Deutsches Fernsehen – public TV broadcasting corporation, founded in 1961

Chapter 1

The philosophies of broadcasting pluralism

From Kiel opposite the Danish coast, to Munich in the foothills of the Alps; and from Aachen on the Belgian border to, since German unification in 1990, Frankfurt-on-the-Oder on the Polish frontier, the broadcasting system of the Federal Republic is one of the largest and most powerful in Western Europe. In 1989, the broadcasting system in West Germany alone had an annual income of £2.9 billion a year.[1] Some fifty-six per cent came from the £76 (DM 228) paid annually by each set-owning household in the FRG, while a further thirty-seven per cent, came from the sale of airtime. The remainder came mainly from overseas sales and dividends of the two major public broadcasting networks, ARD and ZDF (see App. X).

FROM ALLIED CONTROL TO PUBLIC BROADCASTING DUOPOLY

Despite its size, the FRG's broadcasting system is not a huge monolith. At the end of the Second World War, the Western Allies deliberately broke the centralised broadcasting system of the Third Reich into smaller units. In the American zone the broadcasting organisations were regional, based in Bremen, Munich and Stuttgart. In the British zone, the authorities set up a zone-wide broadcasting corporation, NWDR, based on the model of the BBC; while in Rhineland–Palatinate and Baden–Württemberg in the South-West, a smaller version, Südwestfunk, was set up by the French authorities. The stations which served only one *Land* were set up by *Land* law, while those which served more than one *Land* were constituted by inter-*Land* treaties. A relic of Allied control has survived in Berlin in the shape of RIAS. This German-language radio and television station was under the authority of the US

Information Service but received ninety per cent of its income from the federal government which thereby acknowledged the importance of the station's presence for the city of Berlin which was divided during the cold war.

By 1949, when the Basic Law for the Federal Republic was drafted and agreed, broadcasting had become the responsibility of the West German Länder (see App. I). By the early 1950s, the *Land*-based stations joined together to form an association, which attempted to combine the organisation of a nation-wide broadcasting service with *Land*-based editorial freedom. The *Arbeitsgemeinschaft der öffentlich-rechtlichen Rundfunkanstalten der Bundesrepublik Deutschland*, or ARD as it is now universally known, formed the first network of public broadcasting corporations in the FRG. By 1955, it had nine members. The largest, which provides over a quarter of the network programming, is WDR in Cologne which seceded from NWDR. The next largest are NDR, based in Hamburg, and BR based in Munich, which provide roughly a sixth each. SDR in Stuttgart, HR in Frankfurt, SWF in Baden-Baden and SFB in West Berlin each provide between eight and nine per cent, while RB in Bremen and SR in Saarbrücken contribute a mere three per cent each. In addition, there is a complex system of financial equalisation which guarantees the smallest stations enough money to finance their programme quotas (see App. II).

For each broadcasting organisation, a *Rundfunkrat*, or broadcasting council, is appointed and/or elected according to provisions laid down in the relevant *Land* law. Although the details vary from *Land* to *Land*, the normal procedure is to establish a three-fold tier of control. The broadcasting council, which is responsible for the general policy of the organisation, has some twenty or so members, usually a mixture of politicians and representatives of employers' organisations, trade unions, youth groups, sports associations and the churches. It appoints an *Intendant*, or director-general, and a smaller *Verwaltungsrat*, or administrative council, to supervise financial matters.

By the late 1950s, new broadcasting frequencies were becoming available in the UHF band. But the *Land*-based nature of broadcasting meant that the ARD system suffered from two disadvantages. First, it was an institutionally fragmented organisation, ill-designed to act as a national champion. Second, although several of the ARD broadcasters augmented their revenue by selling airtime, advertisers had no way, either through the broadcast media or through the press, of advertising to the whole of the Federal Republic. In addition, the federal government wanted to get its hands on broadcasting. In 1959, therefore, Chancellor Adenauer attempted to set up a private company, financed by state loans, to use the new frequencies. But the *Länder*, which argued that the proposal was unconstitutional, referred the whole question to the Federal Constitutional Court.

In an epoch-making decision, the Court agreed. Adenauer's proposal was rejected, but from the ruins of the Constitutional Court's rejection a new phoenix emerged, *Zweites Deutsches Fernsehen*, the second German television channel, ZDF. The new organisation was authorised by another inter-*Land* treaty, signed this time by all the *Länder*. Like the ARD stations, ZDF is also a public broadcaster, supervised by a three-tier control system. It is financed by thirty per cent of the licence fee, augmented by the sale of airtime on a nation-wide basis.

At the same time, the Court accepted federal jurisdiction for the external services DW and DLF, which the *Bund* had set up already in 1960. While both are financed from the federal budget, DLF receives an additional allocation, in recognition of its status as a truly national broadcaster to both halves of Germany. Both stations have a public service control structure, and along with RIAS they are associate members of ARD.

For the next twenty years ARD and ZDF happily co-existed side by side. In 1964, the two television networks were augmented by a series of *Land*-based third channels, run by the ARD stations. Radio too continued to be run by the ARD stations organised on a *Land*-wide basis. In the mid-1970s, however, cable and satellite technologies provided new distribution opportunities. The traditional duopoly could no longer be justified by the shortage of terrestrial frequencies. Instead the new electronic media gave privately organised groups a way into broadcasting. Conservative politicians seized the opportunity and passed new laws legitimating private, wholly commercially funded broadcasting; and by 1984 a dual system of public and private broadcasters was beginning to emerge.

But the decision of the Federal Constitutional Court in 1961 had done more than reject Adenauer's proposal for a private television company. It had placed broadcasting firmly on the federal constitutional agenda. Broadcasting and its regulation were too serious to be left in the hands of the politicians. The guiding concern of the Court was the role played by broadcasting in the formation of public opinion, the constitutional platform of ideas which the politicians sought to represent and to interpret into legislative and administrative action.

THE CONCEPT OF PLURALISM IN THE FEDERAL REPUBLIC

The key concept which has underpinned the thinking of the Federal Constitutional Court has been that of pluralism. In the FRG, pluralism has a political and a socio-cultural dimension. It arises from liberal theory, which sees society as a series of conflicting interests which compete in the policy-making process.

> Political pluralism is a doctrine of *functional federalism* (as against monistic absolutism) on the basis of a variety of independent associations, at least an expectation that such groups existing in reality could help to ensure civil liberties and make the state serve human needs.[2]

This competition of interests is intended to bring about a balance of power. Federalism is to protect different interests, views and ideas from being suppressed by a dominant regime. This concept of pluralism permeated the West German constitution, the Basic Law, which was created in 1949 under Allied supervision.[3]

Article 9 of the Basic Law guarantees as civil rights the free formation of associations and public assembly. Power is divided vertically, through the principle of federalism, between the *Länder* and the *Bund*.[4] Article 20 of the Basic Law separates horizontally the legislature, the executive and the judiciary; and Article 21 safeguards the free formation of political parties. The role of the eleven self-governing entities of the *Länder* is to maintain cultural, economic and historical diversity and to provide a check to the central legislature and government of the *Bund* in Bonn.

Central to broadcasting regulation is Article 5 of the Basic Law, which expressly guarantees the free formation, expression and dissemination of public and individual opinion, and the institutional freedoms of broadcasting and the press. The same article also secures the freedom of art, science, research and teaching. In order to prevent state centralism and the homogenisation of mass communications and education, the areas outlined in Article 5, including broadcasting, are part of *Länder* jurisdiction.

The German Federal Constitutional Court, which interprets the civil rights and other legal norms laid down in the Basic Law, described the West German ideal of pluralism, which informed its broadcasting decisions, in the following terms.

> The permanent process of the formation of public opinion and will flows into the act of parliamentary election which is decisive for the building of state competence . . . [but] the right of the citizen to participate in the political decision-making process is not expressed merely through the act of voting, but also by influencing the permanent process of the formation of political opinion, the formation of 'public opinion' . . . Public opinion influences the decisions of the state agencies. Furthermore, groups, associations and various societal formations try to influence government action and legislative decision-making in the interests of their members. But above all, between elections, the political parties influence the constitutional bodies in their decisions, particularly parliamentary resolutions.[5]

The free formation of individual and public opinion, for which broadcasting and the press are instrumental, is 'a fundamental building block of the free democratic order since it guarantees intellectual conflict, the free discussion of ideas and interests, which is vital for the functioning of the state'.[6]

This interpretation of pluralism modifies the liberal model, widely accepted in Anglo-Saxon thinking, in several respects. In the Federal Republic, the political parties are permanent institutions of public life and are constitutionally assigned the strongest pluralist role. Over and above interest groups, the contemporary political parties are seen as the political voice of a majority of citizens cutting across particular interests. The classic idea of liberalism, that of social groups defending civil liberties against an absolute ruler, has thus been replaced by the concept of the all-embracing democratic state, the social and legal state (*sozialer Rechtsstaat*), which gains its legitimacy through political representation of its citizens in parliament. This strong reliance upon political parties naturally means that factional politics permeate every aspect of West German life, including its broadcasting system.

The Constitutional Court regarded not only political parties, but also other associations of interests, as 'intermediary forces' which precede parliamentary decision-making and are necessary for the democratic formation of the public will.[7] Therefore, non-partisan interests have also been institutionalised and hierarchised in order to carry out a number of state regulatory duties, such as the allocation of public funds to charities, collective bargaining, and public insurance. Last but not least, they have a mandate to participate in the regulation of broadcasting.

In practice, these developments tend to lead away from the liberal model of group pluralism towards a brand of neo-corporatism. A harmonious view of interest group pluralism does not do justice to the political realities in the FRG. The West German system is characterised by 'sectoral pluralism', where participation in the policy process is largely confined to those sectors with the greatest economic and political clout.[8] The scope for the democratic formation of the will in the public sphere has also narrowed with the growing complexity of modern public policy. The public will is increasingly decided by the executive and the administration.[9] Indeed, the state bureaucracy and whole batteries of well-informed, legally trained civil servants, the so-called *Referenten*, steer and transform interest group demands, and become the main information sources of the politicians themselves. This also affects broadcasting regulation. In the process, the scope for parliamentary decision-making has been reduced.

The system of group political bargaining tends to marginalise weak and unstructured interests. Citizen initiatives have sprung up as a reaction to the rigidities of the system, but they too tend to achieve their aims through established institutions, such as the political parties. For example, there is a strong connection between the free radio associations and the Greens.

The declared purpose of the Basic Law is to maintain political, social and economic stability. Political culture is therefore 'basically consensual and suspicious of any form of direct democracy and plebeian participation.'[10] The free expression of opinion, enshrined in Article 5 of the Basic Law, is therefore constrained by Article 18, which tolerates dissent only as long as it is not abused to fight against the free democratic order. Thus radical onslaughts on the dominant ideology of the Federal Republic can be construed as illegal. As a result, change has tended to remain within, and mediated through, the institutional system. Last but not least, redress for the citizen against unjustified state action is provided by the elaborate system of administrative courts.

PARTY POLICIES AND THE NEW BROADCASTING TECHNOLOGIES

In 1984, the established duopoly of ARD and ZDF was ruptured by the introduction of private broadcasting. Behind this push was an alliance of conservative and liberal political interests, which, by the end of 1982, governed most of the eleven *Länder* and the *Bund*.

Once in government, the CDU adopted the mantle of pluralism as the justification for its broadcasting policy. This would cater for the needs of the democratically responsible and active citizen (*mündiger Bürger*) who would no longer be exposed to the public service 'monoculture'.[11] The declared aims of CDU media policy were to develop cable and satellite technology in order to stimulate national economic growth, by providing export opportunities and employment potential; to strengthen the domestic market to compete with future transfrontier satellite signals which could not legally be prevented from being received in the FRG; and finally, to ensure more positive reporting for the party's political philosophy and its policies than it was getting from the public broadcasters, which it called 'red broadcasting'.

For the FDP, the new technology would steer broadcasting towards the free market. The citizen would be the consumer of a variety of, possibly local, programmes upon demand. At the same time, the party intended to monitor and balance the social effects of media use and to strengthen the cultural output of the public broadcasters. The influence of both the political parties and the state in the control organs of the public broadcast corporations was to be reduced.[12]

The SPD had long opposed the introduction of private commercial broadcasting. This was both for ethical reasons and to prevent public opinion from being shaped by a few media moguls. But it too had to recognise that the new technologies offered new opportunities for economic growth. At its 1984 party congress, therefore, it adopted, against strong rank-and-file opposition, a new pragmatic approach. It would accept a controlled private broadcasting sector whilst giving priority to the development of the public system. The new approach essentially responded to the interests of SPD-controlled Hamburg, with its heavy concentration of media industries and its intense competition with Munich and West Berlin for investment in media production.

The city feared that the conservative *Länder*, through their moves towards deregulation, would monopolise the investment and employment opportunities arising from private broadcasting. In the face of political realities, its 'refusenik' attitude had shut the SPD out of any positive contribution to shaping the emerging new broadcasting order. After 1984, the SPD therefore concentrated on implementing alternative regulatory models to those developed in CDU- or CSU-dominated *Länder*.[13]

The Greens, who became a coalition partner in the West Berlin *Land* government, strongly emphasised local communications with active citizen participation. New radio projects should be non-commercial trusts or charitable associations. The public service system should be strengthened and made more accountable. In common with the FDP, they wanted it to be less dependent upon the influence of the political parties and the state – a demand in reaction to the strong dominance of the parliamentary factions of the CDU, the CSU and the SPD in the broadcasting control bodies.[14]

Whatever the policies of the individual political parties, it was unlikely that they could be implemented without the involvement of the Federal Constitutional Court. Since its first landmark decision handed down in 1961, the Court has handed down no less than four further rulings on broadcasting regulation. On every occasion, it has sought to preserve, if not to broaden, the political ideal of pluralism enshrined in the Basic Law. This legal structure has also given rise to a particularly German mode of broadcasting regulation. 'In no other Western country but the Federal Republic would the law be employed so massively as a battleground and weapon for changing the order of broadcasting.'[15]

RULINGS ON BROADCASTING BY THE FEDERAL CONSTITUTIONAL COURT

In the FRG, broadcasting regulation, like all areas of German life, is regulated by a highly formalised legal structure, reaching down from the Basic Law and its interpretation by the Federal Constitutional Court to specific broadcasting legislation in the individual *Länder*.

The Federal Constitutional Court, *Bundesverfassungsgericht*, at the top of the legal hierarchy, interprets the Basic Law in legally binding terms. It provides general guidelines that the *Länder* and federal legislatures have to meet, but only rules on matters of public interest. Important for media policy is its authority to adjudicate on conflicts of legal authority between the *Bund* and *Länder*, and on the consistency of parliamentary law with the Basic Law, or with international law.

The Basic Law and the Federal Constitutional Court decisions override any other jurisdiction. Thus, when the Court rules on the constitutionality of individual *Land* or federal state (*Bund*) acts, its decisions assume general legal validity. *In extenso*, it protects and redefines the political ethos underlying the constitution.

The Court cannot rule on the broadcasting order on its own initiative. The question has to be appealed by an interested party. Any private legal or natural person, including in some cases the public broadcasting corporations, has the right to appeal to the Court to protect a constitutionally guaranteed basic right; but complaints against *Land* or *Bund* laws can only be lodged by at least a third of the members of the *Bundestag*, or the federal or *Land* governments. Relevant cases can also be referred by a lower court.

No court operates in a legal vacuum when interpreting ideals expressed in legal terms. In order to be effective, the judges have to take actual developments, political practice and legal theory as well as public debate into account. Thus, the decisions of the Constitutional Court necessarily reflect the economic, social and political relations of the 'real world'. But in recent years the Court has increasingly been criticised for laying down specific rules itself and thereby transgressing into the area of legislation which is a parliamentary prerogative in the FRG.[16] Yet, it has also been accused of keeping its decisions too general and vague to be effective.[17]

Recourse to the judiciary, in particular the Constitutional Court, by parties with conflicting interests in broadcasting has been especially rampant when there has been a lack of consensus among politicians as to media policy. Once the constitutional and practical foundations of the broadcasting order had been established in the 1960s, there was broad consensus in media politics as to the legal framework within which the cultural sphere was to develop. This collapsed in the late 1970s when the development of cable and satellite technologies, and the associated introduction of private commercial broadcasting media, challenged the traditional legislative framework. As a result, the

Constitutional Court has been increasingly called upon as an 'ersatz legislator';[18] and its decisions have assumed quasi-statutory quality. Over the years, it has handed down six fundamental decisions on broadcasting, in 1961, 1971, 1981, 1986, 1987 and 1991.[19]

The Basic Law and the free formation of opinion

Article 5 paragraph 1 of the Basic Law lays out the basic guarantee of freedom of opinion in the Federal Republic.

(1) Everyone shall have the right freely to express and disseminate his opinion by speech, writing and pictures and freely to inform himself from generally accessible sources.
(2) Freedom of the press and freedom of reporting by means of broadcasts and films are guaranteed.
(3) There shall be no censorship.[20]

Paragraph 2, however, limits these rights 'by the provision of the general laws, the provisions of law for the protection of youth, and by the right to inviolability of personal honour.'[21] If the restrictions contained in paragraph 2 conflict with the basic right contained in paragraph 1, in each ruling the objective benefits for the democratic order as a whole have to be balanced against the disadvantages limiting the freedoms contained in paragraph 1.

The inherent function of Article 5 is to safeguard the formation of both individual and public opinion. It is principally inspired by the liberal tradition of freedom of opinion where individuals are seen as defending their rights against the state. But this is mitigated in West German constitutional theory by an acknowledged element of social responsibility of the state towards the individual. Consequently, the free formation of opinion is to enable the individual not only to participate in the democratic process of the state, but also to find his or her place in civil society and its underlying culture. This assumes that individuals can freely inform themselves on public affairs and voice their opinions through a public medium. The public medium then takes on some control functions for the social order, protecting not only the state but also the individual. The Federal Constitutional Court expressed this philosophy by defining broadcasting as a 'medium and factor' in the process of opinion forming.

The dual concept of public opinion which emerges from the interaction between individual rights, civil society and the democratic state is mirrored in the provisions of Article 5. Generally, the Basic Law, including this article, is based upon the idea of *subjective* rights, i.e. safeguards for the freedom of the individual including legal persons. Article 5 even forms part of the human rights section of the Basic Law. But its drafters also included a notion of *objective* rights, namely safeguards for the democratic state, its institutions and its social order. In Article 5, these find their main expression in the second sentence of the first paragraph, which is important precisely because of its objective character in protecting the freedoms of broadcasting and the press and giving them the status of democratic institutions.

The Constitutional Court interpreted the term 'freedom of reporting by means of broadcasting' extensively as 'freedom of broadcasting' by analogy with 'freedom of the press'.[22] It thereby confirmed all broadcasting as a public institution: the 'provision of broadcasts is a public duty', it has ruled ever since its first broadcasting decision in 1961.

Sentence (1) of Article 5 provides guarantees for the freedom of information, protecting communicators and receivers alike. It covers the subjective right of the individual to freedom of expression. Advertisements are also protected, but only in their content, not their profitability. Restrictions on advertising time are therefore considered constitutional. Freedom of information in both its communicating and receiving forms only extends to all *generally accessible sources* of information. The scope of access is limited by both public and civil law, such as laws for the protection of the state, or the penal code. Thus broadcasts, including advertisements, may be forbidden if they are seen to harm moral, social or individual rights. Laws against tobacco or alcohol commercials, or against broadcast advertisements on Sundays are thus legitimate.

For broadcasting, the 'crucial test of the system's efficiency and acceptability' comes when sentences (1) and (2) are interpreted as functionally different ways of achieving the constitutional aim of the free formation of opinion.[23] Two opposing interpretations have been used in the legal debate either to justify or to restrict access to the broadcast media by private broadcasters.

If sentence (2) is subservient to sentence (1), i.e. the rights of the individual take precedence over institutional safeguards, this interpretation would imply a free market of broadcasting by inferring an absolute right of access. It would permit regulation for the individual exercise of broadcasting activity, including economic structural regulation to prevent market failure. It would exclude, however, any formal rules to secure specific forms of control, organisation or programming.

However, sentence (1) is widely interpreted as not granting a right to obtain access to a source which is not yet generally accessible.[24] It is merely a protection from state interference. For example, it does not mean that the state has to provide the citizen with cable so that he or she can receive all available satellite broadcasts. Cable operators or programme providers have not been able to invoke the principle of freedom of reception against *Land* regulations limiting access, since cable has to be made specifically accessible before it can become a means of general reception. On the other hand, cable distribution must not limit the choice of terrestrial and direct broadcast signals normally received by the citizen.[25]

Traditionally, there has been a division of media powers. A privately owned press and the public broadcasting sector complemented each other. Although it has been questioned whether the press can fulfil its democratic function under only lightly regulated free market conditions, for historic reasons it has never been given a comprehensive legal framework.[26] In contrast, because of the belief in the persuasive power of radio over the masses, which seemed to have been demonstrated during the Third Reich, the normative framework for broadcasting has always been deemed to extend beyond the creation of merely structural conditions. Thus, as the Court stated in 1961 for the first time, the provision of broadcasts was a 'public duty' for which institutional safeguards were required.

So far, it has been held that without institutional guarantees the state could not prevent the formation of a dominant opinion, whether political, social, economic or cultural. This in turn would constitute an infringement of the rights of the individual to participate in the free flow of public information.[27] The underlying assumption is that in order to participate in the social life of the Federal Republic the individual must have access to the whole spectrum of opinions and ideas and that these can only be secured under an institutionalised framework of regulations. Despite the other individual rights protected by the Basic Law, such as the free exercise of a profession or trade, the Constitutional Court has not yet explicitly declared an individual right to broadcast.

Broadcasting between *Länder* and *Bund* regulation

As a result of the separation of legislative powers between the *Bund* and the *Länder* it is the latter who are individually and severally in charge of all cultural matters including broadcasting. All *Länder* have a clause similar to Article 5 in their individual constitutions. They have inferred their broadcasting authority from Articles 30 and 70 of the Basic Law which stipulate that the *Länder* have to assume responsibility for all those areas that the Basic Law does not assign to the *Bund*. Each *Land*'s jurisdiction ends at its boundaries, however.

The 1961 judgement of the Constitutional Court confirmed *Land* responsibility for broadcasting in absolute terms. 'The content of Article 5 and its guarantee of the freedom of broadcasting are of such fundamental importance for the entire public, political and constitutional life of the *Länder* that they may demand of the *Bund* not to interfere.'[28]

Article 73(7) of the Basic Law, however, gives the *Bund* control over telecommunications, and Article 87(1) delegates this right to the Deutsche Bundespost (DBP). In its 1961 judgement, the Court ruled that the DBP was responsible for frequency allocation and management, for all aspects of transmission technology including cable and satellites, and for the operation of broadcast equipment but not studio operations. It also had to abstain from infringing the media-political authority of the *Länder*. The assumption was that technology was neutral and was merely a 'service' for the cultural, *Länder*-regulated side of broadcasting. But the development of cable and satellite in Germany has shown that technology can be used by the *Bund* to influence developments in media policy.

Thus there is no integrated communications authority in the FRG, like the Federal Communications Commission in the USA, to regulate content, organisation *and* technology; and such a body would not be possible without changes in the Basic Law. In 1986 the Constitutional Court acknowledged, however, that the possibilities of supraregional and international transmission might simply override *Länder* sovereignty. The *Länder* were therefore called upon to harmonise their regulations for national broadcasting. Although this requirement reduced the autonomy of the individual *Länder*, it was nevertheless meant to maintain the principle of federalism.

By the time of the 1986 judgement, the *Länder* had been unable to co-ordinate their satellite regulation and there were calls for a national satellite authority.[29] The Court clearly tried to prevent the *Bund* from encroaching on the regulatory powers of *Länder* by appealing to them to allocate jointly the channels of the German Direct Broadcast Satellite (DBS), for example by means of an inter-*Land* treaty. Likewise, it bemoaned the variations in the *Länder* rules for relaying national broadcasts in cable networks, which reduced market incentives for private satellite broadcasters. It therefore urged the *Länder* to agree on certain common minimum conditions for cable retransmission of broadcast signals and, above all, to harmonise advertising regulation. As in 1961, the Court invoked the 'federation principle' requiring the *Länder* to co-ordinate their actions in order to prevent harm to the Federal Republic. Common action seemed especially important as most *Länder* intended to establish private commercial broadcasting, and rules had to be made to prevent the private broadcasters making their own.[30]

The Court's dual appeal was accepted by the *Länder* when, in April 1987, they concluded the Inter-*Land* Treaty that created a common basis for all forms of nation-wide broadcasting, both public and private.

But the federal state has further powers, over and above the role played by the DBP, which may impinge on broadcasting. Under Articles 16 and 17(11) of the Basic Law, the Ministry for Economic Affairs controls competition policy and the homogeneity of the licence fee across the FRG. Article 75(2) empowers the Ministry of the Interior to supervise the press and film industries. Under Article 73(1) the Ministry for Foreign Affairs co-ordinates international media relations, while further federal powers include copyright protection (Article 73(9)) and youth protection legislation (Article 74(7)).

Regulation under the aegis of balanced pluralism

The Allies, who controlled broadcasting at the end of the second World War, had insisted that broadcasting should be independent of state influence, and that all socially relevant groups could find their views adequately represented in the programmes. As interpreted by the Court in 1961, this meant 'to represent in due proportion all significant political, ideological and societal groups'.[31] In its first broadcasting decision, the Court thus confirmed and thereby institutionalised the Allies' implementation of democratic pluralism.

> Article 5 of the Basic Law requires the enactment of statutes that organise the providers of broadcasts so as to ensure an effective participation of all relevant forces in their organs, giving them the opportunity to air their views within the overall programme schedule. [These statutes must] contain obligatory content guidelines to guarantee a minimum of balance, objectivity and mutual respect.[32]

Importantly, the Court affirmed that the broadcasting system had to be established, modified and regulated only on the basis of *Länder* legislation. Executive action by one or more *Länder* governments was not constitutional without parliamentary sanction. In its 1991 decision, the Court reaffirmed that decisions vital for the structure of broadcasting, such as the allocation of frequencies to the public or private sector, must not be left to the *Land* government, which is not a pluralist body.[33]

By using the existing public broadcasting system as a paradigm, the Court established in 1961 the three interlinked aspects of pluralism which, it ruled in all later decisions, would also have to be enshrined in private broadcasting. These were pluralism in control, in organisation, and in programme content. Further, the formation of individual and public opinion was not merely activated by 'news broadcasts, political commentaries or series on past, present and future political problems, but also by radio or television plays, musical presentations or entertainment broadcasts'.[34]

In its decision in 1971 the Constitutional Court declared, by a narrow majority, that because of their special public service status, the broadcasting corporations were exempt from paying value-added tax on their licence fee revenues. The judges reiterated that broadcasting was 'a matter that concerns the general public', and programme production and distribution were primarily undertaken for social, not commercial, ends.[35]

In its decision in 1981,[36] the Court accepted the principle of private commercial broadcasting provided the legislators also enforced in the private sector the three interlinked aspects of pluralism which it had identified in 1961. It was on this basis that the conservative *Länder* started to introduce private broadcasting legislation in 1984. But even conservative broadcasting policy was not aiming for pure 'deregulation'; the 1981 decision was thus felt to have opened the barriers without dropping them altogether.[37]

The Court's decision in 1986[38] was fundamental for the restructuring of West German broadcasting into a dual system which combines public service and private commercial structures. The Court had been asked by the SPD members of the *Bundestag*, the lower chamber of the federal parliament, to rule on the constitutionality of the 1984 broadcasting act of Lower Saxony. The Court decided that it was only prepared to accept the Lower Saxony proposal provided that eight provisions were removed, and a further twenty-nine were given the specific interpretation to them laid down by the Court.

The Court emphasised the continued need to regulate for pluralism for three reasons. Firstly, the technologies of cable and satellite, and the newly discovered frequencies for low-power terrestrial broadcasting, each of which provided the channels for private broadcasting, could not yet guarantee universal reception. Universal reception, however, has traditionally been an integral part of the public service concept. Secondly, the economics of the market were only likely to permit the development of a very limited number of new stations, especially in television, where entry costs were still high; and the press sector, which was used as a paradigm, had not proved a sound model for a liberal broadcasting system, as it had serious concentration problems. And thirdly, pending EC legislation made it likely that foreign satellite signals would tend to depress quality. The Court therefore set the following guidelines for the regulators to respect, and it elaborated them in its 1987 decision on constitutionality of the private broadcasting acts of Baden–Württemberg in 1987 and Northrhine-Westfalia in 1991.[39]

* The public broadcasting system, but not individual corporations, was to be the 'cornerstone' of German broadcasting. Because of its specific organisational set-up and programme remit, it represented the pluralist forces of West German society. It was therefore assigned the task of providing 'the functions of broadcasting that are essential for the democratic order and cultural life in the Federal Republic'. Its duty was 'the provision of basic services' (*Grundversorgung*), i.e. to supply comprehensive programme services. These included not just political and informative elements, but also entertainment,

music, sport and education, as well as universal geographical coverage.[40] In its decision a year later, the Court also confirmed the right of the public broadcasters to expand, subject to legislative provisions, into new technological and programming areas. Furthermore, their duties had to be guaranteed by adequate finance.

* The private system, in contrast, had only to ensure a 'minimum' standard of pluralism (*Grundstandard*) in respect of its organisation and programme offerings. This was clearly a concession by the Court to the precarious economic position of the emerging market. The minimum was not defined precisely, although the Court did demand 'the highest possible degree of pluralism' in the private sector as a whole, which meant that all views, including those of minorities, must be given a 'chance' to find an airing. In its 1991 decision it reiterated that the standards for private broadcasting did not necessarily have to be inferior to those of the public sector, as long as they did not significantly hinder or preclude the activities of private broadcasters. Although the court implied in 1986 that it did not anticipate private broadcasters offering a full range of high-quality programmes, if they did offer information programmes, they would be obliged to inform objectively, comprehensively and truthfully. Imbalances in the presentation of information would only be acceptable if they were 'of minor importance', or 'not aggravating'. Furthermore, the minimum standard had to include a right of reply and a respect for human dignity.

* Importantly, the Court specified that the *Land* legislatures had to prevent powerful media players from gaining 'a dominant influence upon the formation of opinion'. This was to take precedence over the rules of the federal anti-cartel law. The rules were not only to restrict multi-channel ownership but also press/broadcast cross-ownership. Moreover, the fewer channels there were, the more pluralistically organised the individual broadcaster had to be. Significantly, the Court ruled that '[o]pportunities in the market place may relate to economic freedom, but they do not relate to freedom of opinion.'[41]

* The statutory control of the private sector pluralism requirements, through licensing and programme monitoring, was ideally to be the duty of a panel of experts, external to the broadcasters. Not only should those experts be recruited from all socially relevant groups, but they should be independent of

the state. The Court thus affirmed a system of controlling West German private broadcasting that was modelled closely upon that of the public sector. It conceded, however, that the external control bodies for private broadcasting would have less power than the internal control bodies of the public sector. The latter were responsible for the development of the overall programme output, while the former were only supervisory and reactive, since once a private broadcaster had been licensed the regulatory body could only intervene if a contravention took place.[42]

Despite the emphasis of the CDU/CSU and FDP on competition in broadcasting, the private broadcasting legislation has been essentially constrained by the Federal Constitutional Court in this respect since it rejected unfettered deregulation for both the public and private broadcasting systems. In all its decisions the Court has seen broadcasting as contributing to active citizenship, rather than transforming the audience into consumers.

Because of a traditionally strong reliance on constitutional norms, and in order to reduce the legal insecurity which characterised the private broadcasting debate in the Federal Republic, the *Land* legislators repeated, almost word by word, the Court's basic formulations on pluralism and tended to take over those rules from the broadcasting acts of Lower Saxony and Baden–Wüttemberg that were specifically sanctioned by the Court. The different geographic, economic and political situations within the various *Länder* have nevertheless produced broadcasting acts which meet the criteria of the Federal Constitutional Court in a number of different ways.

THE ROAD TO THE 1987 INTER-*LAND* TREATY

One of the principal outcomes of the 1986 judgement of the Constitutional Court was the signing in 1987 of a new Inter-*Land* Treaty. It is now a major plank in the regulatory framework for broadcasting in the FRG. Its underlying objective is to create a constitution for the 'co-habitation' of public and commercially funded private broadcasting. Although the Constitutional Court was an instrumental factor in bringing the negotiations over the Treaty to a conclusion, negotiations over the Treaty had started several years earlier in 1984.

The CDU/FDP federal government had been promoting an

extensive nation-wide cabling initiative to distribute both German and foreign satellite channels since 1982; and the FRG's direct broadcasting satellite, TV-Sat, was being built for a start in late 1986. One objective behind these initiatives of the CDU/CSU and FDP coalition partners was to create commercial opportunities for private broadcasters.

For the *Länder*, the technological developments meant that broadcast signals would be able to cross the *Land* boundaries and thus the regulatory competence of each *Land*. A common agreement between the *Länder* was the only way to achieve their various policy objectives for the 'new electronic media', whilst simultaneously preventing the *Bund* from prejudicing their media policies. However, as is often the case in the FRG, agreement on these policy objectives was difficult to achieve. At the heart of the argument between the CDU/CSU and SPD *Länder* was the political desirability of introducing commercially funded private broadcasting and the future role of the public broadcasting corporations.

Between 1984 and 1987, all eleven *Länder* in West Germany had introduced legislation for private commercial broadcasting in the form of cable trial laws, final broadcasting legislation or at least preliminary cable relay acts. These statutes differed widely in their licensing conditions, advertising rules, and their requirements for youth protection and programme diversity. The private broadcasters, both German and foreign, lobbied strongly against having to adhere to all of them as they would have made their commercial activities insecure and unprofitable. Instead, they wanted a common framework of national regulations.[43] Thus the *Länder* had to agree, not only how to allocate the new cable and satellite distribution channels, but also how to harmonise the conditions under which public and private broadcasters could operate.

After sixteen rounds of difficult negotiations stretching over more than three years, an Inter-*Land* Treaty was eventually signed on 1/3 April 1987, and subsequently ratified by the parliaments of the *Länder*.[44] Although it was the latest in a series of treaties, such as those which have established ZDF, or regulate the licence fee system, it was far broader in scope.

Even though the Inter-*Land* Treaty is important as a piece of legislation which reaffirms *Länder* authority for broadcasting, in view of the heated and prolonged arguments which surrounded the negotiations, it is difficult to see it as more than a face-saving compromise. It hardly develops a new philosophy for broadcasting in the FRG that will be able to steer it through the changes brought about by commercialisation and competition at both the national and European levels.

The pressure points

As early as October 1984 the Minister-Presidents of the *Länder*[45] had reached a compromise on a common broadcasting bill, with an emphasis on the regulation of national satellite broadcasters.[46] But despite the agreement to a common text by the SPD executive and the SPD Minister-Presidents in Bremen, Hamburg, Hessen and Northrhine-Westfalia, the SPD rank and file considered it too favourable to the private broadcasters. They rejected it because it did not secure the demands of the 1984 SPD party congress. The four SPD Minister-Presidents thus had to withdraw their assent.[47]

Exactly a year later, another major attempt at compromise foundered on demands by parts of the CDU/CSU to finance the regulatory authorities for private broadcasting from the licence fee; and on the staunch defence by Hessen's SPD government of the right to fund HR's regional third programme from advertising. Eventually, the entrenched ideological positions around these issues led to a political stalemate. The public showed less and less sympathy for the seemingly arcane politicking.

From stalemate to agreement

During 1986 and early 1987, five developments turned the political stalemate into a negotiated Treaty. First, the CDU and CSU-led *Länder* threatened the unity of the public broadcasting system, which depends on the production and transmission of common programmes under the ARD umbrella, supported by a complex system of financial equalisation.[48] A redistribution of licence fee monies from the six largest to the three smallest ARD stations in Berlin, Bremen and Saarland ensures their survival and the scope of programme output. The arrangement is therefore an integral part of the Inter-*Land* Treaty which sets the level of the licence fee (*Rundfunkfinanzierungsstaatsvertrag*).[49]

When the ARD introduced its satellite TV channel, Eins plus, the CDU- or CSU-led governments of Baden–Württemberg,

Bavaria, Lower Saxony and Rhineland–Palatinate promptly announced their withdrawal from the licence fee treaty. Despite court rulings in Baden–Württemberg and Bavaria which affirmed that, contrary to the assertions of their *Länder* governments, Eins plus was a legal venture, most conservative *Länder* continued to withhold permission to relay it by cable within their *Länder*, and accused ARD of wanting to block cable channels to the detriment of potential private broadcasters.[50] However, ZDF, which contains a strong contingent of conservative party politicians on its television board, was allowed to broadcast its TV satellite service, 3Sat.

The second milestone on the road to the 1987 Treaty was the threat of federal government action. The DBP, which had planned a 1986 start for the West German DBS, TV-Sat, saw its investment at risk since the disagreement between the *Länder* prevented the legal rental of the DBS channels.[51] This concern was strengthened by the DBP's need to amortise its cable investment, which also risked being delayed by the different *Länder* rules for relaying satellite programmes. In a step of doubtful legality, the federal government therefore empowered the DBP to allocate the TV-Sat channels itself, according to the interests of the majority of the *Länder*. In this manner, it was able to exert considerable pressure upon the *Länder*.[52] This was all the more intense since the geographically expansionist nature of satellite technology combined with the 'misery of broadcasting regulatory law' had already led to calls for a *Bund* broadcasting authority.[53] But any invasion by the *Bund* into their area of legal competence has traditionally been an anathema to all *Länder*, and tended to trigger a strong reassertion of their authority, if necessary in the courts.

Third, the failure of the treaty negotiations had also dealt a blow to the media-economic policies, or *Standortpolitik*, of some *Länder*, whether CDU, CSU or SPD-led. *Standortpolitik* basically meant that each *Land* tried to attract or protect investment in its domestic media economy. The regulatory authority for private broadcasting would favour licence applicants if they promised to site specific economic activities in the *Land*. The *Länder* tried to outbid each other for the investment favours of private television stations, especially the two largest, SAT 1 and RTL plus.

In 1986, it became clear that a number of regional terrestrial frequencies could be made available to private television stations, which would compensate them for the low cable penetration rates. The *Länder* now saw a new opportunity to develop their individual *Standortpolitik*, since the allocation of terrestrial, *Land*-wide licences did not require the approval of other *Länder*. The new terrestrial frequencies did not substantially cross the boundaries of *Land* jurisdiction, and thus would not require common licensing standards. This meant that the chances of a common treaty, which was originally meant to regulate national satellite-based stations, again decreased. The risk that national private television broadcasters would seek satellite-to-cable licences from those *Länder* with the least stringent requirements had been balanced by the desirability of increased terrestrial reach.

But the federal government still needed to find licensees for TV-Sat with its five direct-to-home satellite channels. TV-Sat was only attracting lukewarm interest from the two main private television stations, RTL plus and SAT 1, which were the only viable candidates. The terrestrial frequencies which were now available would increase the audiences for private television far faster than TV-Sat, since the DBS employed the complex new transmission technology, D2-MAC, for which there was as yet no demand. To solve this conundrum, the CDU and CSU *Länder* now decided to grant the new terrestrial frequencies to TV-Sat licensees.

Two separate provisional inter-*Land* treaties legalised this arrangement. One was signed between the southern *Länder*, Bavaria, Baden–Württemberg and Rhineland–Palatinate; the other by the northern *Länder*, Lower Saxony, Schleswig-Holstein and West Berlin, joined shortly afterwards by Hamburg, the only SPD/FDP-ruled *Land*.[54] Apart from creating the conditions for licensing two of the five DBS channels, these treaties also gave the green light to allocate the terrestrial television frequencies to the holders of the DBS licence. Predictably, the existing major private broadcasters, SAT 1 and RTL plus, obtained the licences. In this sense, the partial treaties had created a regulatory situation which the 1987 Treaty had to recognise.

But the urgency with which the provisional Northern and Southern Treaties had been concluded fell away when space technology failed repeatedly, and TV-Sat was finally lost in space. Its replacement could not be launched until August 1989. By then, the DBP-owned medium-power satellite, Kopernikus, which not only permits direct-to-home reception similar to TV-Sat but which also uses the conventional, cheaper PAL transmission standard, was in orbit, and became the West German 'hot bird', i.e. the satellite which carries the most programme services which can be received on the same antenna dish. Far from achieving the status which the struggle over the drafting of the Treaty originally indicated, the West German DBS has now effectively been written off as a trial project.

Fourth, the negotiation process was considerably helped along by the 1986 decision of the Federal Constitutional Court. From the accepted principle that the *Länder* must act so as to avoid harming each other or the *Bund*, the Constitutional Court inferred an obligation on the *Länder* to co-ordinate their satellite-to-cable relay rules. It also pointed out that it considered the regulation of DBS to be a common task. Importantly, the judgement clarified several contested points in that it confirmed SPD demands for substantial guarantees for the public broadcasting system, for standards setting a minimum degree of organisational and programming diversity and for the prevention of media concentration in the private sector.

The final event to pave the way to compromise was the federal election of 1987. It narrowly confirmed the endorsement by the electorate of CDU/CSU/FDP politics and destroyed SPD hopes for a change in the political climate, which had been fuelled by earlier *Land* elections. Both sides were finally exhausted by their war of attrition and had to acknowledge the existing balance of political power. The final Treaty was agreed within six months.

General provisions of the Treaty

The Treaty entered into force on 1 December 1987 and can only be renounced after 31 December 1998. It is a mixture of policy statement, general rules and respect for the separate *Land* powers. It aims to

> set the norms for a dual system of broadcasting. Its concern is to provide both the public and private broadcasters, under conditions of fair co-existence, with the opportunity to satisfy the task of broadcasting, to enhance the diversity of information and to be equal to the future demands of national and international competition.[55]

On the one hand, this guarantees finance for the public broadcasting system and promises it a share in 'all new media technologies'. On the other, private broadcasters are to be assured both adequate resources, particularly from advertising, sponsorship and pay-TV, and sufficient transmission capacities, including terrestrial television frequencies, for national, *Land*-wide, and local programming.

The Treaty therefore covers a wide range of topics which include

* the use of satellite technology;
* the finances of the public broadcasting sector;
* advertising and youth protection for both sectors;
* programme standards for national private stations;
* concentration by national private broadcasters;
* the finance of the control authorities for private broadcasting; and
* the relay of national and international programme channels.

On the basis of the Inter-*Land* Treaty, the *Länder* have since agreed that a single *Land* may allocate any satellite channel supplied by the DBP, provided the other *Länder* do not object.[56] Thus, informal arrangements have come to replace the complexities of the Inter-*Land* Treaty negotiations.

However, in spite or possibly because of the rulings of the Federal Constitutional Court and the Inter-*Land* Treaty, the broadcasting order in the Federal Republic appears far from settled. The root of the problem is the conceptual incompatibility between the constitutional principle of pluralism which is inspired by socio-political and cultural ideals, and the economics of market-led forces. The Federal Constitutional Court did point to the gap between the two concepts in its judgements, but failed to take account of the fact that they are functionally divergent. In order to preserve constitutional continuity and to ensure the effectiveness of the legal norms in the real world, the Court developed a hybrid concept. Private economic concerns were to be regulated through paradigms derived from a public organisational model inspired by a social purpose. Consequently, it triggered a tension between two regulatory philosophies both of which aim to secure institutions in the Federal Republic: specific broadcasting regulation for cultural, social and political purposes; and economic regulation in the name of the free market. Emblematically, the broadcasting debate mirrors the contradictions inherent in the German concept of the 'social market economy'.

Together with the two earlier inter-*Land* treaties which set up ZDF and which re-balance the broadcast licence fees, the nine acts setting up the ARD stations and the acts regulating private broadcasting in each of the eleven West German *Länder*, the 1987 Inter-*Land* Treaty forms a complex web of twenty-three pieces of legislation which regulate domestic broadcasting in the FRG. To this must be added the legislation currently being promulgated to regularise the broadcasting arrangements in the five new Eastern *Länder*, which we discuss in detail in Chapter 8. This is the price which the FRG has had to pay to achieve a balance between *Land* regulation and federal harmonisation in its re-regulation of broadcasting. But before we can examine more closely the similarities and differences between individual West German *Länder*, we must analyse the role played by the federal government in reshaping the broadcasting infrastructure.

Chapter 2

The regulation of signal distribution

All broadcasting depends on the distribution of broadcast signals from the broadcaster to the receiver. Traditionally signals have been broadcast terrestrially, but increasingly other methods of distribution are being used, such as satellite broadcasting and cable transmission.

There are a number of areas in the FRG where the *Bund* is involved in broadcasting, either alone or jointly with the *Länder* (see App. III). The most pertinent of these is its control of broadcasting distribution which, unlike in the UK, has traditionally been regulated and operated as a state monopoly by the Deutsche Bundespost (DBP). For twenty years the DBP has been the sole provider of transmission and distribution facilities for all private broadcasters. They have not been allowed either to build their own facilities or rent them on their own terms.

The state monopoly has been justified legally by the principle of separating control of the broadcasting infrastructure from the content carried, or from network usage. This principle is designed to ensure universal reception and equal access to the network for all users, be they terrestrial, cable or satellite broadcasters. The policy has its roots in a democratic theory of the separation of powers and a public service which aims to provide a geographically universal, homogeneous and socially desirable service.[1]

Apart from its socio-political role, distribution technology, be it over-the-air, by cable or by satellite, is a necessary resource for any broadcasting activity. Distribution costs influence broadcasting economics at all levels. In short, the means of distribution can precondition political choices about the social and economic organisation of broadcasting.

The DBP's monopoly of the distribution infrastructure goes back to 1923 and the early days of radio. But since the 1970s it has had to face three major challenges caused by the development of broadband cable and satellite technologies. First, the technologies created legal uncertainties since they straddled two separate legal traditions: technology-oriented telecommunications law and socio-cultural broadcasting law. Second, they provided outlets for new broadcast channels and thus created opportunities for the *Länder* to introduce private, commercially funded broadcasting. And third, economic policy during the 1980s focused on information technology, including cable and satellite, as a primary structural resource, but simultaneously tried to reduce government spending, bureaucracy and regulatory intervention. So the DBP had to play a facilitating role, while bracing itself for the liberalisation of the telecommunications sector.

BROADCASTING UNDER ALLIED RULE

At the end of the Second World War, broadcasting was instrumental to the Western Allied occupation forces, not just to disseminate information to the population, but also to spread the Allies' ideological message of democratic 're-education'. Their broadcasting policy was essentially informed by the fear that centralised state control over any sphere of public life would facilitate the resurgence of fascism.

Although it is often thought that after the German defeat the West German state was rebuilt from scratch, the building blocks used came from the ruins of the Weimar Republic. As a result, historical administrative structures and beliefs in the benefit of public regulation were allowed to seep into the new ideological foundations. This was especially true for broadcasting.

Both the *Länder* parliaments, instituted by the Allied military governments, and the telecommunication officials wanted to continue the state monopoly for uniform postal and telecommunications services including broadcasting. The declared rationale was that the state should maintain control over the technical aspects of broadcasting to achieve a unified communications structure and international co-ordination.[2] This rationale was strengthened when the legislators re-introduced a centralised telecommunications authority under *Bund* jurisdiction, headed by the Federal Minister for Posts and Telecommunications.

But by 1949 the Allies had all passed legislation to deprive the telecommunications authority of all its broadcasting assets (i.e. transmission facilities and studios) and to hand them over to the evolving *Land* broadcasting corporations. Accordingly, the DBP was forbidden to participate in broadcasting except to collect the licence fee for the *Länder* governments, to provide the landlines necessary for broadcasting and to run a troubleshooting service to prevent signal interference.[3]

The Allies' motives were more political than technological. The transmission of broadcasts by the DBP itself could have had considerable operational, technical and economic advantages. However, these had to be sacrificed in order to safeguard the political future of the evolving West German democracy.[4] For the US authorities, the broadcasting system should 'neither directly nor indirectly become a pawn of the government' or 'the tool of a specific group or personality', but it should 'serve the people as a whole in a free, equal, open and fearless manner.'[5] Similarly, the British proposed an independent corporate broadcasting system whose importance lay in 'its freedom from control by the state or political parties'.[6] In setting up the broadcasting corporations without the involvement of the DBP, the Allies severed the public organisation of broadcasting and its programmes from a centralised power structure, in an attempt to avoid any future totalitarian control over the media such as had characterised the Nazi regime.

When the German Basic Law was passed in May 1949 it was accompanied by the Occupation Statute which remained in force until 1955. The Statute required that any legislation of the occupation authorities, enacted before the Basic Law, should remain in force until repealed or amended by the occupation authorities. This included control of telecommunications and broadcasting by the Allied High Commission. The Basic Law did not prescribe a specific broadcasting structure therefore, and took as its reference the structures established by the Allies that were already in place.

Although a consensus existed that the regulation of broadcasting content was a cultural matter, which came under *Länder* juris-diction, the abolition of the centralised control over broadcasting, by divesting the telecommunications authority of its technical and licensing powers, met with strong political opposition. Between 1949 and 1953 the Allied High Commission opposed all attempts by the federal government to establish an overall federal jurisdiction for broadcasting.[7]

If the post-war German politicians, all of whom had their roots in the Weimar Republic, had their way, the old system under the Reichspost umbrella would have been rebuilt. But the Americans and British, later joined by the French, forced the German parliaments which they had instituted to create a broadcasting system which was independent of the state.[8]

Predictably, once the federal government had obtained full telecommunications sovereignty in 1955 the quarrel over broadcasting jurisdiction flared up again, and finally led to the first broadcasting judgement by the Federal Constitutional Court in 1961.

THE 1961 JUDGEMENT OF THE FEDERAL CONSTITUTIONAL COURT

Although the 1961 judgement of the Federal Constitutional Court essentially resolved a *Bund/Länder* conflict, it also defined the powers of the Federal Ministry of Posts and the DBP over broadcasting.

In the 1950s new UHF television frequencies became available, creating opportunities for a second and eventually a third chain of television transmitters. The ARD corporations were planning to set up additional programme services and started trial transmissions, but their monopoly was challenged. Advertisers and newspaper publishers lobbied conservative politicians for a private commercial broadcast organisation along the lines of ITV in the UK. The federal cabinet, led by the CDU Chancellor Adenauer, introduced a bill for private television into parliament. But it was rejected in the upper chamber, the *Bundesrat*, where the *Länder* are represented. Although the *Länder* used a rhetoric of cultural autonomy to justify the rejection, they were naturally also interested in maintaining their political influence over all broadcasting.

Even so, the federal government eventually set up a state-owned television company under private law, called Deutschlandfernsehen GmbH. Importantly, the government revived the old argument that the setting of organisational parameters came under Article 73(7) of the Basic Law, which grants the *Bund* exclusive jurisdiction for telecommunications. It argued that broadcasting regulation could not be separated into technical infrastructure and social organisation. Radio waves crossed the territorial boundaries of the *Länder*, and thus gave the *Bund* a natural right to regulate. Telecommunications, to which broadcasting belonged in this view, came entirely under its single regulatory responsibility. In order to maximise the efficient use of the frequencies, it argued that the technical licences had to include obligations affecting the organisational structure. What the government meant was that programmes should be delivered by private providers and broadcast by the DBP on its own transmitter network, which it had already started to establish.[9] The cabinet, supported by the DBP's administrative council, had explicitly authorised additional funds for this purpose. The push for DBP-operated stations did not only reflect the political aspirations of the government. It also reflected the DBP's traditional interest in retaining a larger share of the licence fee and reasserting its sovereignty over the broadcasting infrastructure.

But the Federal Constitutional Court took a different view. It denied that the *Bund* could infer from Article 73 any right to regulate the organisation, programming or cultural content of broadcasting.[10] Organisational and cultural arrangements came under the authority of the *Länder*, in line with Article 30 of the Basic Law. Referring explicitly to the intentions of the Allies, the deliberations of the drafters of the Basic Law and the standing practices of the *Länder*, the Court confirmed most of the extant regulatory framework, which meant that it translated a specific historic development into a constitutional principle. Significantly, it emphasised that while the constitutional freedom of broadcasting demanded its independence from the state, this did not prevent the DBP from managing the broadcasting infrastructure. Indeed, the Court specifically ruled that

> Posts and telecommunications as in Art.73(7) of the Basic Law, notwithstanding the reception of broadcasts, only includes the technical transmissions of broadcasts but excludes what is termed studio technology. . . . The jurisdiction of the *Bund* for telecommunications . . . also permits regulations that give the *Bund* the exclusive right to erect and operate broadcasting installations.[11]

But the ruling did not definitively stipulate a DBP monopoly for the broadcast infrastructure. Since the *Bund* is sovereign in telecommunications matters, the Court indicated that it might establish a public operating entity separate from the DBP which could build and own transmission equipment.[12] But until 1989, the government left the telecommunications act of 1928, which secured the DBP's monopoly, unaltered.

Through the Court's decision, the federal government officially regained control over the regulation and operation of transmission equipment, except for the transmitters already owned by the ARD corporations.

The Court justified its decision by referring to both territorial interests and the public interest. Frequency allocations, decisions on the location and performance of transmitters and the monitoring of interference across the whole of the FRG, all had to be made in accordance with technological requirements: 'The interests of the public require radio traffic to be regulated in a manner which can only be carried out effectively by the *Bund*. This also applies to broadcasting.'[13]

With hindsight the decision was criticised, however, as threatening to impair the independence of broadcasting from the state.[14] Remarkably, the Court itself had seen no conflict with the principle of freedom from state influence. It had argued that, unlike the early days of radio, technology now played only a subordinate or 'service' role as opposed to the primacy of the organisational and cultural concepts of *Land* broadcasting law. Under this solution, the central state, viz. the Ministry of Posts and Telecommunications, was automatically barred from influencing broadcasting policy decisions. Since then, the service role of the DBP has been accepted as a constitutional principle by both the *Länder* and the DBP, but their interpretations as to the scope of their rights differ.[15]

The exact boundaries between *Länder* and *Bund* regulatory competences are not precisely embedded in statutory form, nor are the procedures for negotiation. The Court's decision did not supply formal criteria for the relationship between DBP, the *Länder* and the public broadcasting corporations. Perhaps more significantly, the Court did not anticipate that new technologies of broadband cable and satellite would again bring broadcasting policy questions to the fore.

On the other hand, the ruling did enable the federal government to develop a homogeneous geographical broadcasting service for all systems, while allowing costs to be re-balanced between densely and sparsely populated areas. It has even been suggested that the development of such a publicly accessible, uniform infrastructure may impose legitimate restrictions upon the cultural policy decisions of the *Länder*.[16]

THE IMPACT OF THE DBP'S CABLE AND SATELLITE POLICIES

By January 1990, 24.5 per cent of the 25.7 million West German households were connected to cable, a growth of nearly two per cent in the last quarter of 1989.[17] About 800,000 private satellite dishes were in use in both parts of Germany by the end of 1990, serving individual homes or private cable systems.[18] From 1982 to 1989, the DBP invested a total of £3 billion into coaxial cable systems to distribute broadcast signals, a figure which excludes the costs of cable laying.[19] Now the FRG has the highest number of cable connections in Europe, an achievement which was only possible through massive state investment.

The introduction of cable and satellite was triggered by the economic problems of the 1970s and early 1980s. The attempt by the state to develop new information technologies was a response to the economic crises that had begun in 1967 and which led to inflation and marked unemployment in the early 1970s. Later in the decade, they triggered massive efforts by the SPD/FDP federal coalition government at economic and financial management, but by the end of the decade state intervention seemed to have failed and there was a new recession.

The new CDU/CSU and FDP coalition, which came to power in October 1982, curbed public spending on social services and aimed to create favourable investment conditions for private enterprise. One weapon in its strategy was to use the monopoly position of the DBP to expand the broadcasting infrastructure. It advanced three arguments for developing cable and satellite broadcasting in the FRG. They were a mixture of technological, industrial and socio-political rationales. All three were administratively and legally justified by the DBP's monopoly powers.

The global importance of advanced communications technologies had already been identified by the SPD/FDP coalition. Accordingly, it had set up two federal commissions, the *Kommission für den Ausbau des technischen Kommunikationssystems* (KtK) in 1974, and the *Enquete-Kommission 'Neue Informations- und Kommunikationstechniken'* in 1981. Their aim was to analyse new information and telecommunication developments, and to assess not only the economic potential of the new communication technologies, but also their legal framework and their likely political and social impacts.

In 1976, in its final report, the KtK concluded that cabling should only be used for residual coverage of television signals.[20] It did not recommend a national cable grid because there was no explicit or urgent demand for it. But to explore the innovative potential of cable for broadcasting purposes it did recommend that trial projects be set up, which would not only test the technology but would also try out new interactive and local forms of communication. But in general the KtK still emphasised the economic impact of new communications infrastructures rather than their political and social implications. This was probably due to the industrial interests represented on the KtK; and the technical criteria that the commission had to evaluate, which came from the DBP and the manufacturing firms in the electro-technical industry, who were the parties most interested in cable.[21] Indeed, at that time, the DBP was already experimenting with coaxial cable distribution for television.

Although the KtK recommended cable trials for purely technological reasons, it also recognised the implications for *Länder* broadcasting regulation. Cable created new distribution facilities which had to be licensed. It was important to decide whether and how private commercial broadcasters should be granted access, and whether to use the licence fee to finance the trials. These problems delayed a final decision on the cable trials until November 1980. The *Länder* governments in their turn stressed the need to assess the social and cultural effects of cable broadcasting, and highlighted the need for new forms of communications and media research.[22]

In an appendix to the cable trial decision, however, Ernst Albrecht, the CDU Minister-President of Lower Saxony, refused to wait for the result of the cable trials, which were due to start in 1984, before his *Land* enacted an alternative broadcasting policy by legalising private commercial broadcasting. The DBP thus received a signal which encouraged it to cable areas beyond those needed for the trials.

Because of ideological differences between its members, the majority of whom were members of the federal parliament, the *Enquete-Kommission* did not produce any recommendations and the change of government in 1982 cut short its deliberations. Its central argument was that the West German telecommunications market was economically decisive, since seventy to eighty per cent of telecommunications equipment was sold at home and it was an important testing ground for exports. Moreover, the DBP was its largest purchaser.[23]

Satellites would be most effective in conjunction with the small cable networks or existing MATV systems, but individual reception was not envisaged. Although the commission foresaw a national fibre-optic grid for the future, there was disagreement on the desirability of the short-term development of coaxial cable for television distribution, over and above the few already existing small, separate networks. At that time, cable had only twelve channels compared to the later broadband networks which offered up to thirty. The KtK conservative members were motivated by an industrial-political rationale. German telecommunication cables manufacturers, and the brown goods sector of the electronics industry in particular, were suffering from stagnation and severe export problems which, it was hoped, could be ameliorated by the short-term expansion of copper cable systems for television distribution. They therefore stressed that the *Länder* had to create the regulatory conditions for new programme channels so as to make the desired expansion of cabling cost-effective.[24]

For the SPD/FDP members, economic growth lay in individual switched communications, since they preferred an integrated national fibre-optic grid. A prior investment in coaxial television cable would be a waste of national resources. This stance was also motivated by social and political concerns, since they feared some *Länder* would use coaxial cabling to introduce private commercial broadcasting to the detriment of the public broadcasting system.[25]

By 1983, when the new CDU Minister for Posts and Telecommunications, Christian Schwarz-Schilling, made nation-wide cable distribution his aim, the future for the large companies lay in optical fibre, rather than copper cable. But coaxial cabling was expected to create new market opportunities for small and medium-sized enterprises, especially those involved in connecting the cable and in servicing MATV. Although the commercial benefits of cable television had become merely marginal for the large companies, in its cable decision the DBP took into account that the promotion of small and medium-sized enterprises had traditionally been a declared part of the industrial strategy of the Federal Republic, and that as a state enterprise, the DBP had to boost employment in the telecommunications sector. Finally, cabling was expected to stimulate the German media economy by opening the market to new private sector entrants and boosting the broadcast advertising market.

THE DBP/*LÄNDER* RELATIONSHIP

At the administrative level, any decision by the DBP to develop broadcasting technologies has an impact upon the cultural policies of the *Länder*, since it forces them to respond to changing technical infrastructures. A technical decision on whether to use copper coaxial or optical fibre for cabling, whether a cable system should have a capacity of twelve or thirty channels, or whether it should have a tree-and-branch or switched star structure, was bound to have a vital cultural impact. Not only do such technical decisions condition the form of communications, whether passive distribution or interactive communications, pay-per-view or subscription television, but they must also change the regulatory framework, since they raise new questions about diversity and competition and can therefore change the political and economic landscape of broadcasting.

Ever since Adenauer's private broadcasting plans, the DBP monopoly has offered a way for the federal government to influence, or even infringe on, the *Länder* sovereignty for broadcasting. The grey area, left by the Federal Constitutional Court, in the division of powers between the *Länder* and the DBP, has allowed the DBP to influence their policies through its technological push. Because of their differing broadcasting philosophies, the eleven *Länder* have been vulnerable to this 'push' unless they can present the unified front necessary to enforce a proactive, comprehensive broadcasting policy required at the national level.

Cable and satellite

Although, as a public enterprise, the DBP was interested in exploiting the potential of cable technology, between 1970 and 1982 it had to adopt a very cautious political attitude as to how this was to be deployed. Unlike the CDU, which governed in the majority of *Länder*, the SPD-led federal government was opposed to private broadcasting.

The DBP made its first moves into cabling through its regulatory powers over reception equipment. From 1970 onwards the DBP had introduced and operated MATV systems, which were small cable systems with a capacity of up to twelve channels. This technical decision triggered a regulatory dilemma. MATV, which required only a DBP technical permit, offered spare channel capacity. Upgrading the reception equipment, in addition to all of those which could not be received with conventional off-air aerials, would have been technically possible but the DBP cautiously refused to do so without appropriate instructions from the *Länder*.

The *Länder* had not challenged the DBP's practice of relaying the standard terrestrial signals in its early MATV and cable systems. Indeed, a later court judgement confirmed that the constitutionally guaranteed freedom of reception required that when cable replaced aerials it had to carry all the terrestrial signals receivable at that location.[26] Thus the DBP had the right to relay, without specific *Land* permission, all programme channels that could be received there terrestrially with conventional receivers.

In practice, however, it was the DBP which determined the standards for 'general availability' by setting a minimum field strength for off-air signals, or by refusing to boost them. Thus the DBP obtained at least some discretion in determining the carriage of programme channels. At that time, this meant that the DBP only relayed public stations, but ignored transfrontier commercial services, such as RTL Radio. The DBP therefore attracted criticism for interfering with the freedom of reception.[27]

Criticism arose, too, when the DBP tried to expand massively into broadband cable in 1979. It proposed cabling eleven towns with the declared aim of improving reception of the available public services, although it kept pointing to the programme multiplying potential of the improved technical standard (up to thirty channels). These cable 'islands' were meant to be 'anchorage points' for a national network.

But this strategy was felt to pre-empt the SPD's media and technology policies. In September 1979, the federal government therefore imposed a total halt on broadband cabling. It justified its decision in social and cultural-political terms: the new electronic media should not prejudice fundamental socio-political policies, such as social integration and the democratic formation of opinion, before the cable trials as envisaged by the KtK had been concluded. Moreover, since *Land* regulations on the relay of additional programmes did not yet exist, the DBP would be overstepping its 'service' function by relaying additional channels.[28]

However, the need to make up for an anticipated drop in investment in the telephone network, and to pre-empt massive job losses in industry, meant that the DBP was allowed slightly to circumvent the cabling stop. Localised cabling was allowed if it improved reception in areas of high interference; for new housing estates; for cable trial systems; or if it was requested and subsidised by the local authority. By December 1982, before the new federal government's cabling offensive, some four million households were already connected to large private MATVs serving over a hundred households each, and another 0.3 million households were connected to DBP cable systems.[29] The first leg of a national cable grid had thus already been put in place under the SPD/FDP coalition.

Ironically, despite the federal government's professed concern for *Länder* autonomy, the CDU and CSU *Länder* governments considered the 1979 'cabling stop', and not the cabling itself, to be an infringement. In principle, they had welcomed the cabling strategy. Not only did it allow private commercial broadcasting to be introduced, but it also coincided with their desire to become more deeply involved in all telecommunications policies since mass communications (*Länder* jurisdiction) and individual communications (*Bund* jurisdiction) were expected to converge and would probably bring with them economic benefits. For reasons of regional structural policy, the CSU and CDU governments of Bavaria and Baden-Württemberg even claimed that, as a part of its service function, the DBP was obliged to instal cable networks at their request[30] – a point of view which was diametrically opposed to the DBP's official concept of cable not as a broadcast, but as a public telecommunications service over which it had the sole regulatory say.

The federal government aroused further *Länder* opposition when it insisted, in its 1981 media policy resolution, that political decisions on the use of the new media concerned not only the *Länder* but also the *Bund*, with its responsibility for implementing a strategy for information technology.[31] This time all the *Länder* expressed fears that government control of DBP policies would overstep the bounds of its purely technical authority for broadcasting, and they sought more extensive information and consultation procedures.[32]

But the attempts by the federal government to shape broadcasting policy were even more pronounced under the 1982/83 CDU/CSU/FDP coalition government. This was possible because of a specific political constellation: the CDU media spokesman, Christian Schwarz-Schilling, still fresh from chairing the *Enquete-Kommission*, was appointed Minister for Posts and Telecommunications. The majority of the *Länder*, which normally provide checks and balances against federal government domination, now had a CDU- or CSU-led government themselves; and the *Länder* were openly urged by the federal government to follow the CDU's media policy.[33] This constellation was so favourable that a *Financial Times* article, apparently unaware of the constitutional framework, credited the Minister with dismantling the 'public sector broadcasting monopolies in television and radio'.[34]

Not surprisingly, by the early 1980s, the cautious social and political arguments for cable television, based on the expansion of local communications and participation of the citizens in the communications process, which had informed the debates around the KtK, were replaced by a conjuncture of economic and political and social rationales. This is clear from the federal government's justification for cabling:

> In the interests of *diversity of opinion*, [the federal government] considers it not only desirable, but also necessary, that the population will, on demand, be provided with the infrastructure to distribute television and radio programmes via broadband cable networks. . . . Equally, it is the opinion of the federal government that the new information and communication technologies, in particular broadband cabling technology, are important from an *economic point of view*.[35]

Without paying much heed to the fundamental socio-political questions raised by such a move, the new Minister adopted the position taken by the CDU members of the *Enquete-Kommission* and launched into building a national tree-and-branch coaxial copper cable grid. Although he insisted that the cable only created the technical infrastructure and did not therefore influence broadcasting policy, he nevertheless gave clear indications as to how it should be used. According to him, the investment of the huge sums was justified because public broadcasting was occupied by radicals and the left, so that it could no longer work towards social integration.[36] Before coming to power, however, the CDU had declared that the state had 'neither a claim nor a right to desire to intervene directly in the play of media forces or indeed to join in as an active participant'.[37]

Until 1989, the DBP's legal and operational monopoly covered the up-link, space segment and down-link for telecommunications and direct broadcasting satellites. The CDU/CSU/FDP government saw satellite capacity as the main way to increase the number of programme services that could fill and help sell the existing cable networks. The Ministry of Posts and Telecommunications insisted that only by relaying an increasing number of German and European channels could cable be marketed cost-effectively.[38] The *Länder* were virtually forced into allowing new programmes, if they did not want to stand accused of putting a major public investment at risk.

In April 1980, the West German and French governments had concluded a DBS treaty. The then SPD/FDP government had seen DBS mainly as a technological trial, therefore programming, the government suggested, should be provided by the existing public broadcasting services.[39] Significantly, the DBP did not invest in DBS as a broadcasting venture until after the change of government in 1982.[40] The SPD/FDP government was thus careful not to pre-empt political decisions regarding broadcasting policy.

Nevertheless, the *Länder* declared the technological decision to proceed with DBS to be 'inadmissable media-political domination'. At no stage had they been involved in any of the planning and negotiation procedures for the building and use of the German DBS.[41] The DBS agreement was indeed important for the future of broadcasting policy, since it was signed at a time when CLT, the Luxembourg commercial broadcaster, planned a DBS with programmes beamed to the Federal Republic. This was causing a major political rumpus among the *Länder*. The subsequent disagreement among them, as to the desirability of private commercial broadcasting and the future of the public broadcasting corporations, prevented the emergence of a common satellite policy. But meanwhile the media landscape was changing fast as commercial television was relayed through the cable networks.

The failure of the *Länder* to formulate a comprehensive common regulatory framework had effectively allowed the Ministry of

Posts and Telecommunications to take the initiative in the field of telecommunications satellites. The DBP needed programme services that would help it to increase cable connections and reach its profit targets. It claimed that, in addition to the locally receivable terrestrial broadcasts which it was already relaying, it also wanted to relay programme services which, the DBP argued, would not need to be licensed by the *Länder* since they could be received over the air anyhow, albeit via technically upgraded reception aerials. Although the *Länder* approved without discussion the relay of these programmes, they considered that telecommunications satellite programmes and any channels which reached the cable head end via microwave links did still require *Land* authorisation.

But the DBP had already rented two channels on the Eutelsat F1 satellite[42] and acquired six channels on the Intelsat V satellite which needed to be filled with programmes. No national legislative framework existed for this. The Ministry of Posts and Telecommunications thus blamed the *Länder* for wasting public money, arguing that the satellite rentals of £4 million a month for the unused Intelsat channels alone delayed by a year the break-even point for its cable investment.[43]

Many of the conservative *Länder*, which were in favour of private commercial broadcasting, were already drafting private broadcasting laws. Bavaria, Rhineland-Palatinate and West Berlin had made provisions for private broadcasting in their cable trials, although only on a limited regional basis. Lower Saxony and Schleswig-Holstein had also legislated for private broadcasting, but on a *Land*-wide scale. Not surprisingly, therefore, the authority which carried out the cable trial in CDU/FDP-governed Rhineland-Palatinate made a decisive move in 1984 which was to open the national cable market to German private broadcasters. It allocated one of the two Eutelsat channels, officially only intended for reception in its cable trial, to a private broadcast consortium (from 1985, SAT 1). But the signals could of course, cover the territories of all the other *Länder* as well.

At the same time, the DBP declared that it would redistribute the new German satellite channels, and any other programmes carried on the Eutelsat F1 such as Sky Channel, in cable systems other than the two trial networks in Rhineland-Palatinate and Munich which already carried them. The DBP justified this as 'an operational trial' – a concept which has frequently been used by the DBP to introduce a new service unspecified in the usage and tariff regulations. In this way it could test the market for new services without being bound by a tight administrative framework. Even so, the DBP was already engaged on erecting new satellite earth stations, an investment which could hardly be justified for a mere trial run. The 'operational trial' rationale was thus criticised as prejudicing *Länder* broadcasting policies in general.[44] In particular, the DBP's move towards national distribution was felt to have predetermined the shape and characteristics of the West Berlin cable trial since it reduced the economic desirability and technological capacity for local and interactive cable broadcasts.[45]

The following year, the Ministry of Posts and Telecommunications went further by allocating one Intelsat V channel to the commercial broadcaster Musicbox, without even asking the *Länder*. Again, its justification was that it was only to be on a 'trial basis' until the *Länder* reached an agreement on satellite channel distribution. Nevertheless, the DBP had created a *fait accompli* and had reshaped the boundaries for *Länder* policy decisions.

The DBP decisions caused a storm of public protest, and it was accused of acting as a broadcaster itself.[46] The *Länder*, who only a year earlier had confirmed their authority for licensing satellite-to-cable channels, felt this was an infringement of their sovereignty, in spite of any political affinities they had with the federal government.[47] It became clear that if their regulatory authority was not to be undermined by the *Bund* they had to respond and pass legislation in answer to the DBP challenge. A spate of Land-specific legislation followed, with some *Länder* passing preliminary enabling acts (*Vorschaltgesetze*) before drafting a comprehensive regulatory framework for private broadcasting. Finally, the 1987 Inter-*Land* Treaty reaffirmed *Länder* authority for the allocation of all broadcast satellite channels. However, they were still dependent on the DBP to make satellite channels available for broadcast use.

The Treaty clearly restates that the DBP is only allowed to redistribute programme channels in accordance with *Land* legislation, and most *Land* broadcasting laws explicitly assert the *Land*'s right to decide which programmes are distributed.[48] The DBP's contracts for the down-link of the signals with the interested broadcasters must contain a corresponding provision. Although the Treaty allowed the DBP (or private cable or SMATV operators) to redistribute any nation-wide programme channel that complied with the provisions in the Treaty, the DBP, the private cable operator or the broadcaster was still required to notify the *Land* regulatory authority of its redistribution plans, and the authority might, under certain conditions, withhold permission or stop the relay.

The *Länder* claim it is their responsibility to decide which broadcasters may use the available cable channels and local systems. The problem, which may grow with the rise in the number of European satellite channels, is to decide which cable channels are reserved for broadcasters specifically licensed by the *Land* authorities and which are to be used by the DBP to relay services which originate outside the *Land* itself.[49] In a few *Länder* the regulatory authority for private broadcasting is entitled to draw up a usage plan for both cable and terrestrial frequencies. However, since all such regulatory decisions by the *Länder* still require the DBP to make the frequencies or channels available, conflicts between the DBP and the *Land* regulatory authorities have been inevitable.

Theoretically, channel availability is decided upon by the DBP regional telecommunication centres, according to strictly technical criteria. However, the commitment to technical decisions does not prevent a certain degree of political conditioning. In 1986, in its contribution to the federal government 'Programme for Improving the Conditions for Private Broadcasters' the Ministry of Posts and Telecommunications declared that it would move the two main private programmes in the cable networks, SAT 1 and RTL plus, to frequency bands where they could be received by older television sets without specific satellite adaptors which were still being used in forty to fifty per cent of the cabled homes. The measure was expected to double their reach. This had clear political implications since it could oust the two public satellite channels, Eins plus and 3Sat, from the first tier of programming, and thus reduce their reception.

The implementation of technological policy is not straight-forward, especially when the Ministry is caught between its business interests and party-political allegiance. In the case of Eins plus, the ARD satellite programme, some CDU *Länder* opposed the extension of public broadcasting, claiming the channel was illegal as it required a licence, and ordered the DBP not to redistribute it in their *Länder*. The DBP obeyed with an explicit deference to *Länder* authority, despite wanting to increase cable attractiveness with new channels, and even though a court decision had confirmed that the channel was legitimate. Since it was a public broadcasting offering, it did not require a licence from the *Länder*. The ARD argued, however, that contractually the DBP had guaranteed redistribution by a certain date to a given number of households, which included cable connections in the CDU *Länder*. Eventually the DBP could refuse redistribution no longer. On another occasion, the DBP pointed to gaps in its distribution infrastructure in order to justify the slowdown of the cable relay of Bavarian television's third channel, a measure which coincided with an unsuccessful effort by the Bavarian CSU government to take out an injunction against the nation-wide distribution of the channel.[50]

Nevertheless, the regulatory authorities assume that DBP network operation will be the rule also in future. Indeed, despite political disagreements, because of its constitutionally guaranteed 'service' role for the broadcasting authorities, the DBP is the best partner for the *Länder*. Legally, the DBP is only allowed to distribute a signal if the broadcaster concerned can prove to the DBP that it has a licence from one of the *Länder*, or in the case of a foreign broadcaster or a SMATV operator, if it can satisfy the DBP that it has acquired all rights and permission for broadcasting in the Federal Republic.[51] Through the hierarchical structure of its public cable network, the DBP is able to control the access to the market of any broadcaster according to *Länder* law. It can thus enforce the must-carry rules for terrestrially receivable programmes, the cable distribution of all licensed services and, importantly, the discontinuity of distribution.

Terrestrial transmissions

Traditionally, the DBP and public broadcasting corporations negotiated their frequency requirements and transmitter sites and powers between themselves. They were then merely endorsed by the *Länder* governments or parliaments. But with the claims of the private broadcasters to terrestrial frequencies this self-regulatory situation changed. Now, the *Länder* have become much more involved. The DBP officially assigns broadcasting frequencies to the *Land* governments; they, the parliaments, or the private regulatory authorities, now decide on the allocation of the frequencies to either the public or private sector. There are no nationally uniform rules to decide which institution is in charge.

The regulators have to advertise the licences on the basis of the frequency and transmission parameters, including location, which are all given by the DBP. But these also determine the coverage areas and hence the commercial potential of the licence. Many *Länder* are now aiming to adapt the technical data and transmitter locations to their political approach to broadcasting, and to redefine the coverage areas. The regulators either claim that the actual coverage areas do not achieve the promised reach, or else that the stations could lose their regional or local appeal through an unplanned expansion of the coverage area, thus intensifying competition in a wider market. Failures by the DBP to fulfil the administrative and economic aspects of their regulatory requests, that may well be contradictory, have led to recriminations from both regulatory authorities and the broadcasters.

The DBP is bound to ensure that broadcasters only rent transmitters according to the conditions stipulated in the broadcast licence. Theoretically, therefore, private broadcasters have no say over their transmission equipment and its costs. But, in practice, the licences in some *Länder*, such as Lower Saxony, can be vague, just listing the location of the transmitters and the frequencies to be used. Specifications for transmitter height, performance and direction, which all influence the actual coverage, are left to negotiations between broadcasters and DBP. Other *Länder*, such as Northrhine-Westfalia, are more prescriptive and stipulate the transmitter power and its direction.

The DBP has always maintained that the technical specification of broadcast transmissions is a telecommunications matter and should therefore come under its monopoly control. But the question is now the subject of legal controversy. In the 'Hohe Wurzel' case,[52] the DBP was asked by the regulatory authority of Rhineland-Palatinate to instal transmitters for a new private radio in the *Land*. For economic reasons the DBP decided to broadcast the private radio signals from a nearby transmitter at 'Hohe Wurzel' in neighbouring Hessen. Although the DBP beamed its signal at the intended reception area in the Rhineland-Palatinate, the broadcasts could also be received in the Hessen part of the densely populated Rhine-Main region, which obviously boosted the audience for the advertising-financed radio station.

The Hessen public radio, run by HR, which feared inroads into its own airtime sales, and the then Social-Democrat/Green *Land* government which was opposed to private broadcasting (it came to power again in 1991), contested the DBP move in the administrative courts; and simultaneously the government appealed to the Federal Constitutional Court arguing that the apparently technical decision of the DBP eroded their own specific *Land* broadcasting policies, since the DBP could have equally well erected a new transmitter in Rhineland-Palatinate. Meanwhile, a compromise was reached. Nevertheless, a fundamental decision clarifying the DBP/*Länder* relationship is still necessary.

It is not clear in practice how much scope the *Länder* or the private broadcasters have to influence the technical planning of the DBP transmission service, although it has been known for *Land* regulators to exert successful pressures on the DBP to change transmitter locations and signal strengths.[53] The DBP's scope is restricted by the planning parameters of the ITU; and any changes in transmitter characteristics incur undesirable costs, which undermine its duty to be cost efficient. This is therefore a grey area of regulatory policy which is resolved by informal negotiations.

The DBP has also been expected to provide transmission facilities as soon as the licence has been allocated for the relevant coverage area. It has thus had to invest its own resources before it could finalise a rental agreement with the broadcaster concerned. While most *Länder* are prepared to subsidise this initial capital outlay until 1991 in order to speed up transmitter installation, they also expect the DBP to pass these subsidies on to the broadcasters in the form of rebates.[54]

THE DBP AND ITS RELATIONS WITH THE BROADCASTERS

Apart from frequency management, the economics of both private and public broadcasting are also conditioned by the DBP's technical standards and its associated tariff and usage conditions. Although there was limited *Länder* representation and influence on the DBP administrative board until the DBP was restructured in 1989, the Ministry for Posts and Telecommunications was free to decide on usage conditions and tariffs. Thus the charges for transmitter rentals were laid down in its statutory usage and tariff order. But not all technical developments could be incorporated into the legal framework of the usage and tariff order as soon as they became available, since the DBP needed time to 'test the market'. Hence, the rules and conditions for satellite and cable distribution services were laid down in more flexible administrative rules, even though the latest usage and tariff order only came into force in January 1988. Furthermore, exemptions from the statutory regulations have always been possible, especially for the public corporations.

For historical reasons, ARD and ZDF are exempt from observing private sector tariffs. The charges, conditions of use and co-ordination between the various public broadcasters are based on annual negotiations within a joint commission including the DBP, based upon special rules agreed between the partners in a special administrative agreement (*Verwaltungsvereinbarung Technische Leistungen* 1974). Its most important provision is that the DBP is to charge the corporations at cost for its terrestrial transmission and landline distribution services. Satellite transmissions, special services and the costs of policing the airwaves for licence evasion are all charged separately.

In 1989, the ARD stations paid £138 million to the DBP for all its technical services; and ZDF paid £52 million in 1988. In all, the ARD spent seven per cent and ZDF ten per cent of their total revenues on transmission.[55] Although the ARD requires more land lines to bind all its nine regional corporations together, its share is proportionately less since it has a larger revenue than ZDF and it owns the transmitters for its first television channels and the radio stations. The public stations' proportion is low compared with the distribution costs for private television stations which, according to an official of a private national broadcaster, can account for as much as one third of their revenues, especially if they offer regional opt-outs. Political pressure has already forced the Ministry for Posts and Telecommunications to reduce its original tariffs by about a third for most VHF radio and television transmitters and land lines from January 1989, only a year after the tariff order came into force. The cuts were especially dramatic for television.

The private broadcasters still claim that the DBP rentals are dearer than necessary because of the DBP's unreasonably high technical standards, which prevent cheap transmission and, *in extenso*, programme services. They fear that the DBP's network monopoly, in conjunction with its declared objective of introducing integrated broadband optical fibre services, will delay the development of new potentially cost-saving techniques, such as terrestrial microwave and digital transmissions. The DBP argues, however, that its standards follow internationally recognised norms and have to be strictly observed since the broadcast spectrum in the FRG is overcrowded due to usage by its nine neighbouring countries and NATO forces, although German unification and reduction of the NATO forces have somewhat eased the pressure on the spectrum. It is also likely that the technical standards will be lowered if there is political pressure in this respect from the federal government.

In 1989, the DBP already had to reduce its charges for satellite transponders and cable distribution by approximately sixteen per cent in face of the increased competitive pressures from foreign satellites such as Astra and Panamsat. In an attempt to recover its so far unprofitable investment in satellite earth stations and the space segment, especially its loss of around £117 million for the first TV-Sat, the DBP is now looking to private investment to finance the expensive head-end satellite receivers, in return for reduced cable distribution rentals to broadcasters or satellite operators.[56]

LIBERALISATION OF THE DBP AND CHANGES TO ITS BROADCASTING DISTRIBUTION MONOPOLY

In July 1989 the DBP was liberalised and its control over the telecommunications sector weakened.[57] The main aim was to separate the DBP's policy-making and regulation activities from its operational services. In some areas, the market for telecommunications services was opened to competition; in other areas, the DBP has to provide so-called 'mandatory services' in the public interest and it generally retains its network, radio installation, and telephone service operational monopolies.

The Ministry for Posts and Telecommunications continues to exercise its regulatory responsibilities, such as managing frequencies and regulating standards and usage conditions. In particular, the Ministry is responsible for regulating the policies of the three separate state-owned enterprises, DBP Telekom (for telecommunications), DBP Postdienst (for the postal services) and DBP Postbank (giro and banking services), in line with the general political principles of the federal government.[58] In that sense, the influence of the political on the communications marketplace will remain unchanged for the monopoly and mandatory tasks of DBP Telekom; the Minister for Posts and Telecommunications still defines which services DBP Telekom must offer to fulfil its public-interest obligations, and lays down the conditions and tariffs for them, including the reception and distribution of radio and TV signals.

An 'Infrastructure Council' consisting of eleven members of the *Bundestag* and eleven representatives of the *Länder* from the *Bundesrat* ensures public accountability. This body approves the ministerial distribution and general infrastructure plans and public-interest policies, but the federal cabinet may overrule its decision, if appealed to by the Minister. The Minister thus retains extensive powers of secondary legislation. Hence the effect of the Infrastructure Council will mostly be limited to the negotiation of political solutions. Whether this will extend to disputes over the interface between broadcasting and telecommunications remains to be seen.

The *Bund*, in the shape of the DBP Telekom, retained its monopoly over the broadcasting infrastructure. It has 'the exclusive right . . . to set up and operate radio installations'.[59] These include both airwaves and electrical cable installations. The DBP thus continues to operate the transmission systems. However, DBP Telekom is now free to negotiate the fees it charges the broadcasters for its services by individual private contract, subject only to general conditions. This may mean that large broadcasters are offered rebates, while the distribution costs for the smaller companies can rise. In addition, the special charging arrangements between the DBP and the public broadcasters are also at risk.

The monopoly continues to extend to copper cable networks, but as before the Ministry may grant exemptions for certain routes or districts. The DBP liberalisation, with its strong emphasis on cost-efficiency, may result in a further substantial slowdown in the DBP's cable initiative, which is still not in profit. This initiative has been under attack since its inception, not just for squandering public money derived from telephone profits, but also for having compromised the DBP's public-interest duties for universal service and tariff uniformity.[60] In fact, it was broadcast cabling that had brought about the first erosion of the DBP's monopoly, since economic and ideological reasons had forced the Ministry to allow private partners into its cable operating and retail business.

Since liberalisation, the Ministry has not yet decided whether cable operating and retailing should continue to be a service in the public interest and a DBP monopoly, or whether it should be completely opened to private competition. As an example of things to come, a private cable enterprise indicated already that it intended to profit from the liberalisation spirit. It planned to establish and market its own cable networks, including satellite head ends, in those areas which it would not be cost-effective for the DBP to cable. It hoped that the DBP would allow its network paths to be free of the usual DBP routing prescriptions, and permit lower technical standards. It also envisaged using the networks for the newly liberalised value-added services such as telemetry.[61] It was claimed that the hopes of the cable company to achieve those concessions were based on good political contacts with the Ministry.[62]

In the long run, cabling could also become more competitive through the liberalisation of satellite communications. Satellite reception has been gradually liberalised since 1985. Although satellite receivers and transmitters for audiovisual communications still require a DBP licence, after liberalisation the licensing arrangements will probably be fairly generous. It is open to question whether the future broadband optic fibre networks, which operate not on electrical but on light impulses, will be defined as radio installations and thus come under control of the DBP.

Generally, as with the regulatory authorities for private broadcasting, the relaxation of the DBP's distribution monopoly appears to be not primarily a consequence of the new statutes as such, but rather of the political interpretation of how liberal the regulatory regime ought to be. In future, the digitalisation of broadcast signals, the introduction of private providers of value-added services such as cable text, the liberalisation of access to computerised switching nodes for pay-per-view services, and the further liberalisation of satellite facilities could all raise substantial problems of jurisdiction and control between the DBP and the *Länder*.

Chapter 3

The regulatory structures for public and private broadcasting

Although in theory the *Länder* are responsible for broadcasting regulation, their policies have been shaped by two major factors – the judgements of the Federal Constitutional Court and the infrastructure policies of the federal government. A third factor has been the continuation of the traditional pattern of institutional regulation established by the Western Allied Powers after the Second World War.

Each *Land* has its own geography, its own economic policies, and above all its own politics. Each of these played its part in shaping the detailed manner in which the authorities interpreted the general guidelines for broadcasting regulation laid down by the Constitutional Court, and the opportunities for technological expansion offered by the federal government and the DBP. Each *Land* in West Germany was therefore able to model the private broadcasting sector according to its own policy without having to compromise, as some *Länder* had to when the public broadcasting system was established. Then, three *Länder* co-operated to set up NDR; SWF was, and still is, based on a two-*Länder* treaty; and following the 1961 judgement of the Federal Constitutional Court, ZDF was set up by an inter-*Land* treaty between all eleven *Länder*.

In its 1981 judgement, the Constitutional Court had ruled that private broadcasting was constitutional. For several years prior to the 1986 judgement, the conservative *Länder*, which considered the public broadcasters to be 'red', had sought to turn this ruling to their political advantage. A major proponent of this type of restructuring was Ernst Albrecht, the CDU Minister-President of Lower Saxony. During the late 1970s, along with his colleague Gerhard Stoltenberg of Schleswig-Holstein, he had tried to break up NDR into separate parts,[1] but in 1980, after defeat in the Federal

Administrative Court, both *Länder* had to renew the inter-*Land* treaty which they had concluded with Hamburg in 1955 to set up NDR. Albrecht then switched his attention to establishing a private broadcasting channel to compete with the public broadcasters; and he was soon followed by Schleswig-Holstein. The Lower Saxony proposal appeared to mimic that of the public broadcasters, by setting up a regulatory authority with a pluralist supervisory board. It was this proposal which the SPD members of the *Bundestag* referred to the Constitutional Court. The broadcasting policies and priorities of the eleven *Länder* differed, however, and this led to a variety of private broadcasting structures and licensing and control bodies, the regulatory authorities for private broadcasting.

There is no clear relationship between the geography of the *Länder* and their broadcasting policies. The northern *Länder*, and most of Northrhine-Westfalia, are areas which can be easily and cheaply covered with only a few transmitters. The remainder of the FRG, however, especially Bavaria and Baden-Württemberg, is very hilly, requiring many transmitters. But the actual channel disposition does not always follow the geographical situation (see App. IX).

Both Lower Saxony and Schleswig-Holstein planned to introduce *Land*-wide, not local, stations. This was mainly because *Land*-wide private radio was felt the best to establish the desired competition for NDR. But they were helped by the geography as their flat landscape meant that they only needed a few transmitters.

Hessen, which at the time of the private broadcasting debates was governed by an SPD/Green coalition, refused to license private radios, until in 1988 the CDU/FDP government established *Land*-wide radio. The return to power of the SPD/Green coalition in 1991 may result in a more localised structure. Since it was among the last to legislate for private broadcasting, the Hessen act was already deliberately designed to improve on certain regulatory shortcomings which had become apparent in the broadcasting organisation of other *Länder*.

Other *Länder* were more cautious and held back. The SPD *Land* of Northrhine-Westfalia was reluctant to license private broadcasters until it had fully worked out provisions to guarantee the development of the public broadcasters and other rules aiming at a pluralist structure for private broadcasting. Despite its relatively flat geography, it deliberately opted for a local structure in private radio, and granted WDR another *Land*-wide channel. In Baden-Württemberg, Minister-President Lothar Späth had his eye on the social and economic benefits which could flow from a high-tech strategy built on a massive expansion of cable and satellite communications. But Baden-Württemberg also tried to develop gradually its own concept of a socially responsible media policy that would enrich local community life. The local radio structure that was adopted also fitted in with its geography. By adopting a liberal/conservative approach, the *Land* government tried to offer its citizens a combination of traditional community life and the potential for high-tech international communications.

Both Bavaria and West Berlin based their legislation on cable trial acts which were planned from the beginning to allow a looser experimental regime. As in Baden-Württemberg, the philosophy of the Bavarian CSU was that 'small is beautiful' and it too organised broadcasting on a local basis, particularly as this suited its geography. Even so, the Bavarian legislators also established *Land*-wide private competition for BR radio. Bavarian broadcasting policy, as in so many other areas, is torn between its social catholicism and the liberal quest for economic markets. Finally, Munich competes with Hamburg and Berlin to be one of the major film and television production centres in the FRG. Thus, despite their different regulatory philosophies, Bavaria was as keen as Hamburg and West Berlin to protect these important economic and cultural assets. Other *Länder*, such as Northrhine-Westfalia and Lower Saxony, which suffered from high unemployment, also wanted to build up their media industries in Cologne and Hanover.

The SPD-controlled governments of Saarland and Bremen were committed to the survival of their public broadcasters, particularly since they depended on the financial support of other public broadcasting corporations to keep them alive. Given their small size, and as they are flooded with overspill signals, *Land*-wide broadcasting seemed the only sensible choice. But Saarland also tried to shape the broadcasting landscape in political terms by allowing SR to participate in *Land*-wide private broadcasting, and in return gave it a further *Land*-wide radio channel.

None of the *Länder* private broadcasting acts distinguishes between radio and television, even though the two media have different economic characteristics, and are normally used in quite different ways. In practice, however, the regulatory authorities do make a distinction. Radio, which is less expensive, tends to be used as *the* preferred medium to implement the several concepts of diversity contained in the legislation. In contrast, the economics of television, and the new distribution technologies of satellite and cable, have led to nation-wide services (see App. VII). The result is that concepts of diversity are much harder to implement. Once licensed, local radio is also far more lightly regulated than television, where the political pressures for control are more severe, especially because politicians generally assume television is their image-builder and ascribe to it a far more persuasive impact on their voters. By the time the Constitutional Court handed down its 1986 judgement, therefore, each *Land* had its own view of how to turn the opportunities to offered regulate broadcasting to its own geographical, economic and political advantage.

ORGANISATION AND CONTROL OF THE PUBLIC BROADCASTING CORPORATIONS

The legislation establishing the ARD corporations and ZDF specifies that they are to be non-profit institutions incorporated under public law. They are to be self-governing and autonomous, especially in programme matters. Although subject to formal legal supervision by the *Länder*, their autonomy is guaranteed by the representative nature of their broadcasting councils.

The public broadcasting system has a three-tier structure which consists of a supervisory board or broadcasting council,[2] an administrative council and the director-general (*Intendant*; see App. IV). The memberships of the broadcasting councils range from eleven to sixty-six; and their periods of office from two years, re-electable, in West Berlin, to six years, non re-electable, in Northrhine-Westfalia. The members of the broadcasting councils come from 'socially relevant' groups and associations and the political parties, with wide differences in the degree and extent of political and government participation. The administrative councils are smaller with between seven and nine members. They do not have to be pluralistically composed and often include management experts.

The broadcasting councils explicitly represent the 'interests of the general public'. They take the final decisions on all policy matters and watch over the interpretation of the corporations' programme remit. They have the right to issue guidelines, define long-term programming strategy, appoint the director-general and sometimes his deputy, and deal with public complaints. The administrative council controls financial management. The director-general is responsible for the structure and editorial content of programmes and for preparing the budget.

The public broadcasting control system has been attacked on two main grounds. First, the meaning of social relevance is open to a wide variety of interpretations. It is almost impossible to represent a dynamically changing society with councils whose constitution is, by law, largely static. It *is* possible where a *Land* parliament has the right to elect members of newly emerging social groups, but even here a group has to be large and powerful enough to attract political attention. Therefore, in line with the West German concept of pluralism, the established associations and organisations which are also important players in other parts of the political process dominate the broadcasting councils. This structure excludes from access, or at best marginalises, minorities and poorly organised interest groups, such as citizen initiatives. For example, an analysis of all the representatives on the public broadcasting councils shows there are only three environmentalists, one old age pensioner, three delegates of parents' organisations, one consumer representative, one foreigner, and eleven delegates from charities and social volunteer groups. But there are seventy-eight party politicians, thirty-five representatives from the churches, and sixty-four delegates from industrial associations and trade unions (see App. V).

Particularly problematic in recent years has been the role played in the public broadcasting councils by supporters of private broadcasting. One anachronism, which has survived into the age of competition between public and private broadcasters, is the representation of publishers' organisations on the public broadcasting boards, even though their members have large shareholdings in private broadcasting. Conflicts of interest seem unavoidable. No private company would tolerate a competitor on its policy-making board. There have also been cases where the same member of a *Land* parliament has legally been able to sit simultaneously on the control organs of both the public and the private broadcasters, although the parties themselves tend to avoid this practice.

The strong party political representation is another major point of criticism. Generally, the political constitution of the broadcasting councils reflects the parliamentary majority at the time when the relevant public broadcasting act or treaty was passed. A new government is then naturally inclined to change the constitution, if it feels it can expect a better reflection of its policies. Decision-making on the broadcasting councils is therefore strongly influenced by the political sympathies of its members, even those that represent social groups. The independent members, who often come from the churches, have to confront the so-called 'circles of friendship' of the political parties. Fortunately, however, most members of the broadcasting councils also tend to develop a degree of institutional independence which makes them wary of simply following the party line. Even so, many representatives are criticised for lacking the necessary professionalism to reach independent and informed conclusions.[3]

The political majorities on the boards determine the choice of director-general, and frequently his departmental directors, which can result in political manoeuvring at senior levels. Appointments tend to be made by trade-offs between the CDU and SPD, while smaller parties, such as the Greens and the FDP, are often excluded. Editorially, politicisation means that party politicians can exert an indirect influence upon programmes. This is done through contacts on the councils and in the organisation. The awareness of political influence alone can lead to internal self-censorship. 'The system of party-political membership in public television has been refined for many years. This is one of the reasons why television journalists think of themselves, wrongly, as "microphone stands".'[4]

This potential for direct transmission of political power to a broadcasting organisation is inherent to the public broadcasting system, whereas the private sector is far less open to influence from party politicians. It is not surprising, therefore, that even those politicians who have been bent on establishing private broadcasting are now trying to increase their influence on the public sector, either to make up for the lack of response of the private sector or to rein in the public service system.

The best barrier against political influence is a strong director-general, although the two ARD corporations which have had them, HR in Hessen and SDR in Baden-Württemberg, have recently found their statutes under attack. In Hessen, the CDU tried, unsuccessfully, to cut back the wide-ranging powers of appointment of the HR director-general and chairman of the ARD who, although elected by the broadcasting council because of his alleged

CDU sympathies, displayed a surprising independence. Similarly the CDU Minister-President of Baden-Württemberg tried hard to merge the SDR with SWF, the other corporation which covers part of Baden-Württemberg. Unlike SWF, there are no *Land* government representatives on the SDR broadcasting council, and the SDR's director-general, a former chairman of the ARD, is an independent figure although he, himself, is a conservative.

The large political parties are clearly not interested in changing the system of pluralist representation in broadcasting, and point to the constitutionally guaranteed role of the parties in West German public life. In Bavaria, the SPD and the trade unions were reluctant to support a proposal by the FDP, which was not represented on the BR broadcasting council, to reduce by two thirds the number of politicians and replace them with representatives of social groups including old age pensioners and foreigners. The FDP also wanted to give each parliamentary party the same number of seats on the BR council and the private broadcasting regulatory authority, regardless of parliamentary strength, an arrangement which CDU/FDP-ruled Hessen had already adopted for private broadcasting.[5]

Public accountability

The public has virtually no means of participating directly in the broadcasting corporations' decisions on programme-making. Indeed, a right of access to public broadcasting by informal public groups, such as citizen initiatives, has been denied by the Constitutional Court.[6] The 1981 NDR inter-*Land* treaty (passed by a CDU majority) and the 1985 WDR act (passed by an SPD majority) both made a small step towards public participation by providing the individual with the right to suggest programme ideas or changes, although the right seems more theoretical than of any practical consequence. Lower down the scale, the SFB act is the only one to require meetings of the broadcasting council to be public. Normally, council meetings take place privately, and only if they are controversial do they get mentioned in the press. There is a formal structure to deal with complaints by the public, ranging from the director-general and/or the complaints commission of the broadcasting council to the corporations' legal and petition commission at the appeal stage.

THE STRUCTURE OF THE PRIVATE BROADCASTING SECTOR

Organisational models

Three different legal models have been developed to achieve pluralism, but in practice the boundaries between them have started to overlap. The main system is the mixed model as laid down in the 1987 Inter-*Land* Treaty. It was written into the Treaty because most *Länder* had adopted it in their own legislation. It stipulates that until three private channels are available nation-wide, each channel has to be a fully comprehensive, general interest channel. This means it must contain a balanced mixture of the various opinion-forming elements of entertainment, education and information, although in line with the 'minimum standard' which was acceptable to the constitutional court, this does not have to come up to the standard of the public sector model. If the three private national channels are established, the so-called externally pluralist model applies. In this case, no specific rules for the internal balance of each channel are written into the legislation. It is assumed, as for the press, that the available range of all channels will automatically represent pluralism.

The third model is one of internal pluralism, inspired by the structure of the public broadcasting channels. For this, each channel must be provided either by an organisation composed of many different social and economic interests, or else contain an internal programme supervisory council. Each channel must then be a general interest channel.

Mixed model   Article 8 of the Inter-*Land* Treaty embodies the essence of the West German pluralism requirements for private broadcasting.

> The content of private broadcasts has to express essentially the pluralism of opinions. General interest channels have to grant means of expression to the significant political, ideological [*weltanschaulich*] and societal forces and groups; minority views have to be taken into consideration. Thematic or special interest channels may be offered in addition.[7]

As long as there are fewer than three private nation-wide radio or television channels, pluralism can only be guaranteed by general interest channels. To this end, the regulators have to ensure that diverse interests are represented within the broadcasting organisation itself. They may, for example, require the broadcaster to establish a pluralist internal programming council 'with an effective influence upon programming'. No such provision need be made if the broadcaster is a joint enterprise of several interests none of which has more than half the capital and voting rights. The regulatory authority allocating the licences should also attempt to have programme providers with an explicitly cultural remit included in any joint enterprise, although this clause is not legally enforceable.

Thus the provisions of the Treaty permeate the ideology of pluralism in private broadcasting, although it only lays down minimum conditions. Its minimum requirements may be increased by the *Land* granting the original licence, or franchise, on the basis of which the broadcasts can be redistributed, by cable or satellite, over the whole country. Even a German DBS broadcaster needs a licence from at least one *Land*. In particular, the *Länder* may apply different standards to terrestrial broadcasts under their jurisdiction. This is especially relevant to radio and the national television stations which currently rely heavily on low-power terrestrial television channels to reach their audiences. Nevertheless, once the Inter-*Land* Treaty had been signed, most of the *Länder* laws were homogenised to prevent private national broadcasters flocking to the *Land* with the lowest requirements. The Treaty has therefore established a common base from which to analyse any significantly different regulations in individual *Länder*.

***Länder* variations on the mixed model**   In Hessen, the pluralism regulations apply until there are more than four general interest channels. In Rhineland-Palatinate, if pluralism is not secured by the requisite number of available programme channels, the regulatory authority can try to ensure balanced pluralism by passing programme statutes. In practice this has not been applied because the four different broadcasters originally licensed had each a pluralist internal constitution and offered a balanced programme service.

External pluralism   Bavaria and West Berlin had no firm rules on pluralism. The legislation in both *Länder* was based on their cable trial laws. The West Berlin act ran out in 1990, that in Bavaria will be revised in 1992. For both, pluralism is an unwritten principle rather than a firm rule. In Bavaria, the somewhat pluralistically constituted cable companies accept broadcasts from as many programme providers as possible. Special cultural or smaller providers can get subsidies from the regulatory authority.

The original West Berlin regulatory authority found it hard to enforce positive rules for pluralism. Its cable trial act contained a clause requiring that any broadcaster, which fulfilled minimum civil requirements, had the right to be granted a licence. Only if an additional offering unbalanced the already existing broadcasts could the regulatory authority intervene to limit or redistribute the allocated broadcasting hours. The act expressly specified that the authority was not allowed to regulate programme structure. The newly elected SPD/Green government then passed new legislation containing strong elements of internal pluralism.

Internal pluralism In the two SPD-governed *Länder* of Northrhine-Westfalia and Bremen, and in SPD/FPD-ruled Hamburg, internally pluralist, general interest channels are the only ones allowed. The acts in Northrhine-Westfalia and Bremen expressly stipulate that private broadcasters must distribute programmes to assist the free formation of opinion and promote the public interest. They therefore perform a public duty. The Bremen act specifies political 'balance' in addition to the pluralism requirements; and is generally the closest to public broadcasting requirements. No programme service can take only individual views into consideration or serve one political party or group, association of interests, religion or ideology in a biased way. Bremen can afford such stringent requirements since, because of its small size, it is not attractive for private broadcasters that can cover its territory from their transmitters in Lower Saxony.

These three *Länder* also privilege associations of programme providers and require cultural interests to be given the chance to participate in them. In Northrhine-Westfalia, only non-profitmaking associations, composed of socially relevant groups, are allowed local radio licences. The stations are run and financed from advertising sales by privately organised operating companies, but legally the associations remain solely responsible for editorial policy – although a certain influence by the operating companies which hold the purse strings will be unavoidable.

The regulatory authorities

Constitution and duties   Despite all the criticism levelled at the public-service system of control, the legislators have reproduced its external structures in the licensing and control authorities for private broadcasting. There were two reasons for this. Firstly, the legal situation was uncertain. Apart from pointing to the needs for socially relevant groups to be represented and for independence from the state, the 1986 Constitutional Court decision left the legislators free to make their own regulatory arrangements. However, the Court had confirmed as constitutional the Lower Saxony legislation, which had followed the public broadcasting arrangements, and this was adopted as a model by the other *Länder*, since it avoided legal uncertainties over other models. On the other hand, the Lower Saxony model also allowed the politicians to continue to meddle in broadcasting; but since the regulatory authorities are institutionally separated from the private broadcasters, they can only have limited control over editorial content. Unlike the public sector where supervisory control goes hand in hand with administrative responsibility, in the private sector the two functions are carried out by different organisations.

All eleven *Länder* set up regulatory authorities as autonomous corporate bodies under public law, to license and supervise the private broadcasters.[8] They are not government agencies and not therefore directly open to changes in government policy. Any modifications to their legal structures have to be passed by the *Land* parliaments. It is thus to be expected that the SPD-led coalition government in Lower Saxony, which came to power in May 1990, will, as in Schleswig-Holstein and West Berlin where there was a similar change of government from the CDU to the SPD, amend the broadcasting act according to its policy priorities (viz. guarantees for the public broadcasters; open access channels, and a different constitution of the regulatory authority).

The authorities normally have a three-tier control structure similar to that of German public companies (see App. IV). At the top there is a pluralist supervisory board of between eleven and fifty members (the average is about thirty) to represent the public interest just like the public broadcasting corporations. Their periods of office vary between four and six years; and if there are new *Land* elections the parliamentary or government delegates can remain until their term of office ends, even if they fail to be re-elected. The board licenses the private broadcasters, monitors their programming, implements the cable redistribution rules as laid down in the legislation, and, if not specified in the relevant act, decides how to allocate the money which is available for its various duties.

An executive board, which can either be internal or external to the pluralist board, prepares and implements its decisions. It develops administrative and budgetary policies and can issue emergency orders. In Lower Saxony this board also regulates advertising. In Baden-Württemberg, the executive board issues secondary legislation to allocate the available frequencies and cable channels to the public sector as well as the private sector. Elsewhere, this is normally administered by the *Land* governments. In other *Länder*, however, such as Bremen, Hamburg, Hessen and Rhineland-Palatinate, executive and administrative duties are either the direct responsibility of the supervisory board, or are delegated to the authority's director.

The director heads the administrative office of the authority, carries out its executive policies, represents it in court and at the standing conference of the regulatory authorities, the *Direktorenkonferenz der Landesmedienanstalten*, which co-ordinates advertising, youth protection and pluralism regulations. Programme monitoring, advice to broadcasters, technical co-ordination and above all the preparation of policy decisions for the supervisory board are also major responsibilities of the director's office.

There can be overlapping responsibilities at the interfaces between the tiers. The supervisory boards, and often the executive board members,[9] work on a voluntary basis, and meet only monthly or quarterly, although meetings can be more frequent when a licence is being awarded. To a large extent, the incentive to attend the meetings can depend on the attendance allowance. This ranges from £17 in Lower Saxony to over £330 in Bavaria. The rate for board members was originally so low in Lower Saxony that in some cases they changed their allegiance to the more prestigious NDR broadcasting council; and the members had to be paid more in order to achieve a quorum.

The director is often a lawyer from the *Land* administration, and so possesses the necessary legal and technical expertise. His powers of decision vary from *Land* to *Land*. In Bavaria, where the executive president heads the administrative office, they are very strong. They are weakest in Lower Saxony where orders for broadcasters by the supervisory board are implemented by the *Land* government and the director's function is purely administrative. Generally, because of his intermediary role, the director can assume a strong agenda-setting role for the supervisory board.[10]

Although the constitutions of the various pluralist regulatory bodies differ, party political and government interests are generally lower than those in the public broadcasting councils. Membership is also smaller for well-established groups, such as churches, trade unions, municipalities, and even journalists; and significantly less in science and education. Less well represented groups, such as professional bodies, consumers, charities, and environmentalists have gained somewhat, although the overall bias towards traditional social organisations has hardly changed. The so-called minority interests, such as the anti-nuclear and animal rights movements, are hardly represented at all; and old age pensioners and women, who can hardly be regarded as minorities, are still clearly under-represented. As for the lower socio-economic groups, virtually nobody represents them directly (see App. V).

Despite its slight decline, political representation is still substantial. The Lower Saxony board is an example of a 'weighted' body. According to a conservative member, the statutory social groups were carefully selected to avoid government 'iconoclasm', that is mostly groups with conservative values which were not too critical of private broadcasting. In addition, Lower Saxony is unique since the government cabinet office is the official licensing authority with the right to preselect licence applicants. Political influence is often reinforced by allowing parliamentary factions to select additional social groups according to their strength. This is extreme in Hamburg where the social groups can only prepare shortlists of candidates from which parliament makes the final choice.

In Baden-Württemberg, the CDU government organised an executive board of two CDU, one CDU-inclined and two SPD members, by ignoring the FDP and the Greens. Furthermore, the pluralist supervisory board is the least powerful of all the *Länder* since it can only authorise the executive's decisions, or submit alternative proposals. Even this limited role has to be reviewed in 1991. In contrast, Hessen gave each parliamentary party equal representation on the supervisory board. The cable trial legislation in West Berlin considered pluralist control too bureaucratic and unnecessary, since it was assumed that pluralism would result from individual right of access to the market. As in Baden-Württemberg, decisions were made by a five-member executive board representing the three major parties. The SPD/Green coalition, which came to power in 1989, has now introduced a new regulatory structure to replace the cable trial act which includes a pluralist licensing and supervisory board.

Bavaria, Hessen, Rhineland-Palatinate and Saarland allow direct government participation in the supervisory board and illustrate the pervasiveness of government involvement in broadcasting control, beyond that in the public broadcasting structure. In other *Länder*, as diverse as CDU/FDP Lower Saxony or SPD Northrhine-Westfalia, government influence is increased by the non-voting attendance of a member of the cabinet office during the meetings of the boards. This is officially justified by the goverments' formal legal supervisory powers over the regulatory authorities.[11]

Despite their different political outlooks, pluralism is also inscribed at a lower level in both Bavaria and Northrhine-Westfalia. In Northrhine-Westfalia, local radio associations are made up of voluntary groups. In Bavaria, local cable companies with pluralist boards organise all *Land*-wide and local broadcasting, including terrestrial services. The Northrhine-Westfalian law requires the local radio associations to have an internally pluralist structure, while Bavaria grants local social groups priority access to the cable companies. Significantly, the associations and the cable companies both determine editorial policy.

In most *Länder*, all broadcasting interests, including cable operators, are prevented from sitting on the board. Some of the interests represented are critical of commercial broadcasting, but by including publishers and industrialists on the boards, there is an inherent danger that the supervisory boards may be captured by commercial broadcasting interests; this is especially so in Bavaria, where programme providers are allowed into the local cable companies which transmit and distribute the programmes supplied by licensed providers on a commercial basis.

In Bavaria, clashes of interests between the regulatory authority and the privately organised cable companies, especially the largest in Munich, are programmed into the system. According to Article 111a of the Bavarian constitution, all broadcasting must be publicly organised and run. So, although in practice the Bavarian regulatory authority works much like those in the other *Länder*, it is legally a public broadcaster and is required to assume full responsibility for a pluralist programme output.[12] Nevertheless, its regulatory philosophy is deliberately entrepreneurial and non-interventionist. In practice, therefore, it is the cable companies which make the licensing decisions, which then have only to be approved by the pluralist body of the regulatory authority. Although these regulatory arrangements were repeatedly questioned by the Bavarian Administrative Court,[13] the cable companies still consider the authority's public-interest obligations too restrictive.

Finance and administration   The authorities receive two per cent of the broadcasting licence fee, as stipulated in the 1987 Inter-*Land* Treaty. This secures over ninety per cent of the authorities' finance. In addition, the authorities charge the broadcasters for any administration, such as licensing or reprimanding them. In Hamburg and Schleswig-Holstein, the private broadcasters are also subject to an annual levy of between one and three per cent of their revenues. In Hamburg, this is to finance cultural objectives, such as open channels; in Schleswig-Holstein, it goes towards administrative costs. Television stations subject to a levy can, however, obtain a rebate in return for meeting a quota of in-house productions.

The amount which the authorities spend on administration varies from *Land* to *Land*. Any money not used to finance open channels and transmitter infrastructures (see below) is meant to go back to the public broadcasting corporation which collected the licence fee in the first place. But this is unlikely to happen without political pressure, since the authorities can expand their budgetary needs in line with the funds available. They can also carry forward any unused funds into the following year's budget. But public criticism in Northrhine-Westfalia did force the authority to give part of its unspent money to WDR, to promote a new *Land* film foundation; and Hessen has earmarked between thirty and fifty per cent of the additional licence fee income to promote the cultural activities of HR.

The 1989 budgets (see App. VI) varied from just under £8 million in Northrhine-Westfalia to £0.6 million in Bremen, depending on the number of licence fee paying households in each *Land*, and the legal duties of the authorities.

These disparities are built into the federal system. In public broadcasting, the differences are mitigated by a complex equalisation scheme, but the budgets of the smaller regulatory authorities make it doubtful whether enough money is available for all their public-interest duties, especially programme monitoring and associated research. At the other end of the scale, however, the authority in Northrhine-Westfalia is clearly the most active in spending money and reminding broadcasters of their programme obligations. But the prosperous authorities also have a reputation for overmanning and heavy-handed bureaucracy.[14]

But the licensing and monitoring duties are not directly comparable. The *Länder* with local radio stations, several private terrestrial television broadcasters and open channels normally need more resources, most of which will initially be spent on licence co-ordination. But rather than on financial resources, the establishment of a multiple broadcasting structure and the allocation of money to the various budgetary headings depends primarily on the broadcasting philosophy and tradition in the *Land*.

Infrastructure subsidies   The regulatory authorities have the power to pay subsidies to the DBP in order to set up the specific broadcast infrastructures necessary to achieve their individual broadcasting structure.   But the money, which comes from the additional licence fee, only lasts for four years. The subsidies go towards the erection of new terrestrial radio and television transmitters and/or their operating rentals. Lower Saxony also subsidises television landlines which permit regional opt-outs. This is intended to help the private broadcasters develop universal coverage, which forms part of their public-interest obligations, and to prevent them from cherry-picking by transmitting only in densely populated areas with high advertising revenues. Since the DBP has the monopoly right to erect and operate transmitters, the subsidies are not only to speed up transmitter erection, but also reduce DBP rentals for the marginal transmission sites.

As a rule, the proportions of the licence fee which can subsidise infrastructure measures are specified. Baden-Württemberg and Hessen lay down the minimum to be spent on infrastructure subsidies, while in Lower Saxony secondary legislation requires that ninety per cent of the licence fee income be spent on infrastructures. The Lower Saxony government went even further by passing a decree to prescribe the detailed allocation of the funds.[15] At the other extreme, the authority in Northrhine-Westfalia can allocate whatever funds it deems necessary for infrastructure subsidies.

The arrangements thus vary from *Land* to *Land* according to the regulatory priorities. Hamburg and Saarland exclude transmitter subsidies completely. In 1989, Baden-Württemberg earmarked £3.3 million or some seventy per cent of its total budget for infrastructure tasks. In the same year, Lower Saxony spent, as required, £3.2 million or ninety per cent of its budget on infrastructure. For Northrhine-Westfalia, in contrast, the figure was £0.7 million or a mere eight per cent. Between 1988 and 1989, Bavaria nearly doubled its subsidies, from £1 million to £1.9 million (see App. VI).[16]

Public accountability   In practice, the public accountability of the supervisory boards is extremely limited. The opportunity to experiment with alternative forms of public participation in broadcasting supervision was missed when the new legislation was drafted. As on the public broadcasting councils, the interests of the 'general public' are normally mediated through representatives of group interests. But the delegates of social groups and political parties are primarily accountable to their respective organisations, rather than the public at large; and hence they are often unaware of their responsibilities as 'trustees'. Some laws, however, do stipulate that the board members shall not seek or receive instructions from their delegating groups or parties;[17] and like the broadcasting councils the supervisory boards may develop a degree of independence. Even the Lower Saxony board, that is often thought to be 'on the long leash of the government', has developed a certain independence of spirit.

The public itself is normally excluded from the meetings of the supervisory boards. Only in Bremen and Northrhine-Westfalia may the public sit in on discussions, while in Hamburg the public may be informed of decisions. In practice, the degree of accountability of the authorities depends both upon their financial standing and on their self-image. The authorities in Lower Saxony, Schleswig-Holstein and Hessen are run like state administrations and the public can find out little about them. Those in Northrhine-Westfalia and Bavaria present themselves as public-interest institutions, but they are also public relations conscious bodies, organising conferences and issuing regular press releases and other publications. Ironically, the general public may be best served by party political interests, because they have the means to publicise and question the internal procedures within the boards through their parliamentary links.

The procedures for dealing with public complaints vary. Sometimes, as in Hessen, Lower Saxony and Schleswig-Holstein, there is no mention of them at all in the legislation. Where there is, they tend to be less formal than the corresponding procedures for the public broadcasting organisations. Northrhine-Westfalia, once again, has the most detailed provisions. Public complaints are normally appealed to the executive or administrative office, if they have not been answered satisfactorily by the private stations themselves. In Saarland, the same regulatory authority is responsible for complaints against both the public and private broadcasters.

PROGRAMMING OBLIGATIONS IN THE PUBLIC AND PRIVATE SECTORS

General programme rules

The *quid pro quo* of the public broadcasters' independence from the state, which is written into the relevant acts and statutes, is a firm commitment to the West German concept of pluralism. Both the ARD and ZDF are required to assist in the realising of a free democratic order. Article 10 of the 1987 Inter-*Land* Treaty forbids the misuse of violent material, the glorification of war, incitement to racial hatred, and pornography. This provision, and the specific youth protection rules, apply to all broadcasters, whether public or private, national or local.

The programming responsibilities of the public broadcasters are set out in the various programme guidelines of the ARD corporations and the ZDF. The ARD programming principles, for example, stipulate that, apart from formal requirements for balanced pluralism, obedience to the general law, objective reporting and granting airtime to the churches and the political parties, programming must be as comprehensive and varied as possible. Not only is the audience to be informed, educated and entertained (in that order), but it must be given

> an objective and comprehensive overview of international, national and *Land*-wide events in all essential realms of life. The demand for pluralism is to be especially respected in information broadcasts and those that serve to form opinion. Significant

political statements and analyses, as well as information on new facts and [their] contexts are essential parts of the programme. The duty to inform also requires reports on unconstitutional opinions, events or states of affairs.[18]

The acts, statutes or treaties establishing the nine individual ARD corporations may vary from this in minor ways. Apart from following similar general principles, ZDF's programme guidelines are more overtly political than those of the ARD. Its broadcasts are 'to promote the reunification of Germany in peace and freedom, help to preserve freedom for Berlin and foster efforts aimed at European unification'.[19] This is a slightly different emphasis to the political remit of NDR, where broadcasts are to 'support peace and German unity as well as to extol [the principle of] *social justice*'.[20]

Additional weight is given in the statutes of some ARD corporations to citizen and consumer advice, to the arts and above all to cultural diversity, especially in conjunction with regional diversity.[21] Similarly, BR is required to take into account 'the special character of Bavaria'.[22]

The extent to which the statutes regulating the public broadcasting corporations influenced the pluralism requirements for the emerging private sector depended on the political situation in each *Land*. In Saarland, where there is only one act for private and public broadcasting, the same pluralism principles apply to both.

According to the letter of the law, a pluralist output would also seem to be guaranteed in the private sector. In particular the requirements for local and regional diversity in nearly all the private broadcasting acts indicate the role for the private sector of concepts which have not yet been adequately realised by the public broadcasting corporations, especially in radio. However, the legislation seems difficult to implement in the private sector. Instead of pluralism being an end in itself, as it is in the public sector, these requirements are the price which the private sector has to pay in order to have a licence to make a profit by selling airtime.

The programming requirements for nation-wide private broadcasting are laid down in Article 9 of the 1987 Inter-*Land* Treaty. By and large, they mirror those in *Länder* legislation. The standard laid down in the Treaty is only a minimum standard, which can be increased by the *Land* issuing the licence. Furthermore, the provisions in the *Land* acts continue to apply to regional programmes.

All broadcasts are expected to support the 'free democratic order' and general criminal and civil laws, including youth protection. They are required to respect human dignity and the morality, religions and ideologies of other citizens; and they are expected to promote international understanding.

Information programmes, which are considered an integral part of general interest channels, have to be truthful, objective and comply with recognised journalistic standards. Fact and comment have to be kept separate; and a right of reply has to be guaranteed.

The Evangelical, Catholic and Jewish churches must be given 'adequate' airtime on request. During elections, party political broadcasts have to be allowed; and the time allocated to each party has to be proportional to the number of seats held in the parliament for which the election is being held.

Any general interest nation-wide programme channels 'ought' to contribute to the representation of pluralism within the German-speaking[23] and European cultures including 'an appropriate amount of information, culture and education'. They should contain 'an essential amount of in-house and commissioned productions, including German-language and European co-productions'. There is thus no formal obligation on private national broadcasters to offer cultural programming, although the terms of the Treaty naturally shape the requirements and expectations of the licensing authorities. The private broadcasting acts of Hamburg, Northrhine-Westfalia and Saarland contain nearly identical clauses which apply to all licensed general interest *Land* stations, and give the regulatory authority the right to lay down the requisite amounts.[24]

The private broadcasters have welcomed the lack of firm production quotas. They consider a quota system unfeasible in practice since their staple programming fare is television serials, most of which come from the USA. Their recent agreement to contribute £4 million over three years to the federal film/television production fund under the film/TV agreement[25] can therefore be seen either as a recognition of their cultural obligations, a goodwill gesture to placate politicians or an effort to acquire inexpensively future broadcasting rights to quality films, in an increasingly competitive market. Their contribution is still small, however, compared with the £18.7 million that the public broadcasters ARD and ZDF have pledged over the same period.[26]

Over and above these programming requirements, Hessen, Hamburg and Northrhine-Westfalia prefer licence applicants which grant the most statutory editorial freedom to their staff.[27] This should ensure that accepted journalistic ethics when reporting take precedence over any influence from the channel owners.

Youth protection

Article 10 of the Inter-*Land* Treaty contains identical youth protection provisions for the public and private broadcasters. One of the regulators' main concerns is the protection of minors. All programmes likely to pose a serious moral risk are banned. Any programmes, including music videos, that could prejudice the physical, moral or spiritual well-being of minors must either be encrypted or broadcast between 11pm and 6am. No feature film with a 16-certificate may be shown before 10pm; and no film with an 18-certificate before 11pm. The regulatory authorities or the public broadcasting councils may grant exemptions, especially if films are more than fifteen years old, or suitable cuts have been made. In its guidelines, ZDF assumes that exceptions are possible for films certificated more than five years earlier, or if the broadcasts are of exceptional information, documentary or cultural value.[28] It is unclear, however, whether these exceptions also apply to news and documentary reports.[29]

In practice, there is still some uncertainty in interpreting the youth protection rules. The Inter-*Land* Treaty is caught between two regulatory structures. One, for cinema films, provides a separate control regime for feature films, mainly through self-certification, and through secondary federal legislation for videos, and publishes an index of films banned for minors. The second, for broadcasting, was traditionally based on self-regulation. The federal criminal code also prohibits violence and pornography in the production, distribution and publication of written and audiovisual material.[30] The problem is how to regulate adequately the growing re-use of audiovisual products in different media, be they the cinema, video, television or pay-per-view broadcasts.

On the one hand, the youth protection and pornography prohibitions of the Inter-*Land* Treaty make explicit reference to the corresponding federal laws, but it is unclear whether these provisions then apply to all broadcasting, possibly thus censoring artistic expression. If so, can the regulatory authorities, which are accountable under administrative law, be entrusted with enforcing criminal law, even though this is normally done by the judiciary?[31] There is thus a danger of overlap between *Bund* and *Länder* jurisdictions, given the judiciary's more extensive powers than those of the authorities. If complaints against unsuitable programming are made directly to the federal prosecutor general (*Staatsanwalt*), the broadcasting authorities could lose their powers of self-determination.

This could happen as the regulatory authorities have interpreted the Treaty regulations in different ways. Before the Treaty was signed, all the *Länder* had realised that there was an increase in violence on private television, despite the various prohibitions in *Land* legislation. But each *Land* has its own standards of youth protection, which is hardly surprising since even experts disagree as to how people are influenced by the media. In principle, the broadcasters can make their own assessment of a particular programme, and the authorities only monitor a selection of all broadcasts. The private broadcasters insisted on their right to self-regulation and refused to allow voluntary pre-censorship by the authorities.[32] Given the conflicting regulatory opinions, the broadcasters tended to adopt the most liberal interpretation possible, and there have been a number of Treaty contraventions already.

Although pornography and violence on television did not originally dominate the West German regulatory debate, even conservative politicians who support private broadcasting are now beginning to be worried about some of its more erotic output, although the broadcasters try to meet the 11pm watershed for the more explicit programmes. The regulatory authorities, like the politicians, are therefore convinced of the value of the youth protection rules and have come to realise that 'hopes that the market would regulate itself are completely misplaced'.[33] A working party, consisting of three representatives of the regulatory authorities, a representative of the private broadcasters and an academic expert has been set up to resolve these differences.

Right of reply

In the *Länder* press acts, a right of reply (*Gegendarstellungsrecht*) has been customary; this was integrated into *Länder* broadcasting legislation, both public and private. The 1987 Inter-*Land* Treaty acknowledges that such a right or similar provisions have to be ensured for national, cable-relayed channels, but does not elaborate further, leaving its legal implementation entirely to the *Länder*.

A right of reply is granted to persons or organisations that are directly affected by a factual statement in a broadcast. The right of reply provisions do not necessarily serve to rectify wrongly reported facts, but the objective of the provision is wider in that it is intended to compensate for imbalances of information: as the Latin tag has it, *audiatur et paribus*. The persons or organisations affected have to demand their right in a written statement, addressed to the broadcasting station. The station is legally obliged to honour 'justifiable' demands by reading out the reply over the air free of charge, at the same scheduling slot where the original statement occurred. If the station refuses to broadcast the reply, the persons or organisations concerned can appeal to the administrative court to get an injunction; the regulatory authorities do not directly enforce this right.

The right of reply provisions are however more formal than of substantial importance. First, in law, every editor is obliged to pursue balanced reporting. Second, there is no guarantee that the reply will reach the same viewers and listeners who heard the original statement. And third, redress through the right of reply rules is limited. They only apply to persons or organisations that are wronged directly, i.e. those referred to in the broadcast in question. Other parties interested in advancing further arguments can only make use of the standard complaints procedures; or if they are influential enough, raise the matter with members of the regulatory bodies or the parliamentarians, who can then put pressure on the broadcasters.

All the private stations, both radio and television, applied for licences in the hope of making money by selling airtime. Along the way, they gave undertakings about the pluralist nature of their future programming. The manner in which the ideal of programming pluralism embodied in law is interpreted by the regulatory authorities, and the extent to which the authorities can monitor and control the organisation and the programmes of the private broadcasters, are the questions to which we now turn.

Chapter 4

From legislative theory to regulatory practice

The legislation in each of the *Länder* requires licensees to demonstrate that they can meet the necessary organisational and programming requirements. In addition, most *Länder* require proof of financial stability and a good business plan, in order to weed out applicants with a 'gold digger' mentality. These rules are frequently formulated in vague or blanket terms in the primary legislation, and their effectiveness is determined by the manner in which they are interpreted by the authorities.

Licence applications are requested in the 'official journals' of the respective *Länder*. The application includes the constitution of the applicant organisation, often approved by the federal anti-trust office, a business plan, and a detailed programme schedule. This is the basic document to which the terms of the licence refer.

The authorities do not have to publish the reason for awarding a specific licence, or the text of the licence itself. Since the award of a licence is an administrative act, a decision can be appealed before an administrative court. The court's powers are limited, however. If the authority claims one applicant was selected in preference because its programmes promised more pluralism of opinion, there is little the court can do. A complaint in Schleswig-Holstein, by Tele 5 against the licensing decision for RTL plus and SAT 1, was rejected by the administrative court.[1] But once a licence has been awarded this freedom can also permit the authority to turn a blind eye if economic pressures prevent the broadcaster from fulfilling his promises.

MONITORING

Licence review

Ideally, a regulatory authority needs a range of sanctions to monitor and regulate the programme output of a private broadcaster. The most draconian, and therefore often the least valuable, is the withdrawal or non-renewal of the licence. The conditions for licence renewal vary between the *Länder*.

As can be seen from the following table, except in Bavaria where trial legislation still applies, the maximum licence period in the *Länder* is ten years.

Baden-Württemberg:	The licence period is one to five years, with no explicit renewal provisions.
Bavaria:	The cable companies' contracts with the programme providers are reviewed after four years to enable a possible reorganisation of transmission facilities, and include newcomers. The current licence periods end in December 1992, the end of the trial law.
Berlin:	The cable licences are due for review by July 1990, the end of the trial; the terrestrial licences will end by 1994.
Bremen:	The licence period is two to ten years, with possibility of renewal.
Hamburg, Schleswig-Holstein:	The licence period is five to ten years, with the possibility of renewal.
Hessen:	The licence period is eight to ten years, with the possibility of a five-yearly renewal.
Lower Saxony:	The licence periods range from one to ten years in theory, but all broadcasters are licensed for ten years. There are no explicit provisions for renewal.

Northrhine-Westfalia:	The licence periods range from four to ten years, with no explicit renewal provisions.
Rhineland-Palatinate:	The licence period is ten years, with one review period after five years to enable reorganisation. The radio licences were reissued in 1990.
Saarland:	The standard licence period is ten years, with the possibility of renewal.

Most licences are allocated for the maximum period to allow the broadcasters sufficient time for economic planning and development. However, the disadvantage of long licence periods, often with unspecified renewal arrangements, is that they can keep out new broadcasters with alternative programme policies. The exception is Northrhine-Westfalia, where one of the two private terrestrial television broadcasters has been licensed for four years only, to make way for the third private DBS broadcaster, jointly licensed by Northrhine-Westfalia, Hessen, Bremen and Saarland, which it is hoped will be operational by 1992. The licence giving the greater reach has been awarded for ten years, however.

The minimum licence periods and the renewal provisions vary. Whether the current licensees will have their licences renewed will obviously depend on their record and the degree to which they co-operate with the regulatory authority. If, as seems likely, there are no proven alternatives, most authorities may simply renew the licences in order to maintain continuity.

At the end of its cable trial in 1992 Bavaria will draft new legislation, which could incorporate modifications to its licensing practices with possibly fewer formal pluralism demands. Baden-Württemberg, Hessen and Rhineland-Palatinate explicitly require a legislative review within four or five years to study the impact of legislation on pluralism and the private broadcasting market. These will be far more wide-ranging than an evaluation of the performance of an individual broadcaster, and could lead to modifications in the legal framework. They could also permit a review of new distribution capacities and supranational legislation. The overt reason for the review, however, is to compare performance against promise: 'Despite present experience with private broadcasting in other federal *Länder*, the *Land* legislators still have to rely upon forecasts when licensing private broadcasters and evaluating progress in the broadcast sector.'[2]

Although Hamburg, Northrhine-Westfalia and Schleswig-Holstein do not require a review, they make explicit provisions for media research, the outcome of which could well influence their monitoring and relicensing practices.

The authorities' monitoring powers

The duties of the regulatory authorities do not end when the broadcasting licences have been awarded. They also have to monitor the broadcasters' behaviour. This presents them with quite a different set of problems.

Except in Bavaria, the regulators have no powers to vet broadcasts before distribution; all control is *post facto*, and all broadcasters are therefore obliged by *Land* law to keep copies of their broadcasts for six weeks. Given the large number of local radio, cable and terrestrial television stations, their opt-outs, and the open access channels, only the two largest authorities, Northrhine-Westfalia and Bavaria, are able to monitor the programme services on a continuous basis. The others have to rely on sampling, where most effort is concentrated on the control of advertising rules (see Chapter 6) and youth protection. Programme diversity and quality tend to be neglected because they cannot be judged by a fixed yardstick.

The laws in some *Länder* provide a graded range of formal reprimands or orders by the authority to stop contraventions. Others are less sophisticated. Although the awards of licences and official orders to modify behaviour are administrative acts, regulated by public law, there are different ways of enforcing them. Official orders are normally always preceded by informal bargaining. Sanctions are meted out by the regulatory authority, except in Lower Saxony where the government administration has the executive power. The appeal procedures are highly formalised. If an appeal by the broadcaster to the regulatory authority is rejected in the first instance, the remaining stages are handled by the administrative courts.

Most authorities can impose financial penalties. The maximum fine, specified by law, is generally £16,700 (DM 50,000), but the authority specifies the amount and enforces collection. Only in a few *Länder*, however, can fines be used against a failure to fulfil the pluralism requirements. They are normally imposed for misinformation, or delays in obeying official orders. Sometimes, the authority has the additional power to require a persistent offender to suspend either the entire service, or part of it. In Bavaria and Northrhine-Westfalia, moreover, the offending broadcaster may be required by the authority to announce its reprimand and punishment over the air.

A few authorities, such as Lower Saxony, have no intermediate sanctions of this nature, but have to regulate with only the threat of licence withdrawal, which appears far less effective than financial penalties. Although each law permits the licence to be withdrawn, this sanction is a blunt instrument because it requires severe and repeated offences before it can be justified in court, and so can involve cumbersome administrative procedures. Furthermore, the regulators are reluctant to have an empty frequency on their hands, since this could bring them into conflict with the media policies of the *Land* governments. It is not surprising, therefore, that most private broadcasters in the FRG are convinced that they will never have their licences withdrawn as a sanction.

The authorities must approve permanent changes in the programme output, especially changes affecting broadcasting hours. Northrhine-Westfalia is the only *Land* where this is explicitly stated in law, but all other *Länder* acts require the broadcaster generally to give the authority any information which it needs to fulfil its licensing and monitoring duties. The official criterion for approval is whether the changes affect editorial pluralism, but economic and political considerations also influence the decisions taken.

The respective views of the authorities as to what constitutes a contravention of the licensing terms vary; the Inter-*Land* Treaty has not brought the solution. It merely states that for national broadcasts contraventions have to be dealt with in co-operation with the original licensing authority, which may not recognise the problem however. For example, Pro 7 had to apply for a new cable licence from the West Berlin authority to change from a thematic news channel into a general entertainment channel, although its original licensing authority in Schleswig-Holstein had accepted the change. But Tele 5 was allowed by Bavaria to switch from a music channel to a general interest channel without changing its old licence. The West Berlin authority also refused to allow

Eurosport to replace Sky Channel on its cable networks, on the grounds that Sky Television needed a separate cable licence for its sports channel, for which it had not applied in time. (At the same time, Berlin's refusal allowed Kirch's German-language pay-TV channel to enter the crowded Berlin cable network.) Other authorities have, however, continued to allow Eurosport on their cable networks.

In practice, most contraventions are not clear cut. In these cases, it is difficult to obtain a majority for formal sanctions on the pluralist boards, since their heterogeneity and inexperience often leads to politically cautious decisions in order to avoid conflict. The problem in enforcing these reprimands is that the broadcasters merely tend to make cosmetic changes, which meet the letter, but not the spirit, of the reprimand. The authority is then forced to reprimand several times. It is therefore standing practice to rely largely on informal and repeated talks with the broadcasters to obtain the desired regulatory goal, or at least to reach a compromise, which is possible because of the flexibility incorporated into most of the acts.

CONTROLLING ORGANISATIONAL PLURALISM

The problem which faced the regulators was that the 'ideal' external model presupposed an unlimited number of channels, which were clearly not available in the FRG either in economic or technical terms. In contrast, pluralism through internal organisation is more appropriate when there are only a few channels; these were the circumstances in which the model originally developed. The authorities have basically adopted two ways of allocating their limited channel capacity. One licensed the broadcasting organisation which promised the highest degree of pluralism. The other was a concession to external pluralism, and granted a licence to every applicant organisation which fulfilled minimum requirements. In this model, the airtime was divided between all the applicants; the airtime allocated to each depended on its supposed contribution to pluralism.

Problems have arisen in implementing policy in the internally pluralist broadcast organisation which complements or replaces the external pluralist model in most *Länder*. Most large broadcasting organisations have several partners. In this way, the broadcaster could simplify the initial need to raise capital, but,

significantly, it could also help it to satisfy the pluralism requirements. Licence applicants stood a better chance if they could attract
local partners.

According to the Constitutional Court and the relevant laws,
organisational pluralism is deemed to exist provided no partner
can exert a dominant influence over editorial content. The criteria
for a dominant influence are quantitative thresholds which limit
to a given percentage the capital, voting and/or supplies of
programmes by any one partner. The figures vary according to
the interpretation of 'dominant influence' by the *Land* concerned.
The figure of fifty per cent in the Inter-*Land* Treaty is the lowest
common denominator. Hessen, with ten per cent, has the narrowest
interpretation. The requirement for a pluralist organisation may be
waived however if a broadcaster occupies only a part of a frequency,
as does Tele 5 in Hamburg and Northrhine-Westfalia, or if the
threshold for external pluralism is reached.

In order to prevent editorial domination by one or a few
large partners, another, often supplementary, way of establishing
organisational pluralism is to require an internal programming
committee. RTL plus established an advisory programming committee at the request of the authority in Northrhine-Westfalia,
made up mainly of representatives of its own shareholders. But
the committee's powers over editorial policy are minimal. SAT
1 received a licence along the same lines, but refused to set up a
similar committee since it felt it limited its editorial and economic
freedom. The same was true for the first private *Land*-wide radio
broadcaster in Lower Saxony which the authority unsuccessfully
tried to persuade to establish a programming committee. It
possessed no formal power to enforce its request because it could
not prove the dominant influence of one partner, even though it
considered that output did not meet its expectations.

In *Länder* as diverse as Bavaria, Bremen, and Northrhine-
Westfalia, the legislation also aims to secure adequate outlets
for local cultural groups. The major broadcast licensees, or
cable companies in Bavaria, were therefore required by law to
accommodate within their organisation any such groups and their
programmes, as approved by the relevant authority. But most of
the organisational requirements were not explicitly specified in
the licence, but inferred from the broadcasting acts themselves
which often contain blanket terms. Thus, the regulators have
continually had to compromise to solve the contradictions between

entrepreneurial freedom and their regulatory responsibilities.

Baden-Württemberg, Bavaria, Northrhine-Westfalia, Rhineland-Palatinate and West Berlin reconciled the principle of external pluralism with the scarcity of terrestrial frequencies by specifying the number and type of broadcasters to be licensed for a given frequency or splitting it between the largest possible number of suitable applicants. But generally the authorities wanted the various broadcasters to come to some arrangement on the scheduling of their allocated broadcast hours and financial responsibilities, including the division of transmitter costs. Only if no arrangement was forthcoming did the authorities allocate the hours themselves. Where because of frequency splitting a uniform channel identity could not be achieved, this naturally upset both the broadcasters and their audiences, and led in turn to a shortfall in advertising revenue.

Amendments to the private broadcasting acts in Bavaria and Baden-Württemberg reflect the regulators' concern with this problem. The amended Baden-Württemberg act now stipulates that, as a rule, the authority should select the broadcaster which promises the highest possible degree of pluralism, including 'the highest anticipated proportion of in-house broadcasts on the political, social and cultural life in the coverage area'.[3] The authority may only split the broadcast channel if this guarantees individual broadcasters sufficient advertising finance. Similarly, the Bavarian authority is now explicitly required to ensure that the contracts between cable companies and programme providers are economically viable.[4]

The situation in Rhineland-Palatinate became especially precarious when the four private Land-wide radio broadcasters, which shared the same frequency, made heavy losses, thereby threatening the survival of the four stations necessary for external pluralism.[5] Had only one organisation gone bankrupt, not only would the channel have been silent for most of the day, but also the other broadcasters would have had to meet far more stringent programming requirements. The authority has now re-allocated the frequency to a single broadcast organisation which incorporates three of the former stations. Effectively, internal pluralism has taken over, with the ensuing dangers that the financially strongest partner will determine the programme profile, or that previously distinct programme profiles will merge into a middle-of-the-road service.

More often than not, economic criteria can determine channel allocation, hence narrow external pluralism. Two of the three DBS channels available to German private broadcasters have been allocated to RTL plus and SAT 1, which are also the two main private terrestrial television companies. They occupy prominent positions in all cable networks and can be received directly on Astra dishes. This quadriplication came from a trade-off between the needs of the private broadcasters to build up their audience base quickly, the *Länder*'s *Standortpolitik* desires, and federal government pressure to license satellite broadcasters in order to try out new distribution technologies ahead of foreign competition. Theoretically, once cable and direct-to-home reception reaches the same number of homes as the private terrestrial frequencies, the latter could be freed for other providers. This is unlikely to happen however before the present licences expire, and only if there are other viable candidates offering general interest channels.

To prevent such a narrowing of external pluralism and market access right from the start, Northrhine-Westfalia and Hamburg both licensed Tele 5 as a third terrestrial TV broadcaster. A third or fourth private television frequency will not be available until the mid-1990s and then only reach a maximum of twenty per cent of the population, unless a substantial number of frequencies can be freed following German unification and a reduction in the Allies' communication needs. Tele 5 has therefore had to share its transmissions with the RTL plus and SAT 1, but at less profitable times, i.e. during lunchtimes and at night hours. In Hamburg Tele 5 was also obliged to produce a local magazine to obtain a licence at all. Its transmission costs are disproportionate to its income. Nevertheless, by complying with the split frequency arrangements, Tele 5 will be able to substantiate its claim to be the third national private television station in any future licence applications.

In Northrhine-Westfalia another problem occurred with frequencies shared with RTL plus and SAT 1. There, two individual *Land*-wide broadcasters, DCTP[6] and Tele West,[7] were also licensed. The thinking was to give smaller, as yet untried indigenous stations a chance to establish themselves, in order to be ready to apply for a full-time licence at a later date. For technical reasons, their programmes were relayed nationally via cable, using the RTL plus and SAT 1 satellite channels. This particularly irked conservative regulators, not only because it was allegedly illegal to have *Land*-wide services distributed nationally without a licence, but also because the leftist magazine *Der Spiegel* produced a political magazine under the DCTP umbrella. However, RTL plus, which at first only accepted this regulatory imposition *force majeure*, now recognises its value since it improved its programme profile for viewers and regulators.

RTL plus also agreed with the authority in Northrhine-Westfalia to provide a regular slot for two small 'alternative' local programme providers. This was described in the licence as promoting local cultural and social interests. The relationship between the programme providers and RTL plus is regulated by a contract approved by the authority, but which also gives RTL plus editorial responsibility. In 1989, RTL plus cancelled its contract with one of the providers, Kanal 4, an association of video and documentary film makers, on the grounds that Kanal's reporting contravened the free democratic order which all broadcasters are required by law to uphold. RTL plus also claimed that Kanal 4's reporting was unbalanced, and its internal programming council allegedly agreed. Moreover, the West Berlin authority had questioned the legality of distributing Kanal 4 nation-wide.

Kanal 4, in turn, appealed to the Northrhine-Westfalian authority, which noted that RTL plus was in breach of contract, since its editorial responsibility had given it the means to vet and edit the broadcast before it went out.[8] Finally, RTL plus limited the transmission of Kanal 4's offerings to Northrhine-Westfalia, the statutory coverage area. The higher technical costs that such a move involved were then subsidised by the regulatory authority from its infrastructure budget.

All private national television broadcasters themselves now demand clear and uniform rules on opt-outs, not just *Land*-wide, but nationally, so that the high technical costs can be reduced and a consistent programme profile made possible, without interrupting programme flows that vary from *Land* to *Land*.

The Bavarian regulatory authority also had to balance economic viability against organisational diversity and the precedence given to pluralism by the Bavarian Constitutional Court. Various judgements by Bavarian administrative courts, and by its Constitutional Court, made it crystal clear that the Bavarian authority's responsibilities were not, unlike all the other authorities', limited to the co-ordination and control of the licensees. When a channel was divided between several licensed broadcasters, the authority was obliged to secure balanced pluralism within the overall channel output, whereas balance is automatically assumed to exist under the model of external pluralism in other *Länder* once there are several private stations. The Bavarian authority's powers, which must be used if necessary, extended to determining the broadcast schedule. This must be given priority over the market freedom of individual programme providers. This ruling may well cause conflict with the cable companies, which schedule and distribute the programmes offered and are interested in ensuring that their providers are commercially viable, since their own income depends on that.

In its judgement of 27 May 1987, the Bavarian Constitutional Court ruled that economic questions must not determine the authority's decisions on how to 'create *its* programme service', or how to modify it according to the economic fortunes of individual programme providers. Although entertainment programmes attracted more advertising revenue than educational programmes, this must not influence its licensing decisions.[9] A later decision of the Bavarian Administrative Court modified this judgement. The authority did have to consider the economic consequences of its programming decisions after all. It had to create equal financial conditions for all providers. Otherwise the smaller programme providers, especially those with unconventional offerings (the complaint was brought by a jazz service provider), would dry up and reduce the programme choice available.[10] The Court thus recommended that the authority should pool and redistribute the advertising revenues generated by all broadcasters using the same channel.

The Bavarian regulatory authority is now caught between trying to create a viable advertising market, and the Court's requirement to ensure that the smaller unconventional broadcasters survive. Future licensing decisions will have to try to resolve this conflict. Future practice would then be to license only a few financially strong programme providers that would have to give specific undertakings as to the nature of their programme output. The legal requirement to offer access to local cultural and social non-profit organisations might be fulfilled if the regulatory authority purchased, or ordered the purchase of, a quota of material from these organisations which could be included in those programme channels which lacked them. It would certainly have the power and money to do so.

CONTROLLING EDITORIAL PLURALISM

Once a licence has been granted, the authorities' major problem is to decide how to enforce positive programming requirements without being accused of unconstitutional editorial interference and hampering commercial success. This is where the authorities have to take care, since the governments of all *Länder* are now committed to establishing private broadcasting. Each authority has to decide how to respect this commitment, even if the legal rationale of increased pluralism suffers.

The enforcement of pluralism in programme content is all the more difficult since there is no agreed definition of a comprehensive, general interest programme channel, even though the whole principle of pluralism revolves around this concept. The problem is essentially one of monitoring, since the authority can only base its decision to award a licence upon the promised programme schedule. Experience in other countries has shown, however, that programming promises are unlikely to be fully kept by the licensees, and German authorities have had the same experience.

The Lower Saxony authority, which had licensed only one *Land*-wide radio station, felt there was too much music and not enough information and advice in the station's output. But it ran into difficulties with its definition of the four requisite elements of information, advice, entertainment and education, especially as the Constitutional Court had said that less stringent standards should apply to private broadcasters than to the public channels.

Even Bavaria, which has the widest powers to regulate editorial policy, finds it difficult to implement its concept of pluralism. For example, the authority's radio programming policy failed in Munich, where twenty-nine programme providers share five frequencies. Although the frequencies were relicensed in an attempt to create five distinct programme services, the general formats, mainstream pop and disco plus oldies, and the deliberately casual and often unprofessional style of presentation, are felt to be virtually identical, except at certain times when there are different choices, such as an evening jazz slot. But audiences find it hard to track down these special programmes because of the shortage of programming information on the many different services that occupy the same frequency. The Munich stations want to make money, and to do this they programme for the widest possible range of 16 to 40 year olds. Ironically, it is the CSU politicians who promoted private broadcasting who now complain about the lack of identifiably Bavarian culture in radio.[11]

Nevertheless, in 1987, when the pluralist board was asked to approve the only Bavarian private *Land*-wide radio, most of the board members, led by the churches, rejected its proposed schedule because it didn't have enough business and religious programmes; and the contract with the cable company did not satisfy the church representatives. The board also rejected a proposal by the authority's executive to demand merely a 'due proportion' of religious broadcasts.[12] In subsequent negotiations with the Munich cable company, which was the programme organiser, the churches' detailed demands were met.

The Lower Saxony act also requires that the churches get a 'due proportion' of programme time. The same wording was used in the NDR act. But unlike NDR, where the churches are directly represented on the broadcasting council, and can therefore ensure adequate time, the private broadcasters tend to interpret the phrase 'due proportion' at as low a level as possible. The churches now feel they fare best through informal negotiations with the broadcasters, rather than formally by legal means. In 1987, the Evangelical Church in Lower Saxony spent £327,000 on about sixty-five minutes a week of private radio broadcasts, but only £133,000, less than half that figure, to place four hours of material each week on NDR, which also has a larger coverage.[13]

Similarly, there was no way that the requirements for a 'due' proportion of European and German in-house productions or information programming could be enforced. Media politicians and regulators tended to reject production quotas as these could hamper the economic viability of the private television channels. Even the SPD-led authorities do not prescribe quotas, although nationally the party has tended to advocate them. The regulators rely on the assumption that the need to produce a general interest programme will be self-regulating. This remains to be seen. It may be so if the additional finance injected into quality programming brings higher ratings. Meanwhile, the head of programmes at RTL plus is reported to have said of commercial television: 'Whoever believes in beauty, the good and the truth must not make television.'[14]

As yet, quality is at a premium. In-house productions, including commissions and co-productions and productions using preproduced material, accounted for thirty-five per cent of SAT 1 and forty per cent of RTL plus programmes, compared with around seventy per cent for the public TV stations. The series shown on private TV are nearly all made in the USA (SAT 1 has started to commission its own German series), but the origins of feature films varied, with a higher proportion of (older) German films and less US product on SAT 1 than on the two main public channels. The main film output on RTL plus came from Italy, followed by Germany.[15]

Most of the private broadcasters' in-house material consists of information or education programmes, but it does not have to be broadcast at any specific times. During prime time in 1989, between 7pm and 11pm, only fifteen per cent of the broadcasts of RLT plus and six per cent of those of SAT 1 were information programmes, compared with thirty-three and forty-nine per cent for ARD and ZDF. RTL plus tried to develop a strategy of improving the quality of its output, while SAT 1 was noted to exclude any items from its news broadcasts which covered the political situation critically. But the information programmes of all stations were mostly US-style 'infotainment', which mixes soft news in a magazine format with minimal background information. This makes it even more difficult for the regulators to ensure an adequate supply of information programmes. However, in 1989 the private TV stations offered over four times more light entertainment output including music than ARD and ZDF.[16]

Tele 5 made a conscious effort to be thought of as a general interest television station. While its mainstay was music videos, it stepped up its news output and introduced more sports programmes than either RTL plus or SAT 1; and it offered more children's TV than even the public stations.[17] But although the range of programme categories may have improved, the programme quality remained the same. With its new programme philosophy, it wants to win some of the more lucrative future terrestrial licences by showing itself to be more pluralist. However, there are also self-regulatory pressures of the market, since its present 16–30 audience profile is expected to fall by a couple of millions by the year 2000, requiring a more balanced diet to attract a more varied audience.

In some *Länder*, legislation is more demanding than the Inter-*Land* Treaty, and requires specific local and/or regional cultural output from the licensees. Hessen and Lower Saxony, for example, require 'the representation of political, economic, social and cultural life' in the *Land*, or special local opt-outs.[18] This is how they interpret the idea of federalism.

It is extremely difficult for the regulatory authorities to write positive programming obligations into the licences, since there is very little provision for this in the private broadcasting laws themselves. Experience has shown however that special programming obligations, such as local opt-outs or cultural output, must not only be written into the licence but, to be enforceable, the licence should specify start times, broadcast hours, localities to be covered and elements to be included. The broadcasting acts generally leave the implementation of the licensing terms to the authorities or the broadcasters themselves. But the regulators have had to realise that there are no hard and fast standards against which to measure output in private broadcasting, which has made their monitoring tasks more difficult.

PLURALISM REGULATION VERSUS ECONOMIC REGULATION

It is clear, then, that attempts by the regulatory authorities to ensure pluralism in their licensed programme services can adversely affect a broadcaster's chances of profitability, or in some cases, survival. Economic problems are naturally most severe where legislators have relied on local radio to achieve pluralism, as it is comparatively cheap and offers the largest potential for diversity. By contrast, private television, with its more limited transmission facilities, has been far more concentrated right from the beginning. Positive efforts to achieve organisational pluralism have been few, but the economic policies of the *Länder* played an important role in licensing decisions.

Private broadcasting is expected to play a key role in *Land* economic policy, even if it has meant sacrificing a diversity of players. Licensees were selected accordingly, whether this was explicitly stated in the broadcasting legislation or not. For DBS applicants, a *Land* licence was often dependent on substantial investment in production facilities. The invitation for licence applications issued in Northrhine-Westfalia required the second terrestrial television chain to be allocated to a joint enterprise already licensed as a DBS broadcaster, 'which will carry out an essential part of the studio operations for its television service in Northrhine-Westfalia'.[19] The private broadcasting act in Bremen also gives preference to applicants who 'are willing to promote production facilities for radio, television and film in the *Land* of Bremen';[20] and the Hessen private broadcasting law, passed at the end of 1988, was inspired by the fear of missing out on boosting its small media industry.[21] But only powerful media groups can make such promises. Tele 5, which wants to become the third national terrestrial private television channel, accused the authorities of opportunism and in-trading for preferring companies with the largest economic and political clout.[22]

Meanwhile, it has become clear that many *Standortpolitik* hopes of the politicians were premature; once a station had obtained the licence it would soon move to the most favourable location for its production and administration units. For example, the Berlin cable trial act gave preference to such private terrestrial broadcasters as promised to locate extensive production facilities in the city.[23] In order to obtain a terrestrial licence in West Berlin, therefore, SAT 1 made huge media-economic promises, as it did in other *Länder*, but did not keep them despite repeated reprimands from the regulatory authority's executive board and the Berlin parliament. When the SPD/Green coalition government came to power in 1989, the executive board, although it had a CDU/FDP majority, finally announced the withdrawal of SAT 1's terrestrial licence, apparently confirming SAT 1 criticism that the broadcasting policy of the new government was commercially unrealistic.[24] After even more substantial promises from the satellite station, SAT 1 was eventually allowed to keep its licence. However, SAT 1's decision did not result primarily from regulatory pressure. It complied with the demands because it did not want to lose the new market opportunities offered by the reunification of the two halves of the city. At the same time, Hamburg, where the station had also promised to locate its production facilities, would lose out.

The regulators have also realised that only financially sound broadcasters can contribute to their economies at all. In some *Länder* this meant privileging large *Land*-wide stations. The importance of economic licensing criteria became once again evident in West Berlin. During its cable trial, the city had an open-for-all licensing policy, and the regulatory authority there had no legal power to prevent broadcasters which could not guarantee regular broadcasts from acquiring a licence. The authority expected pluralism to be regulated largely by market forces. It did try to ensure the diversity of services promised by many smaller applicants, and opened up cable television channels for them especially. Even so, about a third of the original television licence holders and half the radio licence holders failed to get on air, went out of business, or merged with competitors. The concentration process was intensified when the authority first encouraged joint ventures, and then allocated the one terrestrial TV channel and the two terrestrial radio frequencies to those broadcasters that were economically most important for West Berlin.[25]

The Bavarian and Baden-Württemberg authorities had problems in marrying their legislative philosophy of the broadest possible diversity of local stations with the need to have a sound financial base. The executive board in Baden-Württemberg had to accept the proposal by the private radio broadcasters to allow the joint operation of several frequencies; and syndication of programmes and advertisements for certain stations. A revision of the broadcasting act, passed a month after the board's decision, made it statutory. Now, programme material can even be distributed by satellite to several radio stations which, although legally independent, form a quasi-network for the satellite distributor; but such networks do not require a broadcast licence.

The Baden-Württemberg authority hoped that its acceptance of non-local sustaining services would induce the broadcasters to concentrate their efforts on local issues. The radios were showing a strong local emphasis because this is where they could compete with public radio. Whether this will last in future, when all the licence-holders have started broadcasting, and coverage overlaps, remains to be seen. If such sustaining services are delivered free in return for the acceptance by the local radios of national brand advertising, as is often the case, the local radios may be inclined to reduce staffing levels and operating capital to a minimum. If this happened, a reduction in both the quantity and quality of locally diverse programme outputs would be inevitable. The Baden-Württemberg regulators admit to a certain helplessness in preventing concentration in programme output, although they realise that this may erode Baden-Württemberg's media policy, which was explicitly designed to create a competitive broadcasting market in order to strengthen medium-sized businesses.

From the ninety local private radio channels originally envisaged in Bavaria, only fifty are expected to be viable, most of which have already been licensed. The authority gradually had to allow neighbouring stations to merge. It had also permitted networks to be built up, which is possible in Bavaria because the same company can hold an unlimited number of local radio licences, provided the service cannot be received in neighbouring areas. The authority was accused of lacking stringent control,[26] but the director of the Munich cable company went further and blamed the entire approach to pluralism adopted by the regulatory authority. Instead of trying to establish diversity by using all the available frequencies, he argued that it should have first defined the local coverage areas that were commercially profitable and then co-ordinated the available frequencies accordingly.[27] Finally, the authority relented and allowed syndication and networking, mainly because pressures towards concentration also emanated from the sole *Land*-wide radio in Bavaria which had been licensed after the local radios.

The authority became more careful in organising local and *Land*-wide TV opt-outs, which are required as part of the private terrestrial television licences. After an economic feasibility study, it ruled that local opt-out licences would only be allowed in areas where technical reach and economic conditions could ensure a channel's financial viability. In so doing, it effectively denied any local coverage at all to some areas. It is questionable whether this policy is commensurate with its public service responsibilities, which demand homogeneous universal coverage. The authority also agreed to prescribe broadcast times and periods for the local TV opt-outs. In doing so, it had to balance economic criteria against the aspirations and investments of many small, experimentally licensed television providers.

As a result of such experiences, the authorities now require broadcasters and new licence applicants to advise them of any outside programme material supplied by other stations or programme distributors. *A priori*, an authority cannot legally prevent a broadcaster from using outside material, as this would infringe the station's editorial freedom. All it can do is to specify a minimum of local broadcasts to be produced in-house, and try to enforce this as best as it can. However, it would probably not withdraw the licence because there are few, if any, alternative broadcasters that are strong enough financially and do not belong to one of the larger German media groups.

The two-column model   In Northrhine-Westfalia, the legislators have developed a unique model which aims to secure simultaneously both editorial pluralism and adequate advertising revenues. This is the so-called 'two-column model'. Licences are awarded to local non-profit associations. They are responsible for a pluralist editorial policy, which an independent editor implements on a daily basis. However, they are all linked by contract to commercial operating companies (*Betriebsgesellschaften*) which manage the stations and generate their revenues through the sale of airtime. Importantly, each station has a local monopoly. The *Land*'s private broadcasting act originally provided for fifty-four radio stations, one for each local administrative unit. But it had to be revised after protests about the uneconomic size of the coverage areas by the newspaper publishers, which were intended to be the founder members of the operating companies. The act now stipulates that the area to be covered by a local station is the administrative unit, 'provided transmission capacities and local conditions permit economically effective broadcasting. Otherwise, different coverage areas have to be stipulated.'[28] After commissioning a feasibility study on the local stations in the administrative units, the regulatory authority finally merged some areas, and reduced the target number to forty-five.

During the first five years, only some twenty-five to thirty of these are expected to be viable.[29] The economic viability of the whole concept is also questionable, however. Even if the expensive transmitter rentals are all absorbed by the regulatory authority, the stations can, to start with, only expect advertising when they can reach sixty to seventy per cent of the population.[30] There may also be competition between overlapping areas. This is why the viability of the local stations has had to be increased by linking them into a network of *Land*-wide programme and advertising supplies. Two sustaining companies have been licensed, one a subsidiary of Kanal 4; the other, which will probably be more successful, is Radio NRW, a joint venture between the same newspaper publishers that own the operating companies, Bertelsmann, the Northrhine-Westfalian media giant, and WDR radio.

The two-column model may be difficult to implement in practice, since it suffers from an inbuilt contradiction between the idealism of the programme policy makers, and the necessary commercial orientation of the operating company. Thus it proved difficult, for the local radio associations in Northrhine-Westfalia to find an operating company, without which they would not be licensed. The two Hamburg local radios which followed the two-column model both ran into financial difficulties, and one of them went out of business altogether. Following the referral of the Northrhine-Westfalian broadcasting act to the Constitutional Court by the CDU and FDP *Bundestag* faction, the Court declared the two-column model constitutional. However, this is bound to conflict with the decision by the anti-cartel authorities which decided against Radio NRW (see Chapter 6). Such judiciary wrangles create uncertainty and can jeopardise the chances of the local radios surviving.

Most authorities intent on local variety have had to bow to the economic realities of the broadcasting market. Despite the elaborate model in Northrhine-Westfalia, the broadcasting act had already to be amended. As long as a local radio association has not been licensed, the *Land*-wide programme suppliers can occupy the local frequencies for up to six months.[31] In practice the two-column model may well turn out to resemble another *Land*-wide station with local opt-outs, beside the five run by WDR.

Many media politicians are now disillusioned with the policy of pluralism. Hopes that growth in the larger commercial stations would stimulate a greater variety of output have proved ill-founded; and small radio stations have failed commercially, for a mixture of commercial and regulatory reasons. The failure of Radio 107 in Hamburg is typical. It was partly attributable to the Hamburg authority which allocated its first licence to Radio Hamburg, which was owned by a consortium of financially strong publishers. The company used its head start to monopolise nearly all the available advertising in the very competitive Hamburg market, which is covered not only by NDR but also by the two private radios in Schleswig-Holstein and Lower Saxony with which Radio Hamburg set up a joint sales operation. Radio 107 was unable to develop an appropriate marketing strategy to counter this, partly because of the heterogeneous mix of large media groups and small industrial interests on its board. When Radio 107 had to close down, it was already offering, according to a study conducted by the Hans-Bredow-Institut in Hamburg, a broad spectrum of cultural programmes, which compared favourably with other available commercial programming.[32]

Clearly, the survival of a pluralist radio landscape also requires the regulators not to distort inadvertently the competitive situation in their local market. Hit 103, a commercial radio in West Berlin, had similar problems with an overcompetitive advertising market, although it was financially powerful since it was owned by media conglomerates such as Springer and RTL. It, too, was licensed only after its main commercial rival was up and running. Despite revamping its programming strategy, and even its name, it lost money and had to close down. As in Hamburg, the lack of a common editorial philosophy among rival shareholders intensified its financial problems. Here too, the regulatory authority had failed to foresee these problems. Ironically, it is doubtful whether the demise of Hit 103 with its undistinctive output of music and news led to a decline in editorial pluralism.[33] Instead, Radio 100, an alternative left radio station, has profited from its demise by taking the station's frequency, on which it already occupied a slot, for twenty-four hours a day.

In Lower Saxony and Schleswig-Holstein, where second *Land*-wide private radio stations have been licensed, there is some doubt as to whether there will be enough finance to help establish them as competitors for the private radios which have been up and running for several years. Saarland and Northrhine-Westfalia explicitly avoided such a competition between private *Land*-wide radios by handing over the available second chain of frequencies to the public broadcasters, along with certain obligations to co-operate with local non-profit broadcasters.

The concerns for financial stability can work against access by radio stations which are not financed by advertising and which some politicians consider ideologically suspect. Although one alternative station, Radio Z, was licensed in Bavaria after many problems, another alternative applicant in Munich, Radio Lora, was refused a licence on the grounds that the station could not guarantee the steady revenue flow required.[34] It unsuccessfully challenged the authority's decision in court. Only a few alternative radio stations have been licensed at all, apart from Radio Z, one each in West Berlin and Freiburg, under conservative governments, and two in Hamburg under its SPD/FDP government. In the latter *Land*, however, one alternative radio was forced to close down because it could not survive under market conditions.

THE EFFECTIVENESS OF THE REGULATORY AUTHORITIES

The provisions in the broadcasting acts can only be effective if the authorities have both the will and the power to enforce them. But their power to enforce the public interest in private broadcasting has been limited, either by law or in practice.[35] The Constitutional Court and the broadcasting acts have only laid down a general normative framework but no specific standards against which to judge pluralism in the private sector. When most of the private broadcasting acts were passed, few legislators or governments in any of the *Länder* had any clear idea of the respective roles of private and public broadcasters within a pluralist society. Instead, they accepted the economic and technological pull of cable and satellite broadcasting. Of the politicians who promoted private broadcasting, many also hoped to promote their own political interests. Because of their inexperience with the practicalities of broadcasting regulation, the broadcasting acts contain general phrases and omissions which have to be resolved through regulatory practice or, in some cases, eventually amended.

The pluralist boards possess wide-ranging powers of interpretation of the concept of pluralism, but legally they do not possess the editorial powers necessary to co-ordinate a comprehensive long-term broadcasting strategy. The one exception is Bavaria, but there 'interventionism' is politically an anathema. Interestingly, it is here that there have been most court cases, precisely because the authority's editorial responsibilities have clashed with the economics of the marketplace. In the other *Länder*, once the licensees have been selected, the authorities' control powers are mainly supervisory and reactive, rather than formative. The legal means which they have to remedy infringements can only yield piecemeal short-term solutions.

Some regulators are happy with their lack of formal powers; this allows for private negotiation and avoids public confrontation. Unlike the public broadcasting councils, their separation from the broadcasting organisations gives them the freedom to be more objective, without the fear of offending political friends. Their regulatory reputation depends on being seen as independent and on their determination to force through public-service ideals within the new economic framework. In this regard, authorities in SPD-led *Länder* appear to be more determined, if not necessarily more efficient, than those in the conservative *Länder*. Frequently, however, there is a feeling of helplessness given the lacunae in the laws and the dynamics of the marketplace. This often leads to a 'wait and see' attitude among the pluralist boards.

The scope for regulation designed to encourage pluralism is

being progressively eroded in favour of market-led decisions. Sometimes, as in Hamburg, a regulator may be disillusioned and cynical.

> For myself, the theme of pluralism was of secondary importance . . . .[R]ight from the start, I predicted the discrepancy between the [licence] application and reality. I also knew that we would get one-sided programming. I was right: Applications and reality do indeed differ.[36]

The regulators tend not to discuss the meaning of pluralism. They rely instead on organisational or economic criteria, or on the market.

> The Cable Council [West Berlin supervisory board] has very rarely discussed the basic meaning of pluralism [*Vielfalt*]; in fact it took rather the form . . . of remarks by the other members that one must not regulate what is on offer, but that this is to be left to the laws of the market . . . All in all, there is plenty of latitude and freedom; as the motto says: 'Let us not be more catholic than the Pope.'[37]

Despite the demand by the Constitutional Court for *Länder* co-ordination, and the apparently co-operative nature of the 1987 Inter-*Land* Treaty, the individual economic interests and broadcasting philosophies of the *Länder* often take precedence over co-ordinated regulation. Consequently, major differences remain between the *Länder* in licensing and monitoring nation-wide stations. These undermine effective national regulation. Slowly but surely, the economics of the marketplace are taking over from the pluralist authorities as the prime regulator of private broadcasting. Apart from the public corporations, the only patches of pluralism in this purely commercial landscape are the alternative radio stations and open access channels which just manage to survive at the margins.

Chapter 5

Alternative forms of broadcasting in the FRG

A measure of the pluralism within a broadcasting system which claims to operate in the public interest must be its openness to the public. The West German philosophy of public control through representative bodies has traditionally prevented direct access by a number of citizens and groups to that 'medium and factor' of public life, the medium of broadcasting, be it over the air or by cable. The idea of granting access to social groups which are under-represented in public life reaches back to Weimar Germany and the early days of radio, when Bertolt Brecht envisaged that radio could 'organise its listeners as suppliers'.[1] By this, Brecht may not only have meant that radio should address the culture of the working classes, but he may actually have thought of turning receiving sets into transmission equipment, a technical possibility which had led the postal administration to introduce stringent control of reception.

The idea of social reporting, where concerned citizens produced their own programmes, gained vigour during the citizen initiatives and grass roots movements of the 1960s and early 1970s, when it influenced public radio programmes and stimulated the birth of alternative media workshops and 'free radios'.[2] When privately-owned commercial radio stations were first licensed in West Germany in 1984, and cable and satellite promised an abundance of new means of distribution, the day for, albeit limited, open access to radio and television broadcasting seemed to have arrived.

SOCIAL REPRESENTATION IN MAINSTREAM RADIO OUTPUT

Direct access for social groups did not materialise earlier because the particular integrative philosophy of West German public broadcasting was only challenged by the introduction of commercial private radio.

Individuals generally had no opportunity to participate in either private or public broadcasting. The idea of direct access is foreign to the West German public broadcasting system, since in theory the system integrates the major social forces into the public communication process by giving them seats on the broadcasting councils. The drawbacks of this approach have been described earlier. Although their programming remit clearly obliges public stations to cover social and minority issues, competitive pressures from private stations have increasingly marginalised minority output.

Commercial private stations broadcast information on social issues by listing events and possibly giving airtime to press releases from interested groups, but it does not normally provide background reporting. In order to prevent the private stations from excessively streamlining their output, some regulators have tried to incorporate non-profit organisations into private mainstream programming. This has happened in Bavaria, Bremen, Hamburg and Northrhine-Westfalia.

THE ALTERNATIVE 'PROFESSIONAL' RADIO SPECTRUM

OK Radio, in SPD/FDP-governed Hamburg, is closest to mainstream private radio. It is fully financed by advertising, but organised according to a variant of the 'two-column' model discussed in Chapter 4. Although a commercial operating company manages the station and sells advertising airtime, the actual licensee in control of editorial output is an association of non-profit organisations, none of which is directly represented in mainstream private radio. In Hamburg, twenty diverse local groups including trade union workshops, a women's organisation and the YMCA are editorial associates and aim to produce programmes that reflect the interests of their individual groups. However, clashes with the operating company have meant that the intended distinctiveness of the programme output has suffered. The company is mainly interested in a return on its capital and therefore wants a streamlined professional output. Otherwise it fears the station could lose out to its six competitors in its struggle for audiences and advertising revenues.

Two other stations, Radio 100 in West Berlin and Radio Z in Nuremberg, are financed through a mixture of membership subscription, individual donations and 'ideologically sound' advertising without which neither could survive. Both were founded, and are operated and financially supported, by a variety of citizen initiatives, social and cultural organisations and individuals with leftist or green leanings. These organisations define the overall editorial philosophy, which is socially committed and aimed at the 'intellectually aware listener'; they also produce the programmes and allocate the programming budget.

Radio Z was only licensed after extensive discussion in the pluralist board of the Bavarian authority, which scrutinised not only the proposed financial arrangements but the station's unconventional programming ideology. These discussions took place even though there are five local radio channels in Nuremberg, which are more than enough to provide balanced pluralism in line with the Bavarian approach. Radio Z broadcasts daily from 4pm to 12 midnight and shares its frequency with other mainstream commercial stations.

Radio Z and Radio 100 both have to rely on voluntary contributions and minimum staffing and salary levels in order to survive. Although they were both licensed under conservative governments, and even though Radio Z has been awarded over £10,000 from an official media fund for its women's and cultural output, they have been repeatedly attacked by conservative public opinion. On both stations, women's and gay groups get regular slots for their own broadcasts. Radio Z also broadcasts regular programmes made by young people and prison inmates; and Radio 100 gave regular airtime to voices from GDR opposition groups. Additionally, both aim to include contributions from third party producers with similar views. For example, Radio 100 gave airtime to striking Berlin students; and Radio Z provides an outlet for productions by a South Africa study group.

Considering the ideological diversity of the programme suppliers, the main difficulties for the stations' chief editors are to ensure a minimum production standard, and to keep the programmes within the bounds of their editorial responsibility without appearing to censor the content. Their task is made more difficult by the occasional ideological quarrels between the founding organisations, which could well endanger the stations' operations.

The fourth alternative station in the FRG is Radio Dreyeckland in Freiburg, which offers an 'open studio' to all interested programme makers. Programme contributions come mostly from its fifty founding members which include a family planning group; the senior citizens' movement, the Grey Panthers; but also a religious organisation. Like the alternative stations in West Berlin and Nuremberg, Radio Dreyeckland had to overcome political resistance from the conservative camp, which repeatedly delayed its opening.

This left-wing ex-pirate is the only station which refuses to compromise commercially. It is solely financed by membership contributions and donations. It operates on a small-scale budget, trying to make a programme with a very high information content. The station is entirely run by voluntary labour and freelance contributions, but there is a danger that the initial enthusiasm with which citizens' groups contributed to the programme will fall away. Moreover, although the station has a distinctive audience profile and attracts a regular listenership, especially among the student community, it does not yet have the necessary membership to guarantee its survival. When, like Radio 100, it managed to get a full frequency allocation after the demise of one of its intended mainstream commercial rivals, this put the station under greater financial pressure. This precarious situation was further aggravated by high royalties and transmission costs, which alone account for a quarter of its total budget of £117,000 per year.

OPEN ACCESS CHANNELS

Open, community or citizen broadcasts are offered either through publicly financed access channels on cable networks, mostly for television, and/or slots on terrestrial radio. Far from being an integral part of the broadcasting system in the FRG, open channels (*Offene Kanäle*) have only gradually been introduced in some regions since 1984. Legislative provisions for open channels exist in Berlin, Bremen, Hamburg, Northrhine-Westfalia, Rhineland-Palatinate, Saarland and Schleswig-Holstein. In Hessen, the regulatory authority may set up open channels in selected local cable networks.

When the discussion about cable broadcasting began in the mid-1970s, cable was mainly seen as a medium of local communications that would offer citizens a new means of access. When the open channels were set up within a private commercial broadcasting framework, their objective, in line with the 1986 Constitutional Court requirements, was to give those individuals, social groups, organisations and institutions that were not sufficiently represented on other private media a chance to air their views. But by then the rationale had changed. No longer were the media to be emancipated from below. Now, a private broadcasting market had to be established. Not surprisingly, therefore, open channels stood accused of being an 'alibi' for a private broadcasting system which was taken over by the economically powerful, before they could even be tried and tested.[3] Their main function is now said to be for training: 'The medium shall contribute to the formation of social knowledge by offering the self-directed use of communications.'[4] Even so, for the first time, they provide individuals with a right of access to distribute their own programmes throughout the electronic media.

The authorities regulate these channels by administrative statutes, thus enabling them to be run autonomously. Access to the means of distribution is normally free to private individuals and non-profitmaking organisations which do not hold a broadcast licence, but in most *Länder* party-political organisations are barred. The open channel participants themselves are legally liable for their programmes. These do not have to meet the content requirements for objectivity and balance required from commercial private broadcasters, but they do have to obey the general law, the youth protection rules and to respect human dignity. This is ensured by vetting from the authority. The programmes are not scheduled according to a particular programming philosophy but on a first come, first served basis, unless several broadcasts have a common theme.

One of the major questions has been how to approach the potential users and to train them to use the broadcast medium. The regulatory authorities themselves, helped by voluntary organisations, offer production equipment, studios and post-production facilities, technical advice and help, all free of charge. But the shortage of spare production capacities is a problem. In contrast, and possibly because of this shortage, the open channel capacities are not being used to the full. Users with their own production facilities are therefore privileged. The authorities therefore try to organise production facilities sponsored by third parties, such as the local authorities, the trade unions, or adult education institutes.

The authorities have also negotiated special broadcasting rights with the collecting societies, and pay the operating and distribution costs. These are not cheap. In West Berlin, the open channel facilities for cable television and radio cost over £0.3 million to set up, and £0.5 million a year to operate.[5] In the 1987 Inter-*Land* Treaty, the Minister-Presidents therefore authorised the authorities to use part of the additional licence fee income for open channels.

The regulatory authorities themselves decide the amounts to be spent on promoting these channels. According to the Treaty, the channels have to compete for licence fee funding with the subsidies to improve the transmitter infrastructure (see Chapter 3; and App. VI). Thus, under their CDU-dominated governments, the *Länder* of Baden-Württemberg, Hessen, Lower Saxony and Schleswig-Holstein regarded the erection of transmitters for private broadcasters as a priority and made no provision for open channels. Meanwhile, the SPD-led government in Schleswig-Holstein has legislated for open channels and earmarked the infrastructure money for their use. Similarly, the new SPD-led government coalition in Lower Saxony is likely to introduce open channels.

The clearest financial commitment to open channels is in Northrhine-Westfalia, where in 1989 the authority earmarked £2.1 million for radio and £1.8 million for cable channels. This was just under half of its budget, and three times the amount it spent on infrastructure subsidies. Northrhine-Westfalia is also committed to training individuals and to citizen initiatives to use the new means of communication, and to accompanying research. Hamburg, in contrast, reduced the amount it spent on open channels from £0.8 million in 1988 to £0.4 million in 1989. The 1988 figure reflected the high start-up investment required for open channels. The smallest *Länder* of Bremen and Saarland, both SPD-led, use up to seventy-five and thirty-nine per cent of their limited budgets to promote open channels. West Berlin spends over forty per cent of its small budget on its open access channels; but it can afford to do so as its open channel was started back in 1985 and benefited from the additional funds for the Berlin cable trial, of which open channels were a statutory part.

In Bavaria, which is torn between socially committed Catholicism and a philosophy of economic liberalism, the situation is again different. Because the regulatory authority is expected to fulfil the duties of a public broadcaster, it is the only *Land* in the FRG where there are direct programme subsidies for private broadcasting. There is no legal provision for open access but the cable companies are required to broadcast fully comprehensive pluralist programming, including access for social charities, religious groups and others. In Bavaria, the funds earmarked in the Inter-*Land* Treaty for open channels, which amounted to £0.7 million in 1989, subsidise almost two thirds of the initial costs of regular commercial or charitable programme providers, especially if they are small or medium-sized enterprises, and provided they can offer home-made cultural, religious, or social-affairs programmes. The subsidies are allocated by the pluralist board for use on production and for financing distribution facilities. In this manner, an organisation for the handicapped, an evangelical programme service and a theatre channel have survived. But since the authority offers neither production facilities nor advice, many citizens' groups would it find hard to raise the initial capital outlay needed. Moreover, there is no guaranteed slot for the programmes of these cultural and social groups within the broadcast schedules organised by the cable companies.

Apart from providing open access channels, in Rhineland-Palatinate the activities of local non-profit radio and television associations are subsidised by a broadcasting trust set up and financed by the *Land*. The open access slots are organised and financed by the regulatory authority itself, although users may be asked to pay a contribution towards the distribution facilities which are provided separately.

In general, irregular scheduling of the open access programmes limits firm audience commitment to what is essentially 'their' channel, and their ratings are very low. Northrhine-Westfalia has therefore attempted to make the best use of the public money spent on open channels by granting the WDR priority access to use these channels on cable systems for live transmissions of parliamentary debates.[6]

To improve the reach of open access programmes, another, often complementary, approach has been to integrate them into terrestrial radio programmes and to allow access to local organisations, but not to individuals, under the label of citizens' radio (*Bürgerfunk*). This approach has been adopted by Bremen, Hamburg, Northrhine-Westfalia and Schleswig-Holstein. Northrhine-Westfalia, for example, requires the non-profitmaking local radio associations to set aside fifteen per cent of their broadcast time, or up to two hours daily, for programmes produced by local cultural or social groups. These requirements form part of the licence, and the regulatory authority supervises their implementation. The associations must also help the groups produce their programmes; but the groups can then reclaim the costs charged from the authority. But although the opportunity to broadcast is available, local cultural and social organisations often lack the resources and know-how to take advantage of it. Often, they may also be partners themselves in the main local radio associations.

Practical problems can arise from the exact timing of citizen programmes on a commercial radio channel. The most popular hours may well be reserved for the mainstream service, thus marginalising the citizen channel, making it difficult to create audience interest. In Saarland, the regulatory authority has therefore included the open channel on a new radio frequency which it allocated to its public broadcaster SR. Users are able to broadcast for up to six hours a week; the authority specifies the broadcast times after consultations with potential users, thus making sure that the broadcasts reach a sizeable and interested audience.

PUBLIC COMMITMENT TO ALTERNATIVE BROADCASTING

Three aspects of the history of alternative broadcasting in the FRG seem particularly striking. First, most alternative radio stations as well as open channels were initially set up by right-wing *Länder* intent on breaking up the traditional public broadcasting duopoly. In that sense, alternative broadcasting has been a by-product of the introduction of private commercial broadcasting. But out of over 130 newly established commercial radio stations there are only four alternative stations, plus the marginal open channels. It is doubtful therefore whether they owe their existence to the libertarian beliefs of the regulators, or whether they are merely the figleaf of pluralism which the Constitutional Court sought to implement, but which in reality masks a considerable narrowing of social representation in mainstream private broadcasting. The regulators themselves sometimes admit as much when asked about the social value of access broadcasting.

Secondly, the legislators supported alternative models of broadcasting in a curious manner. They made scant economic provisions for alternative radio. All stations with non-profit goals have thus to compete for audiences with commercial stations. The alternative radios experiment with new forms of social representation by reworking the traditional public service philosophy, but with the exception of Radio Z they receive no subsidies for programming or operating costs. In contrast, the open access channels have received some £5 million in public funds, although their contribution to public communication has, as yet, been minimal.

The reason for this discrepancy may be that open access channels are considered politically less explosive, because they are much less effective. They could be deemed worthy of public support precisely because they defuse claims for access to broadcasting by under-represented social groups. However, although a few pirate radio stations survive, spreading religious messages or broadcasting folk music, clamour for access to participate in the exchange of socio-political ideas and opinions is rare.

There is a marked lack of interest by regulators and audiences in alternative broadcasting. The German public appears to lack the willingness to get involved in the processes of 'civil society', but relies instead on whatever is provided by public authorities. There is no strong tradition of financial support and sponsorship of interest groups in the FRG. In short, the need for channels to express divergent views has not yet taken root in the public mind and is not very pronounced precisely because German society is socially integrative, a concept strongly perpetuated by the public service tradition of broadcasting.

Because of this, while it is still too early to judge the value of citizens' radio, open television cable channels at least could contribute more to political pluralism if they were employed for the live transmission of parliamentary debates by the public stations. This has already been stipulated in an amendment to the Northrhine-Westfalian broadcasting law.

Thirdly, there is the future of social commitment in public broadcasting. If the media politicians are really as concerned with creating new and diverse forms of communications as they always claim, it is surprising that they do not require public broadcasters to initiate radio workshops and open slots for groups and initiatives with social objectives on the public channels. Since public broadcasting already has a strong commitment to present social issues, such a step would appear logical. The question is however whether the politicians would be prepared to allow the public stations adequate finance for such purposes.

Chapter 6

The regulation of the market

The regulation of the broadcasting market has two main aims. They are to manage competition between the private commercial broadcasters; and to govern the economic relationship of the 'dual system' of public and private broadcasters. According to the 1987 Inter-*Land* Treaty, a fair co-existence between the two halves of the system should strengthen the pluralism of broadcast information and 'respond to the requirements of future national and international competition'.[1]

The private broadcasters compete with the public broadcasters in three areas: for audiences, for revenues, and for the rights to broadcast programmes and sports events. With total broadcast revenues amounting to some £2.8 billion in 1989 (see App. X), competition is intense. In addition, the private broadcasting market is regulated not just by the competition rules for these three areas, but also by merger and anti-concentration rules, which monitor ownership, market access and behaviour.

There are two main philosophies that animate regulation of the broadcasting market. First, there is the 'normative approach' adopted by the Federal Constitutional Court. It takes as its guiding principle, editorial pluralism. By this is meant a diversity of programme output which has to be achieved through *Land* regulation. Competition in the marketplace is not a primary constitutional goal for broadcasting.

> The danger of excluding . . . views from the process of the free formation of opinion must be counteracted; [so must the danger] that those . . . which possess broadcast frequencies and financial resources exert a *dominating influence upon the formation of opinion*. (1981 decision)

[and] 'Opportunities in the market place may relate to economic freedom but they do not relate to freedom of opinion' (1986 decision).[2]

This is the approach which the *Länder* have tried to implement.

The second justification, which underlies competition regulation, is what may be termed the 'numerical approach'. This holds that the terms of entry and the operating conditions of a market have to be regulated so as to permit the largest number of broadcasting organisations, which will then produce the desired programming diversity through the competitive process.

[A] variety of providers will also help enforce the valued principle of the division of powers in the electronic media sector, decrease any dominant position in the market place of ideas and thus reduce the risk of cultural dictate and manipulation.[3]

This approach is underpinned by the prevailing legal and political justification for concentration regulation by federal anti-cartel legislation in the FRG.

From a social-policy perspective, excessive concentrations of economic power through mergers may undermine the foundations of the liberal order of the state. Political democracy and a market economy are inconceivable without a decentralisation of power.[4]

The two approaches operate at different analytical levels. The normative approach is concerned with programmes, their content and effects. The numerical approach is concerned with broadcasting organisation and services or channels. But although the two approaches operate at different levels, they interact in an unregulated and unplanned manner. In its 1986 judgement, the Federal Constitutional Court ruled that the basic programmes provided by the public broadcasting corporations could be supplemented by the private broadcasters, provided they met a minimum standard of pluralism. But it ignored the economic realities of everyday commercial practice; and in particular the threat that intense economic competition can bring to programme diversity, when all programmes do not have an equal market appeal.

THE REGULATION OF ACCESS TO AUDIENCES

Private broadcasters

Access to audiences through the allocation of distribution channels is the prerequisite for the market success of a commercial broadcaster. At the time the Inter-*Land* Treaty was signed, cable and DBS technology were still secondary media. Despite the euphoria of the conservatives and the fears of the SPD, which the age of the new electronic media had provoked, cable up-take was unexpectedly slow. By January 1990, five years after the launch of private television, over six million, i.e. a quarter of all television households, were connected to cable.[5] Although the break-even point for the satellite TV stations was forecast at 4.4 million homes connected,[6] of the satellite broadcasters only RTL plus and SAT 1 expected to break even in 1990, and this was primarily a consequence not of cable but of terrestrial distribution which gave them access to over sixty per cent of homes by the middle of the year.

Indeed, to speed things up, in 1985 both private broadcasters and the *Länder* governments had urged the DBP to discover gaps in the UHF terrestrial television spectrum which the private broadcasters could use. The DBP subsequently co-ordinated over 160 regional areas, giving access to up to seventy per cent of West German households over the air. Article 1 of the 1987 Treaty then required that licences for these regional television frequencies 'should, if possible, be allocated on an even basis throughout the Federal Republic'.[7] This meant that RTL plus and SAT 1, which were there first as viable licensees, could effectively monopolise the use of the new frequencies, with the occasional participation of Tele 5 or, in Munich, Pro 7. There are however significant overlaps between the areas covered by private satellite receivers, terrestrial transmissions and those passed by cable. It is therefore difficult to quantify the real gains in audience reach.

Competition between the private and public television channels is most intense on the cable networks. In 1989, ARD and ZDF together had a fifty-five per cent share of cable viewing time, compared with thirty-four per cent for RTL plus and SAT 1; while in all homes including those with terrestrial reception, the shares were seventy-six and eighteen per cent respectively.[8]

This is not surprising, since at that time the private stations could only be received in fifty-seven per cent (RTL plus) and fifty-two per cent (SAT 1) of all TV homes. Conversely, the major ARD and ZDF services enjoy an average reach of ninety-eight per cent terrestrially (see App. VIII). However, with the increased technical reach of the private TV stations via cable, satellite and terrestrial frequencies, it can be expected that ARD's and ZDF's share in all homes will eventually fall to fifty per cent.[9]

The DBS TV-Sat, which was originally going to make up for gaps in cable coverage through direct-to-home distribution, cannot compensate for the differentials in reach. The private stations have not considered it an attractive option because of its complex and costlier transmission technology, D2-MAC. The market for the new receiving equipment has been extremely slow to develop, and it could be overtaken by high-definition TV. Meanwhile, RTL plus and SAT 1 have effectively been forced to continue with their DBS licence in return for their terrestrial licences, but all private television stations are also trying to improve reception by using the medium-power Luxembourg satellite Astra, although its estimated direct-to-home reception potential in the eleven Western *Länder* is little more than 500,000.[10] Direct reception via Astra and, to a lesser extent, TV-Sat is now quickly building up audiences in the five new Eastern *Länder* (see Chapter 8).

Article 1 of the 1987 Treaty also allows for a third partial satellite agreement, the so-called 'Western Satellite Treaty', which was concluded in June 1989 between the remaining *Länder*, Bremen, Hessen, Northrhine-Westfalia and Saarland, in order to license a third private DBS broadcaster.[11] They envisage a European service, with both private and public participation, which is due to start in 1993. The act in Northrhine-Westfalia reserves one chain of regional terrestrial television frequencies for this provider. It is therefore likely that SAT 1, which only has a temporary licence for these frequencies, will lose audiences from there when the third private DBS station starts broadcasting. Moreover, since the terrestrial television frequencies were awarded to broadcasters which promised to invest in the region, those organisations which have not done so could lose their licence if there are others prepared to apply.

Public broadcasters

The opportunities for the public broadcasters to gain new audiences with extra channels have been restricted by the politicians. The Inter-*Land* Treaty gives ARD and ZDF a DBS television channel each, for an 'additional television programme service with cultural emphasis'. European partners may participate. This legalises the existing services, Eins plus (ARD) and 3Sat (ZDF with Austrian and Swiss public broadcasters). But under the Treaty the broadcasting corporations are now *obliged* to provide such services.[12] Audiences are likely to remain limited because the services now have a specific cultural remit, but they could increase if the services can get terrestrial transmission facilities in addition to cable and DBS. This could happen in Bremen. The terrestrial transmissions there could then also be received in neighbouring *Länder* where they would compete for audiences with the private stations.

ARD and ZDF may also participate in one additional European television venture, 'if their share of programming does not constitute a substantial portion of the whole programme and the programme does not contain advertising aimed at the . . . Federal Republic'.[13] This legalises the planned Franco-German cultural satellite service (La Sept/ARD/ZDF) which was initiated by Baden-Württemberg's Minister-President, Lothar Späth. The ARD, however, fears that this project will impose an additional strain on its already precarious finances, and regards it as politically imposed;[14] and both the public networks object to being restricted to a cultural mandate.

The politicians have also made it virtually impossible for the public broadcasters to expand. Any new national or regional public broadcasting services, other than those already agreed, will now require a special inter-*Land* treaty, and they will be forbidden to sell advertising. Moreover, in the memorandum of understanding attached to the Treaty, the *Länder* declared that regional television programmes which are distributed nationally, currently those of BR and WDR, could not take their national satellite distribution costs into account when calculating licence fee increases. This calls into question the viability of any national distribution of ARD's regional television channels.

THE REGULATION OF BROADCASTING FINANCE

Although the 1987 Inter-*Land* Treaty expressly lays down the receiving licence fee as the 'primary source of finance' for public broadcasters, they can also raise money from the sale of airtime.[15] This complementary source of income is severely restricted, however. Conversely, private broadcasters receive no licence fees directly (indirectly, they profit from it through the infrastructure subsidies), but can raise finance from any other source, of which advertising is the main one. The regulatory ideal, which underpins this, is a clear division between a licence fee funded public sector, and a private sector funded by advertising, as in the UK; even though the private broadcasting authorities receive their funds from the licence fee.

In revenue terms, however, the private broadcasting sector still lags far behind the public system. Although the licence fee accounted for over half the total revenues of the entire broadcasting market in 1989, the public broadcasters also earned seventy-two per cent of the advertising revenues, twelve per cent less than in the previous year. Although the private stations broadcast twice as much airtime as the public stations, they had a mere ten per cent share of the total broadcasting market. Compared with 1988, they nevertheless doubled their share (see App. X).[16] The advertising revenue per minute in private television was less than half that in public television; and the ARD radio stations together earned more from a minute's advertising than the total advertising income in private radio. This shortage of finance particularly affects many local radios; while the few private *Land*-wide radios can survive.

The licence fee system

The 1987 Inter-*Land* Treaty confirmed the traditional licence fee arrangements, including both the equalisation between the ARD corporations and the ZDF's thirty per cent share of the licence fee revenues. The general licence fee is, as before, paid by each household owning radio or/and TV receiving sets. It is therefore still a universal charge, and is unlikely to degenerate into a 'subscription' for public channels in the foreseeable future. As such, it satisfies the constitutional requirement for 'basic services provision'.

Since 1970, the level of the licence fee and the conditions surrounding it have been set by the Minister-Presidents in a special inter-*Land* treaty. Traditionally, it was decided by an arbitrary process of political negotiation between the *Länder* governments for the lowest common denominator.[17] In response to much criticism, the 1987 Treaty now stipulates, albeit somewhat vaguely, that revisions of the licence fee should be made with 'a high degree of objectivity'; and so, theoretically, it does away with some of the political bargaining inherent in the previous system. Revisions are now to take place biennially; the factors to be taken into account for a revision include the 'competitive development' of the existing programme offerings, the potential for efficiency and rationalisation, cost increases in media production, increases in advertising revenue and participation in new technical ventures.

Three more experts were appointed to the KEF, the commission that assesses the financial requirements of the corporations. It now consists of six experts and eight political appointees, but the group of experts has also been granted a right of veto. As before, broadcasters are not allowed to sit on the KEF. Given the political realities, the licence fee provisions are judged by an insider as making 'only very cautious attempts to achieve, if nothing else, a higher degree of planning accuracy for the broadcasting organisations, together with the first steps towards a more objective procedure.'[18]

Despite the licence fee increase of £9.60 per annum (DM 2.40 per month) after January 1990, the public broadcasting corporations predicted programming cuts because of insufficient funding[19] – in 1989, ARD had a deficit for the fourth year running, ZDF for the second year. In its customary defence of the public sector, the SPD is now proposing an index-linked licence fee, although it is unclear what the base-figure would be. But the licence fee provisions of the Treaty may well have to be revised, since the Bavarian Administrative Court has challenged the present system of fixing and apportioning the fee, and referred the case to the Federal Constitutional Court.[20]

Advertising regulation and practice

The general advertising rules in the Treaty[21] apply to private and public broadcasters alike. The difference between the two systems lies in the vital question of the advertising ceiling and the interpretation of the rules by the respective regulatory bodies.

The general rules reaffirm the customary restrictions on advertisements in the public sector.[22] Advertising must be clearly separated from other programme material, i.e. through the insertion of animation; it must not exploit the inexperience of children or young people; advertisers or agencies are not allowed to influence programming; and political, religious, and social advertisements are forbidden, along with tobacco commercials.

Television commercials must be grouped in a block, i.e. at least two spots must be broadcast together. In addition to the commercial breaks before and after the programme, television broadcasts over sixty minutes long may be interrupted only once. This rule now applies to the public stations as well, whereas previously they were not allowed to interrupt their broadcasts with commercials. The Treaty does not specify any class of programme as being exempt from advertising breaks. This rule is bound to conflict, however, with the advertising regulation in the EC's TV Directive (see Chapter 7).

The aim of the rule on commercial breaks is to prevent arbitrary interruptions of broadcasts. In the explanatory notes to the Treaty, a broadcast is defined rather summarily. It cites the example of a feature film or serial, including the commercial break itself as well as the appropriate programme announcements, previews and weather reports.[23] This would allow serials, which generally last for about forty-five minutes, to be interrupted by advertising only once, although much is still in flux and the interpretation of the provision depends on how the term 'broadcast' is defined in the guidelines of the relevant regulatory bodies.[24]

For ZDF, once a broadcast is interrupted by other independent editorial material, such as a news programme or a magazine, or where it consists of two separate episodes, it can no longer be counted as one broadcast. Given the public sector advertising ceiling of twenty minutes (see below), this interpretation is advantageous to the broadcasting corporations since it gives them more opportunities to spread out the same advertising footage. Both the public and the private sectors already tend to have shorter programmes linked by commercials. The *Länder* regulatory bodies can allow sports broadcasts to be interrupted more than once during natural breaks. For instance, they granted RTL plus four commercial breaks in its sports magazine.

Specific public sector rules   On the public networks, television advertising is limited to an annual average of twenty minutes per day, with a maximum of twenty-five minutes on any one day, but there is no advertising on television after 8pm, or on Sundays or public holidays. Advertising is not forbidden on the third regional television channels. The start time of the advertising blocks is unregulated, but ARD traditionally starts at around 6pm, ZDF at about 5.30pm. Most of the advertising spots are therefore concentrated between 7pm and 8pm when peak time begins. Higher ratings mean higher spot prices.

The Inter-*Land* Treaty limits radio advertising to the upper limits of the individual ARD radio stations that existed prior to 1 January 1987, but allows them up to ninety minutes a day, regardless of how they are spread across the four radio channels in each corporation.

This has removed the freedom that most public stations enjoyed in fixing their own radio ceilings. Any change will now have to be agreed among all *Länder* governments. The Treaty thus reduces the ARD's economic freedom and increases the pronounced influence over broadcasting finance of the politicians, since they also set the level of the licence fee. The Treaty also preserves the inequalities between individual ARD corporations. For instance, NDR has been allowed forty-two minutes advertising time by the Minister-Presidents of Hamburg, Schleswig-Holstein and Lower Saxony. They decided to remain below the ninety minute ceiling, even though the upper limit of most other ARD stations exceeds 100 minutes. This is likely to cause problems, not just with the licence fee equalisation arrangements, but also in adjusting the licence fee increases to suit the budgetary needs of individual corporations.

The Minister-Presidents may agree, however, to modify the advertising ceilings for the public stations, provided this does not lead an increase in their overall revenue. This means that an increase in advertising time could compensate for a budgetary shortfall, although it is doubtful whether the money could be used to pay for new ventures. This clause is also dependent on political agreement on the licence fee. If the *Länder* cannot agree on a licence fee increase on two successive occasions, they may withdraw from certain undertakings, vital to the corporations' survival. One of these is the possibility of compensating for a revenue shortfall with increased sales of airtime.

The corporations can still increase their advertising rates, but with growing private sector competition, advertising spots, which were traditionally overbooked a long way ahead, are now harder to sell.[25] When the ARD corporations increased their television advertising rates in 1989, they had to cut them again to meet growing competition from the private stations.[26]

To make up for its substantial losses, the public sector is already lobbying the Minister-Presidents to extend the 8pm watershed. But the chances of success are slim, as politicians of all parties are generally opposed to further commercialisation of public broadcasting. It is an open question whether the restrictive advertising rules can legally hinder the introduction of new services. The 1987 Constitutional Court decision, which was published after the Inter-*Land* Treaty had been signed, ruled that the public corporations had the right to provide additional services. These were to be financed primarily through the licence fee but, failing this, by commercial advertising.[27] Should the politicians explicitly ask the corporations to carry out special tasks, such as a Franco-German cultural channel or coverage of the *Länder* in the former GDR, they will have to provide them with the money to do so.

Specific rules for private broadcasters Commercial advertisements are limited to twenty per cent of the daily radio or television broadcast time, with no time limits or prohibitions on Sunday advertising. Spot advertising is allowed on radio if it is clearly separated from editorial material.

There is no maximum hourly ceiling. The Minister-Presidents placed their faith in self-regulation, since they felt there was a natural limit to the number of commercials which audiences would accept in any one hour. Indeed, the market itself appears to impose restrictions. Although the peak time slots between 7.30pm and 10pm have easily been filled on private television, no private broadcaster has yet reached its daily ceiling of commercial airtime, or wanted to expand advertising during peak viewing time for fear of upsetting the audience which are used to fewer commercials on public television.

The *Länder* regulatory authorities have some freedom to respond to developments not explicitly covered by the Treaty. For instance, they have agreed that teleshopping counts towards the advertising quota. They also decided that it was unlawful for a satellite station to transmit political advertisements. It is unclear, however, whether they can enforce this decision. The politicians could well oppose this, if the private television stations continue to demand payment for party-political broadcasts and refuse to meet their statutory obligation to grant airtime at cost.[28]

According to a major analysis of the regulatory authorities and their practices, the manner in which the regulators interpret and monitor the advertising rules is problematic.[29] Despite attempts to establish common guidelines, each authority still has substantial discretion in interpretation. This can delay agreement. By the time the authorities have negotiated a common position on a given form of advertising, the stations have already introduced a new variant. To date, the authorities have barely even considered the more subtle relationships between commercials and programme content, such as the borderline between advertising and sponsorship, or the practice of scheduling programming output in order to attract specific advertisers. Although this is where most contraventions take place, the regulatory authorities do not have the time or the resources to monitor each radio or television station closely.[30] The permanent body for advertising supervision, which the regulatory authorities have jointly set up,[31] may possibly develop more expertise and clout in this area.

Sponsorship rules

The sponsorship rules of the Treaty apply to all West German broadcasters, but different interpretations apply to the public and private sectors.[32] The Treaty permits sponsorship for broadcasts, but only if 'it does not further the economic interests of the sponsor or a third party' including the broadcasters themselves, serve political or ideological interests in an 'improper' manner or affect editorial independence. The sponsor's name has to be mentioned at both the beginning and end of the programme. Sponsored programmes may not be interrupted by commercials. Product placement is only permitted for 'dramaturgical' or journalistic reasons.[33]

All forms of commercial sponsorship, including product placement, are generally forbidden in the public sector, although sponsorship by cultural, charitable or public-interest organisations is allowed, and has already occurred. The trend is clearly to rely on self-regulation by the corporations, using the very bland 'public or cultural interest' justification. Hence, sponsored events and foreign sponsored programmes can be broadcast, if they are overwhelmingly in the public interest. The ZDF sponsorship guidelines appear to be more liberal than those of the ARD, since they explicitly allow sponsorship through co-operation agreements with other media enterprises such as newspapers, book or music publishers. They also permit deals with other commercial partners for productions that serve the public interest, which would be difficult to fund otherwise.

The sponsorship rules are deliberately interpreted more loosely for the private broadcasters. The guidelines for private broad-casting proposed by the regulatory authorities define commercial sponsorship as a legitimate source of finance, as long as the programme *content* does not *directly* represent the economic interests of the sponsor or a third party. This is automatically assumed to be the case for artistic, cultural or public-interest programmes, but in practice it allows for all forms of sponsorship, except direct reference to the sponsor, whether in writing, in pictures or sound, or by means of the plot within the programme broadcast.

Borderline cases, such as transmissions of sponsored events, which are not explicitly authorised in the Treaty, are bound to arise, and will lead to legal disputes. For example, SAT 1 has already objected to the showing by ARD of a photographic company's logo at the beginning and end of the transmission of a football match sponsored by the company. The administrative court dealing with the case ruled that a broadcast could also include information on the sponsor of an event, provided that it did not resemble an advertisement.[34] But as a matter of principle the court also pointed out that the relevant clause in the Inter-*Land* Treaty was badly drafted, and that an economic interest could only be excluded if the sponsor received no mention at all and had no self-interest in sponsoring a programme or event. This of course denies the intrinsic purpose of commercial sponsorship.

A senior public broadcaster has suggested that, if this opinion continues to be upheld by the courts, the public corporations could be prevented from transmitting any sponsored events at all.[35] Competition in the market for the transmission rights to major sports events has not only meant that the sports associations can now pick the highest bidder, but also that the event's sponsor frequently attaches certain conditions for television coverage to the sponsorship deal. Unless they fulfil these special conditions, the broadcasting corporations could be unable to gain access to major events.

It is also unclear whether the Treaty applies to the practice of barter syndication,[36] or whether it allows information programmes to be sponsored by political associations or trade unions. The intricacies of sponsorship have indeed not yet been fully addressed by the authorities. The dividing line between sponsorship and advertising, in particular, is very fine and will need to be clarified by the courts. Once more, the judiciary appears to be taking over broadcasting regulation from the legislators.

Conditions of co-existence

The financial arrangements for the two broadcasting sectors, as defined by the Treaty, and the regulations arising from them, have already put the public broadcasters in a precarious financial position. This is exacerbated by an increased dependence on the governments of the day.

First, the advertising limitations mean that ARD and ZDF now have less flexibility than before to exploit new technologies. Moreover, their freedom to compensate for cost increases is severely restricted. This is exacerbated by private sector competition for advertising revenue. Consequently, the ARD stations have lost income in both radio and television. Savings can only be made by cutting back on staff and programming costs, with a probable reduction in programme choice.

Second, although the idea behind the advertising restrictions was to emphasise the primacy of the licence fee for ARD and ZDF, it is doubtful whether the licence fee increases necessary to compensate for the losses in advertising revenue would be socially or politically acceptable. Neither ARD, which on average gets about twenty-five per cent of its income from advertising, nor ZDF, which gets about forty per cent, could maintain its current level and standard of programming by relying on the licence fee alone.

Third, in spite of the Treaty provisions, the arbitrary political nature of the licence fee system was amply illustrated in 1988 by the refusal of the Baden-Württemberg government to implement the licence fee increase as agreed in the Treaty. Its justification was blatantly political: the public corporations were 'developing into a state within the state, not least because of the Constitutional Court decisions'; the only realistic alternative to keep them under control, therefore, was the licence fee.[37] Similarly, the cable and satellite lobby viewed the provisions of the Inter-*Land* Treaty with 'pronounced reticence' precisely because they did not curb sufficiently the strong market position of ARD and ZDF.[38]

OWNERSHIP AND CONCENTRATION REGULATION

The regulation of ownership and concentration in the broadcasting market is also a mixture of normative and numerical regulation. The *Länder* justify their approach by referring to the Constitutional Court decision which demanded the highest degree of programme diversity.[39] But unlike public broadcasting, pluralism in the private sector is not an absolute requirement, but deemed by a legal fiction to exist as long as there are *at least* three private national general interest channels. It is *assumed* that competition will then produce diverse programming. According to the Constitutional Court, rather than regulating economic competition directly, the politicians' objective in introducing structural competition rules should have been to secure programming diversity, regardless of any economic implications for the private sector. But the practice is different. Normative regulation of the broadcast organisations is difficult because of the tendencies towards concentration in the broadcasting market. Because of the inherent problem of achieving pluralism of opinion under market conditions, the law often appears not only to be ineffective but also to favour cross-ownership and concentration tendencies.

Putting aside the problem of defining a national general interest channel, it is doubtful whether the FRG can support even three such channels. The two major private television stations, SAT 1 and RTL plus, are only gradually establishing nation-wide distribution. Together with the three public TV channels, ARD 1, the regional ARD III programmes, and ZDF, they form the five basic channels that can be received terrestrially on the same aerial. A third aspirant private television station, Tele 5, is waiting to be allocated national terrestrial frequencies, even though a number of studies have suggested that, even assuming increases in advertising spending as a proportion of gross domestic product, the West German market could only support two private general interest television channels.[40] This means that external pluralism will be very hard to establish nationally. Given these economic limitations, how can the ownership rules for private broadcasting prevent the tendencies towards concentration which will lead further and further away from the pure model of external pluralism?

Foreign ownership

There are no specific limitations on foreign media ownership in the FRG. Foreign investment is basically regulated under West German company law and the federal anti-cartel act.[41] Theoretically there are no restrictions on foreign participation or ownership of a German public limited company or other private company. Any enterprise can trade in the FRG once it has been entered in the German trade register, although non-EC enterprises need a special permit. This must be granted if reciprocal provisions exist in the country of origin of the foreign company. Hence, although all the broadcasting acts require a broadcaster to be licensed under *Land* jurisdiction and to be domiciled in the FRG in order to be legally accountable under German law, this does not apply to the cable distribution of foreign satellite stations.

So far, the few international media groups which have entered West German domestic broadcasting, CLT, Berlusconi's Rete Italia and Canal Plus, have all chosen to work with established German media partners, because they needed their experience and contacts to cope with the complex German broadcasting legislation and its political power structures. Indeed, for reasons of *Standortpolitik*, a broadcast organisation stands a better chance of obtaining a licence, if it has its head office, a subsidiary or production facilities in the licensing *Land* itself. It can then trade on the politicians' desires to secure the economic benefits of new media developments for their *Land*.

Restrictions on horizontal concentration

The legislatures tried to prevent horizontal concentrations, like those in publishing, by introducing relatively arbitrary restrictions on the number and type of programmes that a private broadcaster could provide for a given coverage area. Under Article 8 of the 1987 Inter-*Land* Treaty, which only applies to nation-wide broadcasters, a broadcaster can provide only one national general interest and one thematic special interest channel, on radio and television. This includes regional services that can be received throughout the Federal Republic. All the other interests of a private national broadcaster in another national channel, whether direct or indirect, must be less than a quarter of its capital, voting rights or programme output, since under German company law twenty-five per cent can constitute a blocking vote with substantial influence on company policy. The *Länder* have also tried to prevent any connections between organisations, regardless of their legal form: the acts and the Inter-*Land* Treaty include provisions for 'related enterprises', as defined in company law, to be counted as broadcasters.[42] To establish such connections and assess their effects can be very difficult, however.[43]

The broadcasting acts have generally adopted the provisions of the Inter-*Land* Treaty, and limit channel ownership to four per coverage area, including overspill and cable redistribution from other stations in the same organisation. Although it could lead to syndicated regional or national networks, a broadcaster may own several local licences in the same *Land*, or in different *Länder*, as long as there is no overspill between the coverage areas.

The *Länder* laws also prevent existing broadcasters from holding more that twenty-five per cent in further radio or television channels, although Rhineland-Palatinate permits additional holdings of fifty per cent. Hessen and Baden-Württemberg, however, limit secondary holdings to ten per cent, while Bremen restricts them to a mere five per cent, although one partner can provide up to ten per cent of the station's output.

Although these rules limit channel ownership in a given coverage area, they do not prevent stations from broadcasting the same service on different delivery systems, such as cable, satellite and over the air. According to the criterion of numerical diversity, any new means of distribution should have been used to allow new players to enter the market. But to allow private broadcasters to obtain, as quickly as possible, the high penetration rates which they needed to survive, the *Länder* allowed multiple delivery even though it restricts competition. The numerical regulatory ideal was therefore ignored to establish a private broadcasting market, which was of course the ultimate regulatory goal.

Explicitly or implicitly, the broadcasting acts also allow the regulatory authorities to grant exemptions to the concentration rules in the name of normative pluralism, provided a broadcaster does not exert 'a dominant influence on the formation of opinion'. The interpretation of the phrase 'dominant influence' is clearly a value judgement, but a restrictive interpretation could be deemed arbitrary and would be difficult to substantiate in court.

In general, therefore, the authorities have tended to be permissive in their interpretations of the 'dominant influence' criterion. In Bavaria, the major publishers have been allowed to participate in the only *Land*-wide radio station, despite their multiple interests in local radio.[44] This was possible precisely because of the absence of numerical regulation of broadcast holdings in Bavarian legislation. In practice, the authorities have used the two modes of regulation to complement each other.

Rules on vertical integration

Press/broadcasting cross-ownership   Although broadcasting cross-ownership can develop in several sectors of the economy, it is press/broadcasting cross-ownership that has been the major concern in the FRG. There are good reasons for this. As the German media baron Leo Kirch noted in 1988:

> In the entire world, co-operation between print and television is growing: they support each other and enhance each other. If you are going to make television different, you only have one instrument to speed up the process, and that's the press.[45]

Historically, the relationship in the FRG between the press and broadcasting, which are both protected by Article 5 of the Basic Law, has been regulated by a separation of powers: a public broadcasting system, and a privately owned press. This changed when private broadcasting was introduced. By 1989, more than 290 out of 350 newspaper publishing houses, excluding magazines, were either involved, or planning to be involved, in broadcasting.[46]

In 1986, the Constitutional Court expressed concern over the expansion into broadcasting of the press which was already highly concentrated. In particular, it exhorted the legislators to prevent 'double monopolies' – that is, the monopolisation of public opinion by broadcasters who already held monopolistic positions in the newspaper market.[47] But ever since the arrival of commercial broadcast advertising there had been fears that the latter would erode the financial base of the newspaper and magazine publishers; especially since advertising accounts for sixty per cent of the income of West German newspapers. In order to compensate for the feared decline in these revenues, the publishers have traditionally lobbied the politicians for a stake in broadcasting.

The economic crises of the 1960s and 1970s and the subsequent drop in advertising revenues, followed by the introduction of new printing technology, led to increased press concentration, especially in local newspapers and national general interest magazines. In the last twenty years, concentration has doubled in the daily newspaper market. By 1987, ten newspaper groups, led by Springer Verlag, held fifty-four per cent of the local, regional and national daily market.[48] But the local structure of the press has traditionally been a major feature of German socio-cultural life, so in over fifty per cent of the mergers, take-overs or joint ventures, the local titles have been kept. They can still produce their own local editions while getting their regional and national pages from the main publisher's head office. Another outcome is the preponderance of local press monopolies. Nearly every other citizen can only receive local information from a monopoly daily.[49]

The magazine market is similarly integrated. Since 1972, four major publishing groups, Bauer, Springer, Burda, and Bertelsmann/Gruner & Jahr, have held some sixty-five per cent of the general interest magazine market.[50] They are among the fifty largest publishing groups in the world, with other interests in newspapers, broadcasting, book publishing, and radio and television programme journals.

In 1968 the *Günther Kommission*, an independent commission appointed by the federal government to look into the causes of press concentration, had already concluded that concentration started to endanger pluralism when a publisher controlled twenty per cent of the national daily or general interest markets, while a forty per cent market share actively reduced pluralism. Despite these recommendations, there is still no federal press law regulating press ownership, although the *Bund* has the power to do so under Article 75(2) of the Basic Law. The *Länder* have passed press legislation, but this generally regulates editorial freedom, not organisational or economic structure.

In 1974, after substantial opposition by the German newspaper publishers' association, BDZV, the federal government eventually introduced a law on press statistics. It also tried to improve the market structure of the press through subsidies, such as cheap credits for smaller publishers and financial support to introduce new technology. The federal anti-cartel law also contains a specific trigger for press mergers. All press mergers or take-overs, where a turnover of £8.3 million (DM 25 m) or more is involved (which corresponds to a circulation of between 60,000 and 80,000 copies), are assumed to be undesirable, unless the participants can prove otherwise.[51] These rules have slowed down the concentration process but not stopped it. Today, there are few newspaper publishing companies left in each *Land* below the merger control threshold.[52]

The newspaper publishers and the BDZV have had their eyes on broadcasting since 1957. Not surprisingly, when the *Länder* started to legalise private broadcasting in 1984, they were off to a head start. They could raise capital from their advertising-generated cash flows, and they could use the journalistic and editorial resources at their disposal to wage their own public relations campaign, particularly against the public broadcasters. They also lobbied public-opinion conscious politicians and promoted their own broadcasts at comparatively little cost.

They used the 'erosion' rationale to pressurise politicians and justify their claims for access to the private broadcasting market. Local publishers, in particular, lobbied against the introduction of local broadcast advertising, since two thirds of their income comes from local advertising. But to date the fears of erosion remain unsubstantiated, mainly because advertisers use each medium for different types of advertising.[53] It has been predicted that in time, when private broadcasting is more established, the expansion of national brand advertising on television will lead to a ten per cent fall in the advertising market share of general interest magazines; and that local radio may take up to ten per cent of local press advertising. Even so, there is unlikely to be substantially less revenue, since any decline brought about by a shift from the press to radio or television will probably be compensated by an increase in the overall adspend. The main competition will continue to be between the various private radio and TV stations; and between them and the public stations.[54]

There are other economic motives which underpin the 'erosion' theory. The profits from the expanding but highly concentrated West German print market are mainly invested in multi-media enterprises, which promise extensive economies of scope. As media mogul Kirch noted in 1988, 'the success of the multi-media approach lies not only in increasing the capital structure and economic base of the firm but also in offering a complete range of products which can promote each other on the advertising market.'[55]

A new wave of horizontal integration appears under way in the press because of the new market structures emerging through the publishers' broadcasting interests. The smaller independent publishers are most vulnerable, particularly since the larger publishers can profit from inter-media synergies, such as offering reduced rates for combined press and broadcast advertisements.

The *Länder* rules on cross-media ownership offer a complex mix of enabling and restrictive regulation. All the broadcasting acts contain press-broadcasting cross-ownership rules to prevent what the Constitutional Court called 'double monopolies'. The rules vary from *Land* to *Land*, since they are not covered by the 1987 Inter-*Land* Treaty. They are additional to its provisions that require a diverse constitution for the broadcast organisations. So if a publishing company has a dominant share of the local periodicals distributed in the broadcast coverage area (generally twenty per cent; fifty per cent in Baden-Württemberg), in most *Länder* it cannot own more than half a local station, or supply more than half the programmes. Under the SPD-inspired legislation in Bremen and Schleswig-Holstein, this is reduced to a quarter. These two *Länder*, along with Hamburg, also limit publishers' voting rights in broadcast holdings to twenty or twenty-five per cent, although Hamburg and Schleswig-Holstein allow them to own up to thirty-five per cent of a broadcasting company's capital.

The Hessen legislation, although passed by a CDU/FDP government, is the most severe of all. It forbids a publisher which dominates the local daily market in the licensed broadcast area or a major part of it any involvement in broadcasting.[56] It does not, however, explicitly exclude powerful publishers from supplying local programmes. This clause, which was included after SPD lobbying, largely reflects the failure of other regulatory authorities to monitor or prevent cross-ownership abuses. This was confirmed by the Berlin authority which, in its last report, recommends excluding dominant publishers from having interests in broadcasting altogether.[57]

The effectiveness of the press-broadcasting cross-ownership rules is limited, especially where programmes are offered by a broadcasting consortium made up of publishers. Because of economies of scale, local opt-outs are generally produced under one roof using the same premises and staff. It is impossible to know whether a producer has drawn on information or material supplied by the dominant local publisher in the consortium. It is the same in regional television. The national television stations and the major local publishers, which linked up to provide SAT 1, have formed common local television enterprises to use the stations' capital and national advertising capacity, while the publishers supply local and regional news.[58]

More generally, the effectiveness of the cross-ownership rules is limited precisely because of the privileged position of the press in *Länder* broadcasting. Although the Constitutional Court rejected as unconstitutional any preferential access to private broadcasting by the press,[59] several *Länder* have passed broadcasting acts favouring the press.

Bavaria's private broadcasting act explicitly allowed newspaper and magazine publishers to be licensed as broadcast programme providers. The only restriction on dominant publishers was that they must not supply more than a third of the programming. It also required publishers in the intended broadcast coverage area to be given an 'appropriate' stake in the local cable companies that organise private broadcasting. By easing access for publishers, the law allowed large publishing groups, which own different publishing houses in various parts of Bavaria, to participate. National or regional conglomerates could therefore have a bigger slice of local broadcasting than the local newspaper publishers, who are commonly thought of as the essence of local diversity in the regions.

Northrhine-Westfalia followed the approach of the Constitutional Court by separating programme pluralism from economic competition. Under the 'two-column' model, all publishers in the coverage area of a local radio station, or those that produce the local pages of a regional newspaper, are guaranteed a joint vote on the board of the non-profit programme association which is in charge of editorial policy. They are allowed up to seventy-five per cent of the capital and voting rights of the local operating company which controls transmission and finances the station through the sale of airtime. These provisions are designed to protect the local publishers from potential press advertising losses. Their participation is also deemed necessary to secure the required capital investment, whilst excluding the large national media groups, except, of course, where these are synonymous with local publishers, as in the case of the Westdeutsche Allgemeine Zeitung (WAZ).

There are no provisions to prevent newspaper publishers participating in several local radio channels, even when they are adjacent. So the various local publishers in the coverage area have been able to start joint ventures to raise the necessary start-up capital for the radio stations. As shares in the operating companies have been allocated in proportion to the circulation of the participating newspaper, and since, in many cases, only one or two dominant publishers are present in the intended coverage area, the highly concentrated economic structure of the print sector will probably be reinforced in radio. Editorial pluralism could then suffer from the economic dependence of the programme associations on the publisher-dominated operating companies.

Rhineland-Palatinate was more indirect in its enabling rules. It required socially relevant groups and those applicants who could prove journalistic or publishing experience to be granted priority of access. Both criteria, of course, apply to the publishers. In Hamburg, too, the press was implicitly invited to share in regional broadcasting, since there was no clause to exclude the publishers of the local Hamburg dailies. This was to enable 'those providers that are important in the media area', viz. A. Springer Verlag, the most important Hamburg newspaper publisher, to share their editorial expertise in joint broadcasting ventures.[60]

Similarly, Lower Saxony preferred broadcasters whose programmes could be expected to be professionally produced. In theory at least, this requirement was meant to ensure economic stability for the developing private broadcasting market and to exclude 'amateurs' and 'gold diggers' simply out to make a fast buck. The publishers inspired trust because they were long-established, had a proven track record as information providers and had close links with the political establishment. Even before the broadcasting act was passed, Funk und Fernsehen Nordwest-deutschland, which is mainly owned by an association of local publishers, had been promised a licence by the then CDU Minister-President Ernst Albrecht.

The publishers had no problems in turning these concepts of professionalism and pluralism to their advantage, since the politicians needed to attract investment capital. In its licence application for Lower Saxony, Funk und Fernsehen pointed out that

[y]ears of experience . . . guarantee that Funk & Fernsehen Nordwestdeutschland GmbH & Co. KG [ffn], as a company including all Lower Saxony publishers, will provide radio broadcasts that are made to satisfy the information needs of the citizens of the *Land* and represent, through proven journalistic professionalism, the political, economic, social, cultural and religious events of the *Land*. . . . The editorial resources of its shareholders put at ffn's disposal a unique network of 60 editors who can draw upon information and co-operation provided by about 1000 journalists in Lower Saxony.[61]

However, although private radio managers confirm that 'a professional programme' is what the listeners prefer, they emphasise that newspaper journalists do not necessarily have the expertise to produce 'professional' radio programmes.

Other cross-ownership provisions   None of the broadcasting acts contain any specific references to other forms of multi-media ownership. Between 1985 and 1986 however, take-overs, mergers and acquisitions within the cultural industries, including broadcasting, increased by a factor of eight.[62] European experience also seems to indicate that the liberalisation of broadcasting leads to an increasing wave of consolidation across all media sectors.[63] Today there is a complex pattern of cross-ownership between four major players, Leo Kirch, Bertelsmann AG, the Luxembourg-owned CLT and the Italian Berlusconi empire.

The most noticeable development has been the links between film and private broadcasting. In the FRG, there are only a few players in the market for film rights and distribution. The largest is the Kirch Group. It not only supplies films to both the private and public sectors but, through indirect holdings, the group is the majority shareholder in SAT 1. It is also involved in merchandising, cable marketing, video production, pay-television, radio programme sales, film music publishing, European broadcast ventures and a book club. Kirch's son has a forty-nine per cent stake in the fourth largest national private television channel, Pro 7. Kirch also has a ten per cent stake in A. Springer Verlag, the fourth largest European media group and the second largest individual shareholder of SAT 1; and his group is linked to Bertelsmann AG, the largest European media group, through Premiere, a common pay-TV venture with the French Canal Plus.[64]

Bertelsmann AG, which owns magazine, book, newspaper and music publishing, printing and distribution companies, has stakes in the *Land*-wide radios in Bavaria and Hamburg and, along with other newspaper publishers, a planned stake in Radio NRW, the local radio supplier in Northrhine-Westfalia. It is the major shareholder in a radio news agency, and owns film production and acquisition houses. It is the second largest shareholder in RTL plus, after Luxembourg's CLT.

CLT, in turn, is linked to Bertelsmann AG via a finance company and through its own stake in RTL plus. In addition, it holds a twenty-four per cent stake in Tele 5. Twenty-one per cent of Tele 5 is owned by the Italian media mogul Berlusconi, who in turn is linked to Kirch via common production ventures. These cross-connections do not, of course, prevent companies from competing in areas where they are unconnected. For example, both Kirch and Springer compete when buying film rights. And to close the circle, Gesellschaft für Publizistik, which owns fifty-one per cent of A. Springer Verlag, is, at the time of writing, planning to acquire a twenty-nine per cent holding in Tele 5 (see App. XI).

The changes in media ownership with which the German regulators have to cope are all-pervasive. They stretch from the international down to the local level. But the multi-media activities of local newspaper publishers tend to arouse far less regulatory concern than those of the media giants, although a trend to homogenise editorial output, which their cross-media activities could intensify, is evident in the renewed concentration moves in the press sector. The large regional newspaper groups are now equally active in producing and distributing information both locally and nationally through new technologies such as videotex, often in association with the big media players. Apart from their holdings in private radio and television, they often produce programme material, and own cable businesses as well. More often than not, they also dominate the local press in several areas.[65] Both regionally and locally, all these developments could hasten the loss of regional cultural diversity that has been a traditional element in West German pluralism.

Concentration is also taking place in news production. News agencies, some of which are subsidiaries of publishing companies, package their services for a whole range of often smaller private broadcasters. But no broadcasting law regulates these trends, even though they can narrow editorial choice considerably, especially for audiences who also read newspapers.

Nor do the broadcasting acts keep the advertisers out. In the USA, advertising agencies are generally involved in programme production and broadcasting. It may not be long before, via their European branches, they invest in private broadcasting in the FRG.

The effectiveness of ownership and competition regulation

No company has openly infringed the ownership rules for private broadcasting. Even so, a horizontally, vertically and cross-integrated media market has developed in the FRG. The politicians failed to take into account the extent to which ownership concentration across several media can limit citizen choice in obtaining diverse information and entertainment. The regulatory frameworks therefore appear incomplete.

Yet many *Länder* regulators recognise the importance of limiting ownership. When awarding licences, some *Länder* require licence applicants who form a joint broadcasting venture to apply to the Federal Cartel Office in Berlin (see below) to obtain clearance under its merger control regulations. This does not affect critical changes in ownership after licensing, however. These are especially salient whenever a broadcaster is jointly owned, since during the licensing process the internal composition of an applicant is taken as an indicator of its organisational and thus its editorial pluralism. The relevant authority therefore expects to be advised of any changes in ownership structure, although this is only laid down formally in Northrhine-Westfalia, Bremen and Schleswig-Holstein. In the other *Länder*, the authority may order the ownership structure to be disclosed if and when it deems it necessary. But even if it does intend to monitor closely shareholding changes of licensed broadcasters, an authority can face a range of problems which make its task difficult and its measures potentially ineffective.

Basically an authority faces five problems. First, there is the difficulty of gathering information for which it is often ill-equipped. Under German company law, only ownership changes of twenty-five per cent and over need be made public. The authorities, however, have the wider duty to 'prevent a dominant influence upon the formation of opinions'. None of the laws specify at what level changes in ownership structure will trigger intervention; and the standing conference of the regulatory authorities has been unable to agree upon a common figure. The problem is that any such decision by a regulatory authority could well be contested in court as arbitrary; and the authority would then have to prove that the change would indeed bring about 'a dominant influence on the formation of opinion'. This is a normative rule, and would entail an analysis of the effects of the broadcasts, which would be extremely difficult to quantify in ownership terms, and would therefore be impossible to prove empirically until the proposed change was in place and its effects could be analysed.

The 'dominant influence' clause can, however, be used to sanction concentration. This became clear when the majority partner in A. Springer Verlag set out to acquire a twenty-nine per cent stake in Tele 5, in addition to A. Springer Verlag's over twenty-five per cent direct and indirect holding in SAT 1. According to the twenty-five per cent threshold of the Inter-*Land* Treaty (Article 8(5)), such dual interest in satellite broadcasting would be precluded. However, the regulatory authorities were under pressure to secure the survival of Tele 5, which they regarded as the third private general interest channel required to achieve external pluralism nation-wide. They were therefore inclined to interpret Article 8 loosely by denying that these shareholdings, although beyond the limit, would constitute a 'dominant influence', particularly as the proposed holdings were by different branches of the Springer empire, and other partners in Tele 5 and SAT 1 held counterbalancing stakes. In a practical sense therefore, the provisions in the laws are virtually unusable to establish positive editorial competition, in particular if, as in this case, the Federal Cartel Office approves of a deal which in effect furthers horizontal integration in the broadcasting market.

Second, there can be complex indirect connections between various shareholders and senior executives. The Federal Cartel Office considers the twenty-five per cent threshold for mergers, take-overs and acquisitions, to be too high and has suggested a fifteen per cent trigger instead, particularly as transfers of less than twenty-five per cent share capital often go hand in hand with higher voting rights, or other informal arrangements for management control, such as nominee shareholders, trusts or bearer bonds, which are difficult to prove.[66] None of the broadcasting ownership rules takes account of these practices. As yet, therefore, there is no ban to prevent the son of Leo

Kirch from owning forty-nine per cent of the national television channel, Pro 7, which is heavily supplied with his father's films, but which the Kirch group could not acquire itself because of the multiple channel restrictions in the 1987 Inter-*Land* Treaty.

Third, the requirements in the broadcasting acts for 'professional' and financially sound candidates often encourage concentration. Most broadcasting acts now favour joint ventures between several competing licence applicants, as much a means of securing commercial viability as applying the pluralism prescriptions. The increasing tendency towards networking, where several stations join together to use a common sustaining service, either in the form of general interest programmes within a common music format, or occasionally special interest programmes, makes matters worse.

In the FRG, programme syndication is evolving at all levels. For example, although it has not yet applied for a radio licence in the FRG, Luxembourg's RTL Radio supplies programmes, including advertising breaks, free of charge in order to increase its audience reach. Another supplier of free programmes, Star Sat Radio in Munich, has also built up a European market. In some *Länder*, several local stations are linked into a chain, and programmes are frequently supplied by companies which hold shares in the stations supplied. Although programme syndication is currently most evident in radio, the networking business also shows marked inter-media integration tendencies.[67]

Fourth, current ownership regulation applies to domestic German-language channels. Whether the ownership rules should extend to the redistribution of foreign programme channels has so far not been an issue, but this could change with the advent of the EC internal broadcasting market which the CEC is seeking to establish.

Fifth, it is argued that advertising-funded channels do not contribute to the democratic role of broadcasting, since they are aimed not at the democratic citizen, but the consumer. They could not therefore influence opinion formation unduly. But since opinion formation is the constitutional justification for ownership regulation, these channels at least should be exempt from specific broadcasting regulation, and the ownership rules in particular. Instead, they should only be controlled by *Bund* economic law.[68]

It is clear, then, that the most difficult aspect of broadcasting regulation is to marry the regulation of economic competition with the broadcasting ideal of pluralism. The politicians have been slow to appreciate the importance of the issue. The powers of the regulators to shape editorial diversity through ownership and competition rules remain unsatisfactory. The movements towards media concentration have reduced both the number of private channels and the diversity of their programming, casting doubts on the practicability of the concept of external pluralism. The broadcasting laws are marked by inherent contradictions which stem from the confusion between normative cultural and numerical economic regulation. The regulatory authorities feel increasingly powerless to control the situation. There is therefore a self-perpetuating dynamic: the more the market develops and the regulators lose control, the more justified economic regulation of broadcasting under federal jurisdiction will become.

BROADCASTING AND FEDERAL ANTI-CARTEL LEGISLATION

The introduction of private broadcasting has called into question the legal competence of the *Länder* to regulate the economics of broadcasting, whether private or public. According to Article 74(11) of the Basic Law, economics, and with it the regulation of competition policy, are primarily a matter of federal jurisdiction. By introducing private broadcasting, the *Länder* have created a competitive broadcasting market, but the private broadcasting acts are an intervention in the economics of this market. The question is therefore whether *Länder* regulation should not be restricted to matters of programme content, such as rules on programme categories, violence and youth protection and the right of reply. Since the concept of opinion domination is an abstract ideal that, as has been shown, it is impracticable to regulate for, should the objective of regulation then be to prevent domination of the private broadcasting market, instead of programme output, by a few powerful players?

In play is the interface between the economic and cultural spheres of broadcasting, and whether and how the federal anti-cartel act should supersede or complement specific broadcasting legislation. The anti-cartel rules cannot regulate for a diversity of broadcasting output directly. They can only restructure the advertising, pay-television and programme supply markets. The difficulty is that in broadcasting, economics can influence editorial output. In its 1986 decision, the Constitutional Court had assumed,

somewhat unrealistically, that these two areas could be regulated
separately. This assumption was not shared, however, by the
federal Monopolies Commission, the FRG's expert body on
concentration and its socio-economic effects.[69]

Any application of anti-cartel rules calls into question the
traditional demarcation between *Länder* jurisdiction for cultural
matters, including broadcasting, at a time when there is a growing
shift of powers from the *Länder* to the *Bund*.

The anti-cartel law is implemented by the Federal Cartel Office,
an autonomous federal agency in Berlin. Although its decisions are
based on the anti-cartel law, its general policy directives, and its
associated fact-finding and quasi-judicial decision-making powers,
come from the federal Ministry for Economic Affairs. Indirectly,
therefore, the anti-cartel rules rely on federal government policy,
and by extension, its attitude to broadcasting regulation.[70]

The anti-cartel law generally prohibits all trusts and restrictive
horizontal and vertical trade practices that lead to distortion or
restriction of competition, including informal, non-contractual
agreements. The Cartel Office checks abusive conduct by powerful
or dominant players by resorting to numerical triggers for market-
share or turnover defined in the anti-cartel law. It also vets mergers.
Mergers are presumed to be anti-competitive and are prohibited if
they involve, or would result in, market dominance according to
the legal triggers. But in each case the Office has to prove that
a trade agreement or a merger does indeed create or increase
a dominant position. Take-overs and acquisitions amounting to
twenty-five per cent or more of the shares or voting rights
in another company are classified as mergers. But a merger
is also defined as taking place if one enterprise, directly or
indirectly, gains a substantial influence over the decisions of
another. The act covers both horizontal and vertical integration
and the formation of conglomerates. Since the anti-cartel act was
amended, the Cartel Office now also has the power to ignore the
twenty-five per cent trigger. Merger decisions, moreover, depend
on the Office's definition of the relevant geographical and product
or services market.

The merger rules already apply to joint ventures of companies
intending to acquire a broadcast licence, but because of the
provisions in the broadcasting laws, which try to limit the influence
of any one partner in a joint venture, they are not applied very
often. The merger rules do not, however, cover the diversification

of a company into a different market, such as a publishing enterprise expanding into broadcasting.

The Cartel Office may grant exemptions from the anti-cartel law. These are often for statutory undertakings, for certain industries such as utilities, or for small and medium-sized enterprises which can prove that their action will improve their competitiveness in the overall market, or is justified by the general market structure. The Office may also grant exemptions for 'meta-economic' purposes in the public interest, such as youth, environmental and health protection. Although the Cartel Office does have extensive powers of investigation and search, it cannot enforce these search powers abroad, or obtain an injunction outside the FRG.

Anti-cartel regulation and the private broadcasting market

Since most private broadcasters in the FRG are commercial enterprises, their business conduct is clearly subject to the rules of the anti-cartel law. But since they are also expected to adhere to certain public-service principles laid down in the various private broadcasting acts, unconditional application of the anti-cartel rules may be unconstitutional.[71] The Federal Constitutional Court, moreover, has repeatedly emphasised the primacy of *Länder* regulations for organisation and programming in both public and private broadcasting. It is therefore legitimate for the *Länder* to rely on the Federal Cartel Office only as a secondary instrument.

Nevertheless, the German Monopolies Commission has repeatedly asked the *Länder* to go further and stipulate that when a broadcasting licence is awarded to a publisher it should be vetted by the Cartel Office in order to preclude double monopolies.[72] While emphasising the responsibility of the *Länder*, the Constitutional Court also mused about a corresponding amendment to the anti-cartel law.[73]

The anti-cartel law was recently revised, but the new version does not include any specific media provisions other than the existing press merger rules. Although some parts of the SPD appeared to favour such an amendment,[74] the *Länder* representatives in the conservative-led *Bundesrat* opposed it on the grounds that licence decisions are exclusively a matter for the *Land* regulators.[75] The federal government also repeatedly rejected the Monopolies Commission's suggestions on the grounds that any such expansion of federal economic authority would conflict with the broadcasting jurisdiction of the *Länder*. It argued that the high capital investment needed for entry into the private broadcasting would require most publishers to form joint ventures, which are controlled under the merger rules anyway.[76]

The Federal Cartel Office could theoretically intervene in restrictive practices where private broadcasting legislation is also being circumvented, such as networking, and the pooling of advertising or programme material. It is very reluctant to do so, however. Mergers and practices which would restrict market competition have been tolerated,[77] such as the common sale of airtime by the three main publisher-dominated private radio stations in Hamburg, Lower Saxony and Schleswig-Holstein.

The Office has justified its lenient attitude towards press and broadcasting on two grounds. First, it cannot see any relevant impact on the markets for either broadcast or press advertising. And second, anti-competitive developments in the media market were justified by the general economic interest. The publishers are considered as the necessary stimulus for the growth of the private broadcasting market, which is needed to correct the advantages held by the public broadcasters, in terms of infrastructure, size and economies of scope. As the president of the Federal Cartel Office noted in 1987,

> We do not yet know which of these new broadcasters will remain in the market. So we sometimes say: Just carry on, report back after three years . . . [on mergers of monopoly newspaper publishers]. If it is a borderline case, then we prefer to let it go through. Otherwise we might possibly make short shrift of initiatives which would not have a second chance. We want to support whatever provides opportunities for competition against the public broadcasting corporations.[78]

The Monopolies Commission, however, attached greater importance to structural regulation of the private market. Since external pluralism depended on an adequate supply of new entrants, the private players in this market should not be allowed to set up barriers to entry. Although many private stations were not yet making a profit, entry regulation was especially important since players with substantial economic interests in other media determined the structures of the private broadcasting market.[79] In a later report, the Commission concluded that, in effect, the light touch of the Cartel Office meant that the size of the public broadcasters was the (easy) yardstick for concentration control in the private sector.[80]

The public broadcasting corporations and anti-cartel regulation

The main aim of the Cartel Office has thus been to limit the activities of the public broadcasters. In this, it is supported by the Monopolies Commission. The Commission has repeatedly argued for advertising on public radio and television to be prohibited, in order to prevent direct economic competition between the public and the private sector. This, it is felt, would erode the cultural remit and quality output of the public services but, remarkably, it has not mentioned the distortion of market competition as a reason. It has also suggested that the general licence fee, which it calls a 'compulsory charge', should be abolished for viewers and listeners who exclusively use private broadast services, and that a metered licence fee should be introduced for public programmes. This would approximate to a truer market in broadcasting.[81]

In contrast to the Monopolies Commission, the federal government considers the present structure of the dual broadcasting system a *fait accompli*; in particular, like the national brand advertisers, it points to the anti-competitive dangers of an oligopolisation of broadcast advertising by the large private players. Just like the Cartel Office, it subordinates editorial competition to successful market competition and uses this to justify material restrictions on the activities of the public broadcasters.[82] The Cartel Office has an implicit political mandate from the federal government to intervene in broadcasting. In its 1986 'Programme for improving the conditions of the private broadcasting market', the government appealed to the *Land* legislators and the anti-cartel authorities to facilitate market entry for private broadcasters, not just by expanding the transmitter infrastructure and wielding a light regulatory touch but also by limiting new initiatives by the public broadcasting corporations, especially those financed by advertising.[83]

Those who want to apply the anti-cartel rules to the public broadcasters argue that the effects of the commercial activities of ARD and ZDF on the broadcasting market are too important to be ignored.[84] In 1989, ARD and ZDF had a seventy-two per cent share of broadcast advertising; and their income from programme sales, rights and co-productions was approximately £110 million. These commercial activities at least, the argument runs, should be regulated under the anti-cartel law. But since the corporations' programming activities make them attractive to audiences and therefore to advertisers, it seems impossible to separate their commercial activities from their programming activities. Thus, all their activities should be subject to anti-cartel regulation. Exemptions could then be decided on a case by case basis, under the public-interest provisions of the anti-cartel act. This is the way to decide whether to accept a certain degree of anti-competitive behaviour so that the public sector can provide a basic service.

But the *Länder* and the public broadcasters consider that the Cartel Office's arguments for intervention in public broadcasting are on shaky constitutional ground. The *Länder* acts regulating the individual public broadcasting corporations already limit their commercial freedom.[85] Furthermore, the public broadcasters point to the 1986 decision of the Federal Constitutional Court, which saw the private sector merely as 'complementary', but emphasised the responsibility of the public broadcasters to provide a basic service and to be free to develop new services. Any aim by the regulators to secure or improve the position of private broadcasting should not therefore disadvantage the public sector. The mandate to provide the public with a basic service is thus interpreted as granting them extensive immunity from regulation by federal anti-cartel law.[86]

It was also unrealistic, the corporations argued, to separate the public-interest responsibilities of the public broadcasters from their commercial activities; or to split the broadcasting sector into separate divisions which were purely private and public. The public sector needed its commercial activities, such as programme sales, to make up for deficits incurred through private sector competition, the political pressures on the licence fee and the restrictions on advertising times. Even if their 'fringe' commercial activities were conducted in the market, it would be the duty of the *Länder*, not the Federal Cartel Office, to decide what areas of activity, such as the publication of programme magazines, or participation in satellite channels with private broadcasters, were not absolutely necessary to fulfil their public programming remit.

Furthermore, there is a widely accepted legal view in the FRG, substantiated by the 1971 broadcasting judgement of the Constitutional Court, that the corporations are not being paid for services rendered, as are other public enterprises, but that the licence fee is akin to a share which the public has in the corporations. The broadcasters thus act as a trustee for society, and are not commercial enterprises in the sense understood by the anti-cartel law.[87]

Public/private co-operation

In principle, the Cartel Office, which wants to preserve 'complementarity' or 'fair competition' between the public and private sectors, is hostile to joint ventures between the public and private broadcasters. The *Länder* are divided. The political declaration of intent attached to the 1987 Inter-*Land* Treaty contains a compromise formula: 'the possibilities and limits of co-operation depend on the respective *Land* legislation'.[88] But not many acts contain explicit provisions for or against co-operation. The Baden-Württemberg broadcasting act, which was sanctioned by the 1987 decision of the Constitutional Court, restricts co-operation to co-productions or programme exchanges, while Northrhine-Westfalia and Saarland have specific enabling provisions.

Three co-operative ventures may incur, or have already incurred, scrutiny by the Cartel Office. NDR has concluded an agreement with private radio stations in northern Germany for a syndicate to sell airtime, under the name of NDR plus. NDR can thus maintain its leading position in selling airtime, which had been threatened by the advertising syndicate of the three other major private radios in Northern Germany. The private partners will profit from a guaranteed income. But even the SPD, which normally supports the public sector, criticised this type of co-operation for raising a host of legal and political problems.[89]

Similar criticism was voiced about the other two ventures. SR has a twenty per cent holding in the only private commercial radio in Saarland, Radio Salü. The other major partner is the French commercial station Europe 1, which also broadcasts in Saarland. SR's shareholding, which gives it a substantial say in the programming policy of the new radio, has been justified as a measure to fend off private competition.[90] The other co-operative venture is in Northrhine-Westfalia. There, Radio NRW has been set up to supply a sustaining service of programme material and advertising to the local radios in the *Land*. It is a co-operative venture between WDR, which has a thirty per cent share, Bertelsmann AG, with fifteen per cent and, the remaining fifty-five per cent is held by the publishers involved in the local radio operating companies.

The Cartel Office forbade this venture, on the grounds that it would strengthen the dominant position of WDR in the radio advertising market in Northrhine-Westfalia.[91] Significantly, the Cartel Office ruled that the *Land* legislators did not have a right to waive the anti-cartel rules when they regulated broadcasting. In contrast, the regulatory authority in Northrhine-Westfalia, which licensed Radio NRW, maintained that the Cartel Office had no authority whatsoever to intervene in the execution of the broadcasting laws.[92]

In its decision, the Cartel Office did not address the argument of the regulatory authority in Northrhine-Westfalia that, without such an enterprise to supply programmes and advertising, the local radio stations would be unable to survive. Nor did it consider whether, because of its connections with the local radios via the publishers, the new enterprise may effectively bar entry to any other interested supply company. Nor indeed did the Office forbid the publishers from being involved. Its decision was aimed directly at WDR. Although it considered WDR's position in the advertising market to be dominant, it ignored that it had been built up over the previous two years in fair competition with RTL Radio. RTL Radio had previously monopolised the market in Northrhine-Westfalia. It is still competing. It also set up a German programme supply and advertising company in order to compete, unsuccessfully, for a licence in Northrhine-Westfalia.

Radio NRW has appealed the decision to the administrative court. The involvement of public broadcasters and publishers in private broadcasting was in 1991 examined by the Federal Constitutional Court, to whom the CDU had referred the relevant clauses in the Northrhine-Westfalia broadcasting law.

The Monopolies Commission identified another area of regulation for the Cartel Office when it condemned the exclusive deals for programme and sports rights by the public sector. In particular, it considered the public broadcasters' membership of the EBU, which gives them exclusive rights of access to sports events and to purchase of information programmes, a competitive barrier for private broadcasters. In its *Globalvertrag* decision of 27 August 1987,[93] the Office banned as restrictive to competition a contract that ARD and ZDF had concluded with the German Sports Federation. The contract gave them priority rights to a number of sports events over four years, but it did not extend to the most popular sports such as soccer, golf, horse racing and motor racing, or to any international events.

The corporations argued that their constitutional responsibility to provide a basic service justified the purchase of these rights. But instead of examining these specific broadcasting requirements, the Office only applied market criteria. Yet, even so, the contract was not anti-competitive for private broadcasters as it did not include most popular sports, in which the private broadcasters, as they had themselves made clear, were only interested. The Sports Federation also pointed out that the sports clubs involved were non-profitmaking. They did not therefore, engage in commercial activities in the meaning of the anti-cartel law.[94] Their appeal against the decision failed in two instances; this case, too, may finish up in the Constitutional Court.

But the Cartel Office decided not to intervene when Ufa Film und Fernseh GmbH, a Bertelsmann subsidiary, acquired exclusive soccer transmission rights for its satellite channel RTL plus from the German Football League in 1988. This deal was restrictive for RTL plus's rival SAT 1 and the public broadcasters. The only rights which they could then acquire were secondary rights.

The somewhat obsessive concerns of the Monopolies Commission and Cartel Office over the public corporations' dominant opposition in the rights field surfaced again in 1989, around what can be called the 'Wimbledon' syndrome. Again, Ufa had acquired exclusive European radio and television rights, except for the UK, for the Wimbledon tennis championship. It outbid by far the EBU which had traditionally acquired these rights for its members, most of whom are public broadcasters. This meant that ARD and ZDF could not show the matches, either in full or live. ARD and ZDF, conscious of their mandate to be cost-effective, refused to pay Ufa over £0.3 million to show excerpts, which they considered far too expensive considering that they had only paid £50,000 for the entire championship rights in the previous year. Moreover, they did not want to prejudice negotiations for the free rights to broadcast public events, or at least excerpts thereof. This refusal meant that over fifty per cent of West German viewers, all those not reached by RTL plus, could not watch the championships. There was a public outcry, especially when the singles finals were won by two Germans, Steffi Graf and Boris Becker.[95] Not surprisingly, the sports output of ARD and ZDF dropped by five and seven per cent respectively between 1988 and 1989.[96]

But the Cartel Office generally appears to close at least one eye to the financial strength of companies such as Bertelsmann behind the private satellite broadcasters, which, despite the losses of the stations, enable them to compete for rights and programme acquisitions. Instead, it focuses on breaking the stronghold of the public broadcasters. Exclusive deals by a private station, however, also increase private sector competition and lead to spiralling prices, which cannot be in the long-term interest of the private sector or the regulators either.

RIGHT OF ACCESS TO PUBLIC EVENTS

The 'Wimbledon syndrome' highlighted the importance of legal provisions for a right of all broadcasters to report public events. ARD and ZDF therefore appealed to the Minister-Presidents of the *Länder* to demand free access to public events for news clips; an obligation for holders of exclusive rights to share their signals at cost, for brief reports; and the right to broadcast events of outstanding public interest in full for appropriate fees.[97]

Both the SPD and some parts of the CDU agreed on the need for regulation on public access, and an appropriate amendment to the Inter-*Land* Treaty was passed in October 1989.[98] It is more restricted than the public broadcasters wanted, however. It only provides for free access to public events taking place in the FRG to make brief reports. These are as a rule limited to ninety seconds. If all interested broadcasters cannot be allowed direct access, the broadcaster which holds the exclusive rights has priority, followed by those whose broadcasts can be seen in the regions where the event is taking place. If access is impossible, exclusive rights holders have to allow short extracts of their material to be used by other broadcasters for an 'appropriate' share of the costs. These provisions extend to all European television organisations in the FRG, public or private.

Significantly, this first amendment to the Treaty subordinates the general economic rights in recording and the subsequent exploitation of the event to socio-political broadcasting regulation. The legislators explicitly point out that public-interest restrictions on private property are allowed under Article 14 of the Basic Law. The exercise of private property rights, such as licences or copyrights, may thus be restricted for the sake of freedom of information.

But there are several problems with this provision.[99] First, the high production costs for brief direct reports will limit their use to top events. Second, unless a similar clause is inserted in international, or at least European-level, agreements, the provision will only apply to events taking place inside the FRG. It will not secure access to most of the top sports events that take place abroad. Third, political resistance may come from private television stations and the large sports federations, which fear that the provision could reduce the value of exclusive deals. Such deals are something of a lifeline to the private stations, and they generate substantial and often badly needed income for the sports clubs. Fourth, in the case of shared output, it is unclear how an 'appropriate' share of the exclusive right-holders' costs should be calculated, especially as compulsory licensing of brief reports may reduce the sales value of secondary rights. Fifth, the clause does not really tackle the 'Wimbledon syndrome' since it does nothing to contain the spiralling price rises, and it makes no mention of a right to broadcast at full length and at reasonable cost events of outstanding public interest, which would have to be defined by the *Länder*. And sixth, although the provision would extend to the private stations and give them rights to exclusive deals by the public sector, it is doubtful whether the Cartel Office would consider the right to these brief reports a sufficiently commercial incentive for the private broadcasters to compete in the rights market, since in its view the market is dominated by the public broadcasting corporations. The Cartel Office may therefore be expected to continue to interfere.

THE BALANCE BETWEEN PUBLIC AND PRIVATE BROADCASTING

In its 1986 judgement, the Federal Constitutional Court envisaged a dual order in which the public broadcasters provided a basic service and the private broadcasters augmented this with additional services, subject only to minimum pluralism requirements. In advancing this solution, the Court paid no attention to the economic feasibility of the new order which it was proposing. It considered neither the likely effect of economic competition on the ability of the public broadcasters to continue to provide a basic service, nor the likelihood of private broadcasting surviving public sector competition, particularly in the sale of airtime.

The *Länder*, however, interpreted the dual broadcasting order in a different manner. They sought to establish economic conditions whereby the private sector could survive. To do this, they limited competition within the private sector itself in two ways. They awarded the new frequencies for the terrestrial transmission of television signals to the companies which had already established a lead in relaying television signals by satellite and cable. They also agreed in the 1987 Inter-*Land* Treaty to delay the introduction of external pluralism until at least three private nation-wide channels each offering a diverse programming service had been established. These measures to stabilise the private sector were augmented by measures designed to contain the expansion of the public sector both financially and in the use of new distribution facilities. In their regulatory paradigm, the *Länder* switched from that of the Court, which was the provision of editorial diversity by a publicly organised basic service augmented by a fully regulated private sector, to one based on fair competition between the various service providers.

The economic impact of the dual order on the public broadcasters has been severe, particularly in the sale of airtime, and as a result, programming standards have started to fall. But the Federal Cartel Office, encouraged by the federal government and the neo-liberal ideologies of the Monopolies Commission, went further. It deliberately tolerated anti-competitive practices in private broadcasting, whilst attempting to limit the financial strength of the public broadcasters. Thus the practice of the Cartel Office has shifted the regulatory paradigm of fair competition away from programming on to a market structure where ideally all broadcasters, whether public or private, are to be treated equally.

It can be seen therefore that the dual order envisaged by the Constitutional Court has been undermined both by the regulatory approaches and practices of the *Länder*, and by the economic intervention of the Cartel Office. The Court's initial solution will also be weakened by the developments in the EC, and especially the activities of its Commission.

Chapter 7

The European dimension

The independence of the *Länder* and the complex, hard-fought regulatory compromise of the 1987 Inter-*Land* Treaty are being eroded not only at federal level but also at European level. The approach of the Commission of the European Communities (CEC) to the economics of the broadcasting market is three-pronged. It administers instruments of industrial policy, such as the MEDIA 92 and AUDIOVISUAL EUREKA initiatives. It drafts specific broadcasting legislation, such as Council Directive of 3 October 1989 on the coordination of certain provisions laid down by law, regulation or administrative action in Member States concerning the pursuit of television broadcasting activities, the TV Directive which regulates advertising sponsorship and, to a limited extent, programme standards.[1] And through DG IV, the CEC directorate general responsible for competition policy, it applies the existing competition rules in the EEC Treaty. All are subject to scrutiny by the European Court of Justice. The TV Directive and the competition rules are the main instruments which directly affect broadcasting regulation by the *Länder* and therefore increasingly provide the regulatory parameters for national broadcasting policies.

THE TV DIRECTIVE

The TV Directive was adopted by a qualified majority of the Council of Ministers. It was opposed by Belgium and Denmark, but significantly not by the FRG.[2] It aims to establish an internal market for television broadcast services and the distribution of television programmes. Like the Inter-*Land* Treaty it includes the public broadcasters within its framework.

All services from and in EC member states have to meet the minimum standards specified in the Directive. The areas covered are: the promotion of EC programmes, advertising, sponsorship, youth protection and the right of reply. The member states, however, retain their right to license and monitor television broadcasts.

Television broadcasting is explicitly declared to be a service provided for remuneration within the meaning of the EEC Treaty.[3] From this, the CEC draws its powers to regulate it, either through specific broadcasting regulations, or by applying the Treaty's competition rules. In its 1984 Green Paper *Television without Frontiers*, the CEC had already affirmed that all broadcasts, whether financed by the licence fee or by advertising, were services regardless of any elements of cultural content.[4] The European Court of Justice recently confirmed this view in its 1988 *Vereiniging Bond van Adverteerders and others v. State of Netherlands* (*Kabelregeling*) decision.[5] Even so, the salient role played by public broadcasting in most member states was acknowledged in the explanatory statement to the draft of the Directive. The Directive is 'to guarantee a central and economically healthy role for the public broadcasting service'; but also to 'establish conditions of fair competition without prejudice to the public interest role to be discharged by the television broadcasting services'.[6]

The Directive applies to all broadcasts, public or private, that can be received, directly or indirectly, in one or more member states other than the country of origin. This is the state under whose jurisdiction the organisations broadcast, or where they are situated. In practice, the Directive deliberately includes all possible broadcasts in the FRG, no matter how they are distributed, whether terrestrially, by cable or by satellite. Once they can be received directly in any other EC countries within the satellite footprint, satellite services, such as 3Sat or SAT 1, are covered, even if they are only intended for, and their film rights purchases extend to, German-speaking territories. Depending on the diameter of the satellite receiving dish, 3Sat and SAT 1 can be received in Denmark, the Benelux countries, parts of Italy, France and the UK. SAT 1 can also be picked up in Spain and Eire. Once a television service is distributed by cable in other EC countries, it also comes within the scope of the Directive, even if it is redistributed without the permission of the original satellite broadcaster. The same applies to terrestrial broadcasts. For these, overspill to neighbouring EC countries, which border the FRG, is unavoidable; this is true even for most regional terrestrial television services. The only exemptions are local cable services, such as open access channels.

Each member state has to ratify the Directive by 3 October 1991. This means that the *Länder* will have until then to incorporate it into their regulatory frameworks. In many areas, EC broadcasting legislation will supplant the broadcasting acts of the *Länder*. This is where the problems of jurisdictional competence begin.

In its pragmatic decision of 1986, the Federal Constitutional Court had already taken account of the risks to national regulation from cross-frontier broadcasting. At the same time, the Council of Europe in Strasbourg had started work on a Convention on Transfrontier Television, and the federal government declared it preferred a Council of Europe television convention to an EC directive.[7] Nevertheless, although Germany's federal structure gives the *Länder* the legislative and regulatory authority for broadcasting, the federal government eventually voted for the Directive in Brussels. The decision was based on a cabinet discussion, without either explicit parliamentary approval, or a mandate from the West German *Länder*.

The federal government has been one of the major driving forces behind the Directive since the early 1980s. It wanted to bind the emerging 'pirates of the sky' into a European media order, so as not to endanger fundamental values in the fields of youth protection and advertising. But the Directive was also a convenient tool for the CDU/CSU/FDP coalition to manoeuvre the *Länder* into establishing a homogeneous framework for the liberalisation of domestic broadcasting, and thereby increase the commercial viability of the private sector. The federal government also sees broadcasting as a vital tool in its aim for political integration to accompany the single market in 1993. Prompted by the events in Eastern Europe, the federal government, together with the French, has already announced its desire for political unity.

In contrast, even though it was they who would be responsible for implementing the Directive, the *Länder* had no vote but were only allowed observer status during the deliberations. They had always expressed reservations about the EC regulation. Consequently, when the Directive was agreed, the government of Bavaria, the *Land* with the strongest tradition of autonomy in the FRG, supported by the *Bundesrat*, the ARD and ZDF, appealed against the federal government's agreement to the Directive to the Federal Constitutional Court.[8]

The resulting debate about the applicability of the Directive mirrors the problems which surfaced between the *Länder* and the *Bund* over the application of competition regulation. By extension, the question is how far EC law can derogate provisions of the German Basic Law.[9]

Opinion in the FRG is divided on the applicability of the EEC Treaty to broadcasting. Some argue that, although the EEC Treaty is not universally applicable, its instruments of economic policy should be used to ensure a competitive market. But for those regulatory areas where cultural and social matters take precedence over economic ones, such as programme content, public service responsibilities, and the mode of finance appropriate to these questions, the *Länder* should remain solely responsible.[10] Others have gone further and called for a comprehensive regulation under EC supervision of all broadcasting that is potentially transnational, so as not to impede the creation of an internal market.[11]

The third opinion is that the EC has no explicit competence, either comprehensive or economic, to regulate broadcasting. This is the line taken by the *Länder*. Although the general aim of the EEC Treaty is the economic integration of the member states, this does not justify a creeping expansion of its powers to broadcasting. And although the Single European Act, which amends the Treaties of Rome, aims at a European market for audiovisual products, it does not envisage passing national sovereignty on to the EC in the area of broadcasting.[12] Even the harmonisation of what are basically consumer protection rules, such as advertising and youth protection, cannot replace the constitutionally prescribed 'positive' regulation of broadcasting, which is central to the democratic functioning of the FRG.

The *Länder* thus assert that '[t]he cultural and socio-political function of broadcasting *forbids* a one-sided or merely predominantly *economic view* of broadcasting'.[13] They do not accept that the public broadcasters provide services to viewers for remuneration. To support this, they draw on the 1971 judgement of the Constitutional Court, which ruled that the licence fee did not constitute a payment in return for a service rendered.[14] As for commercial broadcasting, since the pluralist organisation of broadcasting and its programme output are significantly determined by its economic arrangements, according to Article 30 of the Basic Law, the latter also have to remain within the competences of the *Länder*. But not only does the Directive infringe the legislative autonomy of the *Länder*, it also impinges on their control powers and presages the possible establishment of a regulatory authority for broadcasting, within the CEC, above those of the *Länder*.[15] Thus the federal government had no right to vote for the Directive.

But the federal government insisted that its competence in signing the TV Directive only extended to marginal economic aspects of broadcasting and did not infringe the autonomy of the *Länder* to regulate cultural matters. Article 24(1) of the Basic Law does indeed authorise the federal government to pass on to supranational institutions, such as the EC, sovereign rights of the *Länder*. The Constitutional Court has affirmed in various decisions, however, that a transfer must not be allowed to erode the substance of the country's federal constitutional structure.[16] Even though this means that the *Länder* have to retain at least a core of sovereign tasks and competences, the legal adviser of the Bavarian government argues that the *Länder* have, in effect, almost lost their constitutional autonomy due to the formal and practical development of EC legislation.[17] There would be no way of preventing further EC intervention if the EC were to be allowed to claim legislative competence for areas of traditional *Länder* authority, simply on the grounds that a given area has an economic dimension, regardless of other dimensions, such as the cultural and socio-political dimensions of broadcasting, since there is hardly any area of activity which does not have an economic dimension.

Moreover, in view of the Convention on Transfrontier Television of the Council of Europe, which was passed on 5 May 1989, the *Länder* do not see any need for an EC directive.[18] Even so, as a precaution, the *Länder* broadcasting *Referenten* have now started to discuss the necessary amendments to the 1987 Inter-*Land* Treaty, but more pressing problems, raised by German unification, have delayed the negotiations.

The *Länder* prefer the Convention for a number of legal technicalities, even though its provisions correspond closely to those of the TV Directive, which for EC member states assume priority.[19] In its preamble, the Convention specifies its regulatory objectives as: the free flow of information and opinions under conditions of pluralism and equality of all democratic groupings and political parties; and to increase the choice of public programmes, in particular of quality productions in the areas of politics, education and culture. Thus, although it regulates the same material areas as the TV Directive, its rhetoric is much closer to the *Länder* philosophy of broadcasting as culture, instead of a primarily economic activity.

The Convention only acquires force of law once the *Länder*, and not just the federal government, agree to it. In contrast, the TV Directive is absolute in its application, and leaves only its administration and execution to the *Länder*.

The TV Directive allows cable relays to be interrupted for contraventions of the youth protection rules but only after a twelve month probation period.[20] The Convention, in contrast, gives the *Länder* more wide-ranging powers to interrupt programmes, particularly if they do not comply with the advertising guidelines. The signatories may also conclude or adhere to separate broadcasting treaties which expand the rules of the Convention. Under the TV Directive, such treaties might be considered harmful to its goal of establishing 'a common programme production and distribution market' or 'conditions of fair competition'.

The interpretation and control of the Convention rules is supervised by a standing committee which could include representatives of the *Länder* in the FRG delegation, beside the representation from the EC. Arbitration is a negotiated process between contestants and thus leaves scope to take into account national constitutional principles, such as the decisions of the Federal Constitutional Court. In contrast, the TV Directive is interpreted by EC bureaucrats, by national courts, which have to enforce EC law, and finally by the European Court of Justice.

Finally, the Convention applies to the German-speaking countries of Austria and Switzerland, which are both members of the Council of Europe. It is also open for other countries to join, such as the current members of the EBU and the Eastern European countries. Not only do the public broadcasters have established ties with them, but their increasingly capitalist economies are a potential market for the private television stations.

Although the TV Directive takes priority, and its provisions were aligned to those of the Convention, there remain differences and areas of divergence. Thus, depending on the decision of the Federal Constitutional Court, the *Länder* will face the complex task of applying one or both the European regulatory instruments. At the same time, under the provisions of the TV Directive, broadcasters, both domestic and foreign, will be able to challenge from a predominantly market-oriented perspective the broadcasting decisions of both the German regulators and anti-cartel authorities. They can by-pass the 'pluralism-biased' Federal Constitutional Court and appeal directly to the European Court of Justice. The latter can overrule any decision of the Federal Constitutional Court. With that in mind, the German Court can be expected to try to avoid a potential conflict with the European Court and reach a pragmatic compromise between the applicability of national and EC broadcasting law.

The Constitutional Court's final judgement on the TV Directive is not expected until 1991, but in a preliminary decision it has already allowed the federal government to vote for the TV Directive. The Court accepted the argument by the federal government that if it did not sign the Directive it would lose the major concessions which had been negotiated, should the Court eventually find for the federal government. According to the federal government, these concessions were the omission of radio broadcasting, the inclusion of non-EC European productions in the 'European production quota' (see below), the non-binding nature of the quota rules, and the renunciation of a comprehensive European media order.[21]

The provisions of the TV Directive compared to the Inter-*Land* Treaty

The Directive does not bear directly on the organisational, licensing and administrative authority of the *Länder*. It even contains explicit provisions for the member states to lay down more detailed or stricter rules for the television broadcasters licensed under their jurisdiction, especially

> so as to reconcile demand for televised advertising with the public interest, taking account in particular of:
> the role of television in providing information, education, culture and entertainment; [and]
> the protection of pluralism of information and of the media.[22]

This means that in pursuit of the public-service role of television, member states can impose conditions on their broadcasters that are more severe than the Directive's minimum standards for youth protection, advertising or European and independently produced programmes. This justifies in particular a tighter regulation for the public broadcasting corporations than for the private broadcasters. However, the Directive completely ignores the philosophy of the Constitutional Court, that the public-interest role of broadcasting and the special status of the West German public broadcasting corporations demand adequate legal and material positive guarantees beyond the establishment of 'fair competition', guarantees which the Inter-*Land* Treaty concedes at least rhetorically.

The youth protection rules of the Directive are much less specific than those in the Inter-*Land* Treaty, since they allow member states to 'take appropriate measures to ensure that television broadcasts by broadcasters under their jurisdiction do not include programmes which might seriously impair the physical, mental or moral development of minors, in particular those that involve pornography or gratuitous violence'.[23] What is appropriate, however, depends on the different attitudes to pornography and violence which appear to range from the liberal attitude of Italy to the more restrictive view taken in the UK. The FRG lies somewhere in the middle. The youth protection rules in the Treaty are therefore likely to undergo little change.

Modifications to individual provisions of the Inter-*Land* Treaty will be necessary, however, in the field of advertising where the Directive, and the Convention, are simultaneously both stricter and more lenient than the Treaty. The Directive is stricter since it only allows an average hourly advertising ceiling of fifteen per cent in any one day, with a maximum of twenty per cent in any one hour; or a twenty per cent ceiling including teleshopping.[24] The Inter-*Land* Treaty has a daily advertising limit of twenty per cent, but no hourly ceiling, in line with the preferences of most private television stations in the FRG.

The EC rule raises problems for both public and private broadcasters, since it stipulates a fifteen per cent ceiling on a daily, and not a yearly, average. This means there will be no allowance for the seasonal adjustment of commercial airtime customary in West German broadcasting. In the FRG, airtime which has not been sold at times of weak demand can be sold when demand peaks. During 1987 for instance, the demand ratio for SAT 1, between months of high and low demand, was 2.42 to 1; and peak time slots were sometimes overbooked by fifty per cent. Income would therefore be lost by changing to the new system.[25]

Because of seasonal adjustment, the public broadcasters can sell up to twenty-five minutes of commercial airtime at times of peak demand during their two-hour early evening slots, but in times of weak demand it is difficult to sell all the twenty minutes of airtime permitted. Under the rules of the TV Directive, however, assuming that the two-hour advertising slot is not extended, they could sell no more than twenty-four minutes. Under Article 19 of the TV Directive, tighter restrictions to the advertising ceilings, such as those stipulated in the Treaty for the public broadcasters, are permissible; but a relaxation of the quotas is not allowed.

According to calculations by ARD and ZDF, this change could lead to an annual loss of income of £8.3 million (DM 25 m). The *Länder* would then be obliged to make up for such losses if they were to fulfil their undertakings in the 1987 Inter-*Land* Treaty to secure the existence and development of the public broadcasting corporations. They would either have to increase the licence fee again, or they would have to extend the permissible periods for commercial airtime beyond the present 8pm watershed.[26]

Articles 3(3) and 7(6) of the Inter-*Land* Treaty prohibit, for public and private broadcasters respectively, more than one advertising break in television transmissions more than sixty minutes long. But Article 11 of the Directive allows a lighter regime, with one commercial break every forty-five minutes in feature and television films, while other programmes may be interrupted after twenty minutes. Documentaries, information, religious and children's programmes may also be interrupted if they are longer than thirty minutes. Only broadcasts of a religious service may not be interrupted. Some *Länder* may want to take advantage of these laxer provisions to help the private broadcasters to make up some of their losses.

The sponsorship rules of the TV Directive (Article 17) are largely similar to the rules of the Treaty. They also contain the distinctly unrealistic provision that 'the content and scheduling of sponsored programmes may in no circumstances be influenced by the sponsor in such a way as to affect the responsibility and editorial independence of the broadcaster in respect of programmes'.

Like the Treaty, the TV Directive requires the sponsor to be identified at the beginning and/or end of the programme. Similarly it makes no reference to the sponsorship of public events that are broadcast on television. But the Directive is more precise than the Treaty in that it forbids the sponsorship of news and current affairs programmes.[27] In general, the manner in which the EC rules would be interpreted by the *Länder* can be expected to give rise to the same problems and negotiated solutions as the the corresponding rules in the Treaty.

The advertising and sponsorship rules in the Directive do not oblige member states, or in the FRG the *Länder*, to downgrade their own provisions. They are free to impose more stringent or detailed conditions, but nothing more permissive. In the political declaration of intent attached to the TV Directive, the CEC asserts that it would interpret the Directive so as to prevent national broadcasters from migrating abroad and broadcasting back to their original state, merely to escape the more stringent restrictions of that member state. How this objective could be realised in practice is not clear, especially if the competition rules of the EEC Treaty are being applied in parallel. But the Convention is more concrete. A signatory to the Convention may apply its domestic advertising rules to a foreign channel from another Convention country, if the latter's advertisements are intended for the signatory's country (Article 16). The purpose is to prevent distortions in competition that would upset 'the equilibrium' of the signatory's domestic TV system. It is likely, however, that individual *Länder* would consider relaxing their regulations, to allow their domestic stations to redistribute their programming to other German-speaking countries and so avoid discriminating against their domestic broadcasters compared with foreign stations beamed at the FRG.

The other area regulated by the TV Directive and the Convention is the percentage of EC-originated material which is broadcast. The original draft of the TV Directive had provided for a sixty per cent quota of EC programmes. In 1989, ARD and ZDF's output of EC feature films and television serials, including works from other German-speaking territories,[28] let alone television drama, reached between forty and sixty per cent; and although fifty-five to eight-five per cent of the feature films offered by RTL plus and SAT 1 came from the EC, for the mainstay of their programming both channels rely heavily on serials, which are almost all non-European, US productions.[29] This will continue until a market has been established for major European productions that is as cheap as the US market.

It is not surprising, therefore, that the FRG wanted the original quota provisions to be watered down. The final version closely resembles the non-mandatory nature of the cultural provisions in the 1987 Inter-*Land* Treaty. Both the Directive and the Convention now only require that states

> shall ensure *where practicable and by appropriate means*, that broadcasters reserve for European works . . . a majority proportion of their transmission time, excluding the time appointed to news, sports events, games, advertising and teletext services. *This proportion, having regard to the broadcaster's informational, educational, cultural and entertainment responsibilities to its viewing public, should be achieved progressively, on the basis of suitable criteria.*[30]

And the TV Directive adds: 'Where the proportion laid down in paragraph 1 cannot be attained, it must not be lower than the average for 1988 in the Member State concerned.'[31] Moreover, the production obligations of the Directive are explicitly not legally binding, but have instead the character of a political declaration.[32]

Even so, German broadcasters, both public and private, regard the programming rules and the attached CEC's supervisory powers as an infringement of their constitutional freedom from the state.[33] They also object to Article 5 of the Directive, which proposes in a similar non-mandatory form a quota of independently produced informational, cultural, educational and entertainment programmes. The Directive also expects the television companies to contribute at least ten per cent of their *total* programming budget to these independent productions, with the aim of promoting small and medium-sized producers. At an industrial policy level, this requirement is complemented by the EC's MEDIA 92 initiative to develop European audiovisual production and distribution enterprises. Although these arrangements allow schemes such as the FRG's film/television agreement to continue (provided it is not forbidden under EC competition rules), they could also reinforce the tendencies to diversify among the large multi-media companies. In the FRG, it is doubtful whether this provision will contribute much to the stability of the smaller independent sector. The sector is heavily dependent on the public broadcasters, which commission far more than ten per cent of their output from independent producers. Even so, the sector is already in decline because of the financial pressures on ARD and ZDF, and because competition from the production arms of the private broadcasters has led to a fall in revenues.[34]

The summary right of reply provisions in the TV Directive and the Convention[35] are compatible with the corresponding provisions in West German broadcasting legislation since it is left to member states, i.e. the *Länder* in the FRG, to interpret them.

The Convention, but not the Directive, provides the television audience with a right of information to follow events of 'high public interest'.[36] But the provision is very general, and only calls for signatory states to 'examine the legal measures'. The recent provisions in West German broadcasting legislation for the right to report public events briefly go some way to meeting this provision, but they do not deal fully with the right of a large part of the public, which is recognised in the Convention, 'the opportunity to *follow* that event on television'.[37]

West German broadcasters are now faced with an ever-increasing number of broadcasting laws, which limit their freedoms. The EC TV Directive, the Council of Europe Convention, the inter-*Land* treaties, the *Länder* broadcasting acts, FRG and EC anti-trust law and the corresponding decisions of the FRG administrative courts, the Federal Constitutional Court and the European Court of Justice, all limit their freedom. Far from easing regulatory pressures, the changes at the European level are increasing them.

The negotiations over the EC's TV Directive avoided a number of key issues pertaining to the regulation of broadcasting. The main role of the Directive has been to co-ordinate arrangements to allow advertising-financed television services and sponsored programmes to be broadcast throughout the Community. In the final analysis, the provisions in the Directive for the promotion of distribution and production of European television programmes are all voluntary; and the provisions both for the protection of minors, and for a right of reply, allow member states substantial discretion in the manner in which they are interpreted.

So far three key questions have not been addressed in EC broadcasting policy. These are the role played by national copyright laws in transfrontier broadcasting; intra- and inter-media concentration; and the the tensions between EC economic regulation, which draws its authority from the EEC Treaty, and the socio-political and cultural philosophies of broadcasting, which draw their rationales from the national constitutions of most member states. In the FRG, all three issues have become increasingly important.

COPYRIGHT

In its *Coditel* judgement, handed down in 1980,[38] the European Court of Justice ruled that the EEC Treaty could not prevent owners of intellectual property, which was protected by national legislation, from limiting the geographical area over which their works could be broadcast. Since these areas were normally the same as national boundaries, the court effectively ruled that trade in broadcasting between EC member states could be limited by rights holders; and furthermore, if a broadcast was to be relayed across EC national boundaries, the broadcaster had to acquire the rights for all countries covered.

In its original draft of the TV Directive, the CEC therefore proposed that all member states should be required to grant cable operators a compulsory licence to relay internal broadcasts from neighbouring EC countries. But after extensive lobbying the proposal for a compulsory licence was dropped. Cable operators still have to pay for an additional copyright licence to relay broadcasts from neighbouring states; and satellite operators may also have to obtain copyright licences for all countries within their footprint, unless the signals are encrypted and can only be decoded in those countries for which copyright licences have been obtained. In the FRG, DBP Telekom will only relay satellite channels if the cable providers hold all the relevant programme rights. In addition, it pays an agreed lump sum to the West German collecting societies for any terrestrial programme services which are distributed outside their intended coverage area.

After its negative experience with the TV Directive, the CEC has changed its approach. In its Copyright Green Paper,[39] the policy has changed from that of compulsory licensing, which attempted to allow cable and satellite operators the freedom to provide transfrontier services, to *increasing* and *harmonising* the national protection afforded to rights holders. But increased protection is also to be accompanied by EC competition policy in the exploitation of these rights, since this is deemed to be more efficient in economic terms.

EC COMPETITION POLICY

EC competition rules are laid down in Articles 85 to 102 of the EEC Treaty as amended by the Single European Act. The role of competition policy is to strengthen the EC's overall policy of 'promoting a cooperative strategy for the creation of employment, of strengthening economic and social cohesion and of achieving an internal market by . . . 1992.'[40] Since the communications sector is considered essential to achieve the internal market, it has naturally been a focus of competition policy in recent years.

Articles 85 and 86 are used by the CEC's Competition Directorate to prevent potentially undesirable market behaviour, such as cartels or increasing concentration. Article 85 prohibits all business agreements and practices 'which have as their object or effect the prevention, restriction or distortion of competition within the common market'; and Article 86 prohibits the abuse of a dominant position 'within the common market or in a substantial share thereof . . . in so far as it may affect trade between Member States'. Although Articles 85 and 86 only regulate practices 'which may affect trade between Member States', this is interpreted freely and can apply to any transaction affecting the position of competing enterprises in the common market, no matter where the undertakings under investigation are registered.[41]

There are no thresholds for dominance in the Treaty, like the twenty-five per cent clause in the West German anti-cartel law or broadcasting legislation. But a company with a forty to forty-five per cent market share is generally considered to be dominant, even when the relevant market is narrowly defined.[42]

It is normally assumed that the provisions of Regulation 17, which empowers the CEC to take measures to enforce competition rules, includes all sectors of economic activity *unless* the Council defines special procedural rules or exemptions.[43] This has not yet happened for broadcasting. On the contrary, the CEC assumes that broadcasting constitutes an economic activity, and therefore can be legitimately regulated under the competition rules. However, cross-EC holdings can easily slip through the regulatory clutches of the Federal Cartel Office.

As far as the CEC is concerned, the national anti-monopoly authorities are responsible for implementing EC competition law unless the CEC has initiated its own investigation. In particular, the national authorities face the task of preventing a cross-EC holding from abusing its economically dominant position in local or regional (e.g. *Länder*) markets since they are not covered by the EC competition rules.[44]

Competition policy is the only area of EC regulation where

the CEC may issue directives without prior consultation with the member states. Although the Competition Directorate is an administrative body, it is extremely powerful since it performs a judicial role, just like the Federal Cartel Office. It is investigator, prosecutor and judge, all rolled into one. The present conduct of the CEC's competition policy has been increasingly criticised by member states as infringing on national regulatory sovereignty through its application of the competition rules to the public sector, and its neglect of certain meta-economic concerns of state regulation, such as social politics and culture.[45] The development of EC competition policy is an 'institutional struggle in which the Commission is seeking to use the undoubted powers it enjoys . . . to extend its competence to other areas which are still the preserve of the Member States'.[46]

The ARD/MGM/UA case

The boundary which divides the responsibilities of national anti-monopoly bodies from those of the EC competition authorities is therefore distinctly hazy. Certainly, the CEC Competition Directorate has adopted an extremely broad interpretation of activities which affect trade between member states. A clear example of this was its ruling on the acquisition by ARD of the broadcasting rights of a large number of American films and television programmes.[47]

Early in 1984, Degeto Film GmbH, the programme purchasing arm of the ARD, representing all ARD stations except BR, concluded a film licensing agreement with Metro-Goldwyn-Mayer/ United Artists Entertainment Co. (MGM/UA). For $80 million, the agreement gave ARD the exclusive rights to 1,364 library feature films including the James Bond blockbusters, 150 new feature films, all cartoons and 416 hours of television films and series which could be exploited until the year 2013. The licences covered the major German-speaking territories in Europe: the FRG, GDR, Austria, Liechtenstein, Luxembourg, Alto Adige (Northern Italy), German-speaking Switzerland, and all possible modes of distribution. ARD could allocate exclusive sublicences, and did so to the Austrian and Swiss public broadcasting corporations.

The deal was extraordinary in several respects. It bypassed the traditional rights agents, in particular the Kirch group. It was designed to secure a competitive advantage for the ARD before competition from the private television stations would push up prices on the international market for film rights, as has now happened. The term of the licences and the degree of exclusivity enjoyed were unusual for such agreements. They were not so unusual for the Kirch group, however.

In 1986, the Competition Directorate initiated proceedings against the agreement which it considered unjustifiable and leading to an artificial barrier for the other broadcasters. The CEC claimed competence because the agreement covered two, albeit marginal, EC regions, Luxembourg and Alto Adige in Northern Italy. Indeed, if the EC Competition Directorate had not stepped in, it is likely that the Federal Cartel Office would have done so, since the agreement was felt to be unfair to the German satellite stations, which at that time were struggling for audiences and were more dependent on feature films than the public broadcasters. RTL plus in particular was at risk since, unlike its rival SAT 1, it did not have access to the film rights held by the Kirch group.[48] Furthermore, the increasing demand from the private broadcasters offered to film producers and distributors, such as MGM/UA, an opportunity to exploit their products on more fronts than had been foreseen in 1984.

A subsidiary of Turner Broadcasting Systems, TEC, took over the assets of MGM/UA in 1986, including most of the film licences under the ARD deal. UA was split from the main company and continued trading as MGM/UA Co. It took over the remaining rights, including those for the James Bond films and new films.

Although in principle the ARD does not recognise EC authority to regulate the predominantly socio-cultural area of public broadcasting, it conceded the CEC power over the 'fringe' area of purchases of film rights and applied for an exemption under Article 85(3) of the Treaty. This article allows for other meta-competitive goals of the EC, such as regional and industrial policy and technical and economic progress, to justify derogations from the competition rules. For instance, as under the West German anti-cartel provisions, market activities that strengthen the competitive position of small and medium-sized firms would qualify for exemption. Thus Article 85(3) can serve to ease tension that is likely to arise between the application of competition policy and other EC policy goals, such as strengthening the European audiovisual market.

Another exemption from the competition rules is possible under Article 90(2). Article 90 states that the competition rules apply to 'public undertakings and undertakings to which Member States grant special or exclusive rights', including '[u]ndertakings entrusted with the operation of services of general economic interest or having the character of a revenue-producing monopoly'. The underlying principle is to treat public enterprises in the same way as private ones.[49] Article 90(2), however, grants an exemption if the application of the competition rules would endanger the performance of the public service tasks assigned to the public undertakings. However, the ARD did not invoke a derogation under the more comprehensive Article 90(2), since it did not want to put its fundamental legal argument at risk. This was that the corporations as a whole are not undertakings in the sense of the EEC Treaty.

To qualify for the exemption under Article 85, under pressure from the Competition Directorate, ARD and TEC negotiated in 1988 a so-called 'window' solution, which also binds MGM/UA Co. The 'windows' mean that the licences for certain films revert to the licence-holder, who can then allocate them to third parties for exploitation during certain periods. ARD either makes available the copies which are already dubbed, or shares the dubbing costs with the private broadcasters. Although this is distinctly advantageous to the private broadcasters which do not have to bear all the high dubbing costs, ARD is rather laid back about this obligation; it will also ease its own dubbing costs.

ARD also had to relinquish its rights to sublicense. This has mainly affected the Austrian and Swiss broadcasters, who now have to renegotiate their film purchases at source, even though they do not recognise the jurisdiction of the EC authorities.

In 1989, after these changes, the CEC granted an exemption to the deal until 1999 under Article 85(3), thereby acknowledging that the structure of the audiovisual market did not yet allow competitive access for third parties. The exemption was *not* based on an acknowledgement that an extensive agreement of this nature was necessary, if the public broadcasters were to fulfil their responsibilities to provide basic services in the face of increasing competition. On the contrary, the application of the competition rules did not apparently prevent the corporations from fulfilling their public tasks. The CEC justified its ruling in strictly market terms. The 'windows' allowed a certain degree of competition, and the dubbing arrangements promoted access by the private broadcasters. The large scale of the agreement meant that the ARD corporations, which have to work with a restricted budget, were able to acquire more films at lower prices than would have been possible under the standard agreements. As a result, the viewers benefited since more German-language films were shown on television. Last but not least, the agreement was no longer anti-competitive compared with other opportunities to purchase films for the German-speaking market.

So far, the CEC's attempts to deal with the rigidities in the marketplace which arise from national copyright protection laws have only been directed at public broadcasters. In the FRG, this must have pleased the private broadcasters since the main thrust of the CEC's approach, just as that of the Federal Cartel Office, has been to limit the market power of their rivals in the public sector.

It is questionable, however, why the CEC felt empowered to take a decision without looking more closely at the structures of the market in German film rights, in which the ARD's major competitor, the Kirch group, has close links with private broadcasters and other media outlets, which appear to be at least as restrictive as those in the ARD/MGM/UA agreement. According to the CEC itself the Kirch group already holds the German-language rights in some 15,000 feature films and 50,000 hours of television product, including the most lucrative parts of the libraries of the American majors.[50]

EC AUDIOVISUAL POLICY: TOWARDS A COMPREHENSIVE MEDIA ORDER?

In a recently published document, the CEC has outlined its future proposals on audiovisual policy to the Council of Ministers and the European Parliament.[51] This document marks a significant development in CEC thinking now that the TV Directive has been agreed by the Council of Ministers. It is a discussion paper which provides the framework for 'each of the three sections of the audiovisual "triptych"; the rules of the games, the programme industries and new technologies'.[52]

In the field of copyright protection, the paper follows the lead of the CEC's *Green Paper on Copyright* by proposing an increase in copyright protection to a common level in all member states, especially for rental rights in audiovisual works. The initiative for a new directive will

> tackle the problems posed by cable distribution and satellite broadcasting . . . on the basis of extended collective agreements taking into account the growing need for rights to be administered no longer in terms of national territory but in terms of broadcasting areas and taking into account the real audience.[53]

The thrust of the approach is that copyright laws in the EC must be brought up to a common standard, so that the satellite and cable operators can develop transnational markets within the EC in order to compete with terrestrial broadcasters on a more competitive basis. If this policy is implemented in the FRG, the public broadcasters, which, the Federal Constitutional Court ruled, should provide a basic service, can expect to face increased competition from German-language satellite and cable operators based outside the FRG in other EC member states, such as Luxembourg.

The CEC wants to go further, however. First, it wants to promote audiovisual production by examining how it could promote the possibility of independent producers retaining the rights over their works, by 'adapting the rules concerning the acquisition of rights'.[54] There are normally two parts to the pre-financing arrangements when a broadcaster commissions a programme. One part, the network share, covers the right of first transmission within a specified area for a limited period; and the other, the co-producer share, concerns repeat rights and rights of transmission over areas other than those covered by the broadcaster.

In the view of the CEC, the limited nature of the co-producer share

> deprives the [independent] producer of marketing control over his work and greatly reduces his opportunities to call upon the financial markets. This is because the contributions of finance institutions are often based on the successive receipts which they consider achievable from the sale by the producer of his repeat transmission rights.[55]

The intention seems to be to allow a broadcaster which commissions an independent production to retain only the first transmission rights for the production for a limited period in his broadcast area. The remaining rights will stay with the independent producer to establish a secondary market. They could be sold in rival distribution markets, such as video, or satellite and cable, and for subsequent transmissions. The broadcasters could thus be financing the production of audiovisual works which competitors could then schedule against them in the future. For the CEC, '[t]he creation of a secondary market represents a necessary complement to the promotion of independent production since it will create the possibility of profitable production through multiple broadcasts and *the conditions of genuine competition between broadcasters*'.[56]

At the present time, as part of their provision of a basic service, the public broadcasters in the FRG make substantial financial contributions to the film/television production fund which is designed to encourage the production of films suitable for both cinema and television distribution (film/TV agreement).[57] Between 1990 and 1993, they will contribute over £6.3 million per annum. In return, they acquire the entire or at least the major broadcasting rights of those films which they co-produce or co-finance, including long-term rights for repeated transmissions on all broadcast media, terrestrial, cable and satellite. If the CEC proposals were implemented, they would only be able to retain the first television transmission rights for a limited period. The rights for second and subsequent transmissions, along with all other rights, would be retained by the independent producer.

The private television stations in the FRG are also making modest contributions to the production fund over a three-year period, beginning with £1.3 million in 1990. At present this is only a goodwill gesture following pressure from politicians. Hence, the rights co-financed by the private stations will still be available on the market, if they are not acquired by the public broadcasters under the terms of the film/TV agreement. Under the terms of the film/TV agreement, the public broadcasters are barred from co-producing with film companies that depend on them economically, or on whom they have a 'decisive influence', but it is an open question whether a similar provision could in future be enforced effectively in the private sector, since there legal connections between the television broadcasters and larger production companies are increasingly common.

But the CEC wants to go further, to the very licensing conditions required of broadcasters.

For this secondary market to develop, it is necessary that its specific features be taken into account when broadcasting licence decisions are taken in respect of a television channel. This means that the secondary market channels should not have imposed on them conditions difficult to sustain in terms of production proper or programme schedules.[58]

In the FRG, it has been clearly established that it is the *Länder* which license the broadcasters. But, in the name of encouraging independent audiovisual production, the CEC now wants to prevent the *Länder* from requiring any satellite or cable channels to meet any production requirements or programme schedules. Therefore, in the name of free competition between broadcasters, any television broadcasters in the FRG, which are currently required to meet programme and production schedules, would be positively disadvantaged with respect to these secondary broadcasters. The fundamental philosophy envisaged by the Federal Constitutional Court, of a basic service provided by the public broadcasters, which would be supplemented by private broadcasters which were still required to meet a minimum standard of pluralism, would be replaced by a philosophy of unregulated competition between broadcasters.

The preferential treatment which the CEC proposes to afford to the new audiovisual sector goes even further, however. Although it accepts that EC efforts to create a unified market must not be called into question 'by the re-erection of barriers through contractual arrangements contrary to competition rules',[59] it intends to adopt 'a positive approach . . . towards inter-company co-operation' in the field of production.[60] This will permit a substantial number of co-productions to be made, both between film and television organisations and between production organisations in more than one member state. For the FRG, this is most likely to reinforce the integration tendencies in the private audiovisual sector, to the detriment of smaller independent producers.

Although it makes no proposals to limit cinema, video, satellite or cable rights, the CEC proposes three specific ways in which to limit television rights. First, following the lines of the ARD/MGM/UA decision, it intends to limit 'agreements which are excessive in their scope or duration or which impose additional restrictions on the parties'.[61] Second, to ensure that all broadcasting companies have access to attractive programmes, it wants 'to prevent programme material being withdrawn from the market as a result of collective long-term arrangements'.[62] And third, when multinational organisations, such as the EBU, acquire the rights to programmes, then non-members should have appropriate access to the relevant programme material.

All three proposals are designed to ensure that private broadcasters are given access to enough European programmes to compete with public broadcasters. But they do not deal with the growing attempts by the private sector to outbid their public sector rivals for the rights to sports events. In adopting this approach, the CEC is not only seeking to make the rules of the EC marketplace between producers and distributors of programmes more favourable for producers, but to achieve this by restricting the commercial activities of the traditional broadcasters. In the FRG, this means ARD and ZDF.

The CEC also wants to develop a framework for state aids, in line with the provisions of Article 92(3) (c) of the EEC Treaty, which permits state aids 'to facilitate the development of certain economic activities or certain economic areas, where such aid does not adversely affect trading conditions to an extent contrary to the common interest'.[63]

Provided they meet these conditions, the CEC has, 'on numerous occasions authorized the granting of State aids to the film industry'.[64] The CEC now proposes to extend this dispensation to satellite broadcasting services 'because such a trend would help the expansion of the secondary market' in audiovisual works in Europe.[65]

If this proposal is to be implemented it raises a crucial policy question for the EC, and for member states including the FRG. How can member states best aid the expansion of a secondary market in EC audiovisual works?

In the past, the public broadcasting corporations in the FRG have co-operated with the *Filmförderungsanstalt* in Berlin which draws its funds from a levy on sales of cinema admissions and from the film/TV agreement, to provide production funds for German audiovisual works. In an indirect manner, therefore, the broadcasters have acted as a form of state aid to audiovisual production in the FRG. Most of the so-called New German Cinema has been financed in this manner.

But if in future state aid for audiovisual producers is organised to provide programmes for a secondary market in satellite broadcasting services, the new services will be in direct competition with the terrestrial broadcasting services which are expected to co-finance the programmes in the first place. The strategy of ARD and ZDF has been to finance films and programmes which complement rather than imitate those on offer in the international film market. The CEC's proposal is therefore likely to narrow, rather than broaden, the choice of films on offer to the German public. This situation could be aggravated if the licence fee itself is deemed an illegal form of state aid.

At stake here is the relation between the economic objectives for EC audiovisual policy and the socio-political and cultural responsibilities of the broadcasters. This will no doubt be one of the main questions which the CEC will have to address when its proposals for the future framework for state aids to the audiovisual sector are considered by politicians and officials from member states during its consultations planned for 1990.

AUDIOVISUAL OR COMPETITION POLICY?

The EEC Treaty establishes a supranational economic community, but it does not provide a supranational constitution, except in so far as the economic provisions in the Treaty undermine the freedoms inscribed in the national constitutions of member states. There is therefore a structural mismatch between the FRG's broadcasting policy and EC broadcasting policy. The former, which is basically concerned with programme content and its effects on the formation of public and private opinion, derives its authority from the social and political philosophy embedded in the FRG's Basic Law. The latter draws its authority from the EEC Treaty which regulates the economic markets in the sale of airtime and the sale and acquisition of licences to broadcast programmes.

The original draft of the TV Directive contained little reference to the social and political role of broadcasting, but after intense lobbying from the Committee on Legal Affairs and Citizens' Rights of the European Parliament, the TV Directive laid down in its preface that member states are to prevent 'the creation of dominant positions which would lead to restrictions on pluralism and freedom of televised information and of the information sector as a whole'.[66]

This indicated the growing concern of the European Parliament, and to lesser extent the CEC, with the nexus between media competition, concentration, and programme pluralism.[67] However, the

European Parliament also asserted that the TV Directive 'is not *per se* adequate to constitute authoritative and ongoing intervention by the Community, which has hitherto been almost non-existent as far as such crucial issues are concerned'.[68]

The European Parliament was especially concerned with new concentrations of economic power operating on an international scale; increasing cross-ownership in the various media subsectors and in the technical means of transmission; and the rapidly evolving relationship between the public and private sectors with a strong trend away from public monopolies. It thus urged the CEC to take action on an EC multi-media regulation.[69]

The issue at stake is how to marry the provisions of the TV Directive and EC competition rules with the national regulations of member states. For the FRG, this means the various *Länder* regulations and anti-cartel law.

Concentration and ownership control

In 1988, the CEC's competition commissioner declared that he would use his powers to

> maintain access to the market which might be impeded by the operators of cable networks or satellites who refuse to distribute certain TV channels. The vertical integration strategies contribute to the increase of this type of risk for competition.[70]

He also acknowledged that it had 'become a concern of competition policy to enquire and supervise cross-media ownership'.[71]

In December 1989, the Council of Ministers finally approved a merger regulation which now complements the competition tools of the CEC.[72] The CEC now possesses control powers similar to, indeed superior to, those enjoyed by the Federal Cartel Office. Article 21(1) of the merger regulation lays down that '[s]ubject to review by the Court of Justice, the Commission shall have sole competence to take the decisions provided for in this Regulation'.

Its jurisdiction covers all mergers and acquisitions. They are forbidden if they create or strengthen a dominant position which has anti-competitive effects, either across the common market or in parts of it. The threshold is a combined turnover of some £3.7 billion (Ecu 5 bn) by the enterprises involved. A third of this turnover has to come from at least one member state (Article 1).

However, the regulation contains no specific section on

broadcasting. Article 21(3) merely allows member states to retain their jurisdiction for protection of the 'plurality of the media', provided they are compatible with other provisions of EC law. Thus the Federal Cartel Office and/or the *Länder* are still free to take 'appropriate measures' to protect media pluralism. For instance, the Cartel Office can still invoke the special clauses on the press in the anti-cartel act; or the *Länder* apply their own broadcast ownership rules.

The phrase 'plurality of the media' in the merger regulation is indeed open to a range of interpretations by member states, but the CEC appears to interpret the phrase as referring to something like the German idea of organisational pluralism. In its communication to the Council and the Parliament on audiovisual policy, the CEC makes this clear under the heading 'Pluralism and Mergers'.

> Whereas the activities of media operators have increasingly assumed a European dimension, the response to the effects these may have, in certain cases, on pluralism has, for the time being, not gone beyond national limits. National legislation, existing or planned, could be circumvented and would not therefore be sufficient to guarantee pluralism in all cases. Moreover, this situation, characterised by a multiplicity and disparity of national laws, may produce the opposite effect of limiting the activity of operators who could contribute to a growth of pluralism in the Member States.[73]

The Audiovisual Directorate of the CEC, the author of the audiovisual policy document, appears to want to place its ownership and concentration regulation in addition to, or possibly over and above, the EC's competition and merger rules, acknowledging that the application of Community competition law is not able 'to cover all situations in which a threat to pluralism is posed, notably in the case of multimedia ownership'.[74] It proposes a directive 'whose aim would be to harmonise certain aspects of national legislation in this field'.[75]

For the *Länder*, this would affect the regulations on ownership and concentration in the broadcasting acts, and *in extenso* challenge the underlying philosophy of editorial pluralism. Indeed, the CEC does not clarify whether it considers pluralism in the media to extend beyond simply the numerical diversity of players in the marketplace. The general thrust of the remainder of its policy document seems to indicate that the CEC considers that pluralism can only come from opening up broadcasting to increasing competition from the private sector and from preventing mergers which could lead to a reduction in the number of broadcasting organisations. There is no direct attempt, nor could there be given the role of the CEC and the terms of the EEC Treaty, to address directly the role of broadcasting in forming public opinion in the political arena. The Federal Constitutional Court's definition of pluralism is wider in that it encompasses not only the basic services provided by the public broadcasters but also minimum public-interest standards for the private sector, even if the *Länder* have problems in establishing these.

A broadcasting-specific merger and competition directive may be justified, given the multi-media activities of some broadcasters. However, on the one hand, it could only work if it contained competitive safeguards for organisations charged with the responsibility of serving the public by a programming policy based on internal pluralism, which is the situation of ARD and ZDF; and if it respected the public-interest duties of those private stations operating under the internal or mixed models of *Länder* regulation. On the other hand, if the experiences of the *Länder* regulators are anything to go by, a pluralism regulation would only be able to scratch at the surface, leaving the German and EC anti-cartel authorities as the real regulatory force of the private broadcasting market. Over and above this, the pluralism approach of the CEC appears rather rhetorical. Unlike the Constitutional Court and the *Länder* regulators, the EC in general, and the CEC in particular, has a primarily economic remit, but is not charged with considering the political and cultural role of broadcasting in forming public opinion, at least so long as political union, with a comprehensive constitution, does not exist.

POLITICAL VERSUS ECONOMIC REGULATION

As broadcasting increasingly moves from being a national activity to being an international activity, the parameters of the new international broadcasting order are being shaped by a supranational body which draws its authority from a treaty which has within it no political or cultural elements. The economic regulation of broadcasting, based on economic theory, could well therefore take precedence over the political and cultural regulation of broadcasting which is guaranteed in the FRG's Basic Law.

It appears, then, that national authorities, both for broadcasting and economic competition, are losing power to Brussels. This then raises two salient questions.

* To what extent should EC competition rules be used when they conflict with the jurisdictions of member states for socio-political and cultural matters? and
* To what extent should broadcasting regulation in member states, designed to ensure pluralism in programming, be harmonised within the EC? Where should the line be drawn between the jurisdictions over broadcasting of the anti-cartel authorities of member states and the CEC?

The EC anti-cartel rules cannot, and do not aim to, secure the survival of a public broadcasting sector, even though its continued existence is valued by most member states and it is constitutionally guaranteed in the FRG. In short, competition policy is not the weapon with which to forge a positive EC broadcasting policy designed to encourage either economic, or socio-political and cultural, pluralism in the media.

Given the 'democratic deficit' in the EC, between the commercially oriented EEC Treaty and the democratic safeguards enshrined in the constitutions of the member states, in particular the Basic Law, a major structural change may well be needed in the relations between member states and the EC.

A German jurist proposed that in the long term, in order to prevent all broadcasting being handed over to the market forces, what is needed is the creation of a European communications constitution over and above the EC institutions, and the adoption of the German model of pluralist regulation within a 'dual system'.[76] This would provide a positive regulation of broadcasting in line with German constitutional requirements instead of merely abolishing obstacles to free trade in broadcast services using the rhetoric of pluralism and the development of a secondary market for audiovisual products, as the CEC proposes. This could lead eventually to the establishment of European public broadcasting channels, to which all national public broadcasters would contribute. Any adverse effects on programme pluralism from cross-border concentration in the private market could then be matched by a stronger public sector.

Chapter 8

Broadcasting regulation in the five new *Länder*

On 3 October 1990, the GDR acceded to the Federal Republic, and thus ceased to exist. The constitutional framework of the Federal Republic now therefore applies to the five new *Länder* in the territory of the former GDR. The Treaty of Unification between the FRG and the GDR set out the terms of accession and the provisional arrangements which facilitated the integration of the old legal structures of the GDR into those of the Federal Republic.[1]

THE LEGAL FRAMEWORK AND ITS IMPLICATIONS

Two articles of the Unification Treaty were particularly important for the broadcasting order in the five new *Länder*, although it could take some time before the situation settles down.

Article 35 stipulated that the *Länder* would take over the regulation of the cultural institutions which were previously centralised. They assumed the responsibility for their finance, although the *Bund* could promote the cultural infrastructure in the new *Länder* on a temporary basis, in order to make up for cultural differences between the Western and Eastern halves of the country.

In conformity with this, Article 36 laid down that there should be a federal structure of broadcasting regulation and organisation. The former GDR television and radio stations, which were centrally run by the state and the Socialist Unity Party, could continue as 'an autonomous joint institution having legal capacity' under *Länder* control until 31 December 1991 at the latest. The responsibility of this new communal institution was to provide the population in the former GDR with television and radio 'in accordance with the general principles governing broadcasting establishments coming under public law'. There would thus be a public service broadcasting system, responsible for delivering the constitutional provision of a basic service.

Overall control over the transitional arrangements was vested in the hands of a national broadcasting commissioner, appointed by the new *Länder* governments; and a broadcasting advisory council, consisting of eighteen publicly known personalities to act as representatives of socially relevant groups, elected by the new *Land* parliaments and the East Berlin municipal council. Both could influence significantly the manner in which the new public service institution is run. The first commissioner is a CSU member and the former president of the Bavarian regulatory authority which spearheaded the introduction of private broadcasting in the Federal Republic. He was elected by representatives of the new *Länder*, backed however by the administrative support of the federal chancellery in accordance with Article 15 of the Unification Treaty.[2] His election corresponded to the standing practice in the five young and politically inexperienced *Länder* of filling important positions in industry and politics with representatives from the Western half of the country, who had experience in managing the social market economy.

By the end of 1991, the new *Länder* parliaments will have enacted specific broadcasting regulation and set up public broadcasting organisations at a *Land* or inter-*Land* level. After the upheavals in the GDR in November 1989 several proposals were advanced as to how to implement a new broadcasting structure which would also include private broadcasters, even though the Unification Treaty does not mention them. The key question raised by the impending new order is whether the new regulation takes any account of the historical conditions and specific needs of the audience in the former GDR, or whether it will adopt wholesale the structures and associated problems of the FRG's broadcasting system.

There were several proposals for changing the GDR's centralist broadcasting system into a federal system. The process started with a media law commission of the Round Table, the all-party quango which facilitated the transformation to a democratic government, followed by the Directive on the Freedom of Expression, Freedom of Information and the Media passed by the East German parliament in January 1990.[3] This declared a right of freedom of expression and a right to receive and impart information free of censorship. Radio and television, formerly financed by the state, would gradually be transformed into public institutions; and commercial advertisements were forbidden on radio and television until the relevant regulations were adopted by the new *Länder*. A parliamentary Media Control Council would supervise the implementation of the Directive. This body was intended not only to prevent excessive power of social groups or the state in the media, as demanded by the federal German constitution, but also to guarantee the media as having a primarily cultural and not a profitmaking role. The Council, however, had no executive rights, and was soon left behind by new developments.

Both the former state radio and television stations in the GDR, which unlike those in the Federal Republic were run as two separate institutions, had given themselves new statutes. These provided for their transformation to a federal structure with pluralist control, but they also emphasised the need for sound economic prospects for the new *Land*-based stations. Basically they sought to guarantee the survival of the East German television stations, and prevent their integration into ARD and ZDF. In an effort to present a new democratic image, the former state television of the GDR was quickly renamed Deutscher Fernsehfunk (DFF). This was followed by the gradual introduction of independent reporting to meet the wishes of the citizens of East Germany for more objective information on their domestic situation. The news programmes of ARD and ZDF, which had previously been their standard source of information before the revolution, were now not specific enough for their needs.

At the beginning of July 1990, five public *Land* radio stations were established, instead of the previous studios in the administrative districts that had supplied programme inserts to one of the two central radios. They were Radio Mecklenburg-Vorpommern 1; Antenne Brandenburg; Sachsenradio; Radio Sachsen-Anhalt; and Thüringen eins.

According to the Media Directive, the primary source of finance for the reformed radio and television stations was to be the licence fee. In August 1990, the licence fee in the territory of the former GDR was raised from DM 10 to the West German level of DM 19 a month. But in addition, by taking advantage of the current legal vacuum, the East German stations also introduced commercial advertising without any parliamentary regulation. This was a controversial measure which gained only a narrow majority in the Media Control Council. DFF sold thirty minutes of commercial airtime a day, extending beyond the 8pm threshold for the public broadcasters in West Germany; and radio sold about one per cent of its broadcasting time.

In order to demonstrate its independence from ARD and ZDF, DFF commissioned Information et Publicité, Paris, which also sells airtime for RTL plus through its subsidiary, IPA Plus, to sell its commercial airtime. This could be unlawful, however, if the public-service principles referred to in the Unification Treaty are considered to be identical to the public service rules for the West German broadcasting corporations, including those in the 1987 Inter-*Land* Treaty which restrict their commercial activities. The commercial broadcasters want these rules, which limit the competitive impact of the public sector, to be extended to the five new *Länder*. The appointment of a proponent of a dual broadcasting system in Germany as broadcasting co-ordinator makes it likely that this interpretation of the relevant clause in the Unification Treaty will be accepted. However, DFF's contract with Information et Publicité expires on 31 December 1991, by which time DFF itself will have ceased to exist, at least in its present form.

The future prospects for DFF as an independent East German station declined rapidly after the March 1990 elections, which resulted in a conservative GDR parliament, albeit with a weak social-democrat element. However, the civic rights activists, such as New Forum, who had triggered the revolution and had been influential in designing the Media Directive, were not included in de Maizière's new coalition government. The latter established a Ministry for Media Policy which could overrule the decisions of the Media Control Council. Its main task was to prepare the legal framework for the new democratic, federal broadcasting order. Importantly, the Ministry employed broadcasting advisers from West Germany; they were influential in drafting a preliminary broadcasting bill. This was to provide the foundations for the *Länder* broadcasting legislation.[4] It was finally passed in September 1990 but challenged by the *Länder*. Thus, although the Unification Treaty has provisions for some former GDR legislation to be carried forward, the Eastern German broadcasting bill was excluded.

In its espousal of a dual system, and its advertising and programme content regulations, the bill was compatible with the 1987 Inter-*Land* Treaty. It would have set up a state agency for private broadcasters which would facilitate, or possibly predetermine, the subsequent permanent licensing decisions of the *Länder* regulatory bodies. Its main focus, however, was on the organisation of the public service system. It proposed to establish five *Land* broadcasting authorities to develop and regulate all public-law broadcasting activities in what was then still called the GDR. They were to receive the entire licence fee income, which they could then allocate as they chose. The bill was controversial, however, mainly because of its provisions for supervision. It proposed to abolish the pluralist supervisory bodies, which had already been established for the East German radio and television stations. Their statutes were to be rescinded. Instead, the public broadcasting authorities would have consisted of a director with wide editorial powers, appointed by the central government; and an advisory council of five outstanding public personalities, also appointed by the central government. In this way, it was believed, the influence of the political parties on broadcasting could be reduced.

Critics called this bill state-dirigiste.[5] Amazingly, given the involvement of West German jurists in drafting the bill, such a centrally controlled, non-pluralist supervisory structure may have been unconstitutional once the Basic Law was applied in the Eastern *Länder*. Eventually, thanks to the failure of the bill, the *Länder* were free to legislate as prescribed in the Basic Law and interpreted by the Federal Constitutional Court.

The scope of *Länder* legislation is subject to decisions made by the public broadcasting commissioner, and, importantly, by conservative broadcasting policy, since the CDU or CDU/FDP form governments in four out of the five new *Länder*. The broadcasting policy paper by the CDU media commission gives the best indication for the future.[6] It largely reiterates both the spirit and the wording of the Inter-*Land* Treaty. It will not preserve DFF but aims instead to merge the two DFF programmes with ARD and ZDF, in return for full coverage by these two in the five new *Länder*. In addition, the *Länder* are expected, through inter-*Land* agreements, to form not more than two or three regional public radio and television organisations. This latter strategy is also supported by the SPD and the ARD broadcasters. In this manner, the public sector can mainly be financed through the licence fee. All five new *Länder* taken together have fewer licence fee payers than the largest German *Land*, Northrhine-Westfalia. The relevant population of each of the new *Länder* is so small that it would need extremely complex financial equalisation arrangements to integrate a full five-*Länder* structure into the ARD. Whatever happens, the new *Länder* stations will become an additional burden on the ARD finances, particularly because of the increased networking costs. ARD, in return, will expect to take over the commercial advertising sales from Information et Publicité. ZDF, on the other hand, will only have to increase the number of its regional studios in the East German *Länder*.

A further aim of CDU policy is to limit the number of public radio and television stations in order to secure terrestrial frequencies for the private commercial broadcasters. At the same time, ZDF would obtain a national radio channel, that of the former GDR Deutschlandsender whose propaganda role disappeared with unification.

It is open to debate, however, how far the new *Länder* politicians may curtail the public broadcasters in order to favour the private stations, without conflicting with the constitutional requirement for a basic service, which now also extends to the Eastern *Länder*. It can be assumed therefore that all German citizens in both halves of the country have the right to receive, in return for the licence fee and without any extra payment, the ARD, ZDF and regional television programmes and between three and four public radio channels.

There has been no consideration by the authorities of alternative, democratic forms of access media, such as those which sporadically surfaced in the GDR under the patronage of the civil rights activists. One citizens' television channel, Kanal X in Leipzig, was forced to close by the Ministry for Posts and Telecommunications because it was a pirate without a broadcasting licence, although it was tolerated by the municipal authorities. It is still unclear whether the new *Länder* will be more open to such experiments. In a period of transition, the former citizens of the GDR are clearly interested in investigative information and cultural programmes that tell them what is happening and reflect what they feel is their own identity rather than simply accepting a take-over by the West, since they offer a thin ray of hope in a period of socio-political uncertainty.

DISTRIBUTION ISSUES

As in West Germany, the question of technical reach and financial survival of any channel in the Eastern part of the country will be crucially determined by the distribution and reception facilities. Under the socialist regime, the GDR Post Office was responsible for the regulation of both transmission and reception. It collected the licence fee which was then handed over to the government to be re-allocated as a state subsidy to the stations. With the Unification Treaty,[7] all transmission equipment and landlines became the property of DBP Telekom. As in the rest of the Federal Republic, the Ministry will regulate signal distribution. The telecommunications enterprise of the DBP is setting up and operating transmission facilities.

In the 1970s, the socialist unity government allowed the people of the GDR to receive all the Western programme channels that could be picked up over the air, and permitted aerial equipment to be upgraded in order to enhance reception of such programmes.[8] Between seventy and eighty per cent of the seven million television homes in East Germany could receive ARD's first television programme, albeit in moderate quality; over fifty per cent could pick up ZDF; thirty-nine per cent could receive SAT 1 and twenty per cent RTL plus; and, on average, about twenty per cent could receive one of the third regional programmes.[9] Only the areas around Greifswald in the north-east, and the Dresden region in the south-west, were out of range of Western transmitters. It was in these parts of the country that satellite dishes proliferated after 1988, when the GDR government tolerated the private importation and installation of satellite antennae. In the Dresden region alone, fifty per cent of homes own dishes – often connected via self-made MATV systems. Over a quarter of the 800,000 or so satellite receiving dishes are estimated to be situated in the East.[10] FM radio from the West reached about ninety per cent of the population. The powerful overspill of the West German public broadcasters into East Germany was a deliberate political strategy which aimed to provide the East Germans with access to Western democratic values and opinions.

The available radio and television frequencies are now being re-ordered by the DBP so as to allow for the maximum number of broadcasters, but also to facilitate other radio and microwave communication services. In line with the plans of the federal government, ARD has taken over the frequencies previously used by DFF, for which the transmitters already exist, although they will require additional technical upgrading. ZDF continues to broadcast into the East on its existing frequencies and with additional transmitters to complete its Eastern coverage. Another nation-wide television channel for which the transmitter infrastructure already exists will be used for regional broadcasts by the public stations. In addition, there will be two or more further national networks which still require co-ordination. As in West Germany, they may be allocated to private broadcasters. However, the entire transmission infrastructure for these frequencies is not yet finalised.[11] Nor is it clear whether the Federal Republic will be able to retain and use the five DBS frequencies which the International Telecommunications Union assigned to the former GDR in 1977.

Whatever is decided, the onus will be on DBP Telekom to provide the required transmission facilities. This demands substantial up-front investment which it will find hard to make, given its increased profit orientation. As in West Germany, when the terrestrial transmission facilities for the private broadcasters were established, the DBP may want to ask the new *Länder* for subsidies. However, the *Länder* and the future *Land* broadcasting corporations will be short of funds. The DBP and the private broadcasters have therefore been hoping for a continued rapid penetration of the Eastern *Länder* with satellite dishes accompanied by broadband cable networks for the medium term. In this way, the necessary investment can come mainly from the audience, and the broadcasters themselves.

The Ministry also tried to use the demand for West German television in the former GDR to boost its sagging TV-Sat venture. It tried to get ARD and ZDF to replace their transmissions of Eins plus and 3Sat on TV-Sat by their main terrestrial television channels. To do this, it offered them massive discounts on their channel rentals. Similar offers were made to the private satellite broadcasters. These discounts were to be partly financed by the consumer electronics manufacturers who hope to boost sales of TV-Sat equipment, which is selling poorly compared with the reception equipment for the Astra satellite, particularly because of its D2-MAC standard and the associated higher price. ARD and ZDF disagree, however. Any change will have to be imposed on them by an amendment to the 1987 Inter-*Land* Treaty.

While the DBP's TV-Sat strategy may aim at a rapid allocation of vacant terrestrial frequencies to private broadcasters, ARD and ZDF, too, prefer terrestrial transmission on the PAL standard which can already be received by ninety per cent of television sets in the former GDR in either black and white or colour.[12] Dual standard colour sets incorporating both the GDR's SECAM and the West German PAL standard have been on sale in the GDR since

1980. Because of the low penetration of TV-Sat signals, ARD and ZDF have decided also to transmit Eins plus and 3Sat from Astra, the pan-European hot bird, which will ensure a wider reach for these stations in the East than TV-Sat.

CHANGES TO THE COMPETITIVE SITUATION

The additional audience and advertising opportunities in the former GDR are likely to intensify the competitive pressures in the West German market.[13] Although high unemployment rates are predicted in the new *Länder*, and the spending power of their citizens may be lower than that of their Western compatriots, advertisers will nevertheless be able to profit from the demand engendered by the Easterners' need to catch up with Western living standards and their consequent appetite for consumer goods. Thus the market in the Eastern half of the country promises to be lucrative for private broadcasters, even if gains only materialise in the medium term.

The large private commercial broadcasters, RTL plus, SAT 1, Tele 5 and possibly Pro 7, are already staking their claims for the future competitive race for terrestrial television licences. In view of the increasing concentration in the West German television market, these four broadcasters will probably be the only viable candidates. The addition of the five new *Länder* to their networks could provide RTL plus and SAT 1 with the additional viewers which they need to go into profit. But the new market could also give Tele 5 and Pro 7 a chance to establish themselves as national general interest stations, since terrestrial transmission in the five *Länder* would overspill into more than two thirds of the West German television homes.

Competition for the airwaves in radio and television will be hottest in and around the 'island' of Greater Berlin. Not only do the former West Berlin stations reach into large parts of Brandenburg and Saxe-Anhalt, but the German-language US service RIAS, financed by the *Bund*, has lost its propaganda role. It may now change to a commercial radio and TV station.[14] In addition, there are two former GDR radios, Berliner Rundfunk and the youth station DT 64, which, although based in Berlin, cover all of the new *Länder*. DT 64 is likely to survive, possibly as an element of the new national radio.

In order to prevent competition for scarce licence fee resources and the increasingly stretched advertising revenues, several *Länder* stations are expected to co-operate or even merge. The Minister-Presidents of Saxony, Saxe-Anhalt and Thuringia have decided to form one public corporation. The Brandenburg government aims to set up an independent station, possibly in co-operation with WDR, and Mecklenburg-Vorpommern is also looking for prospective affiliations with other ARD corporations without which a station could not survive autonomously. But these plans for strategic alliances may be modified in the course of the parliamentary debates for broadcasting legislation in the new *Länder*.

The private radio licences, which will be advertised in the new *Länder*, are likely to attract newspaper and magazine publishers. Western German, and some European, publishing houses, most of which also have stakes in private broadcasting in the West, are already eating into the Eastern press market. Moreover, some public radio stations in the East have already signed co-operative ventures and deals for commercial sales or programme syndication with West German private radios. The dearth of finance for the new broadcasters in the East may eventually speed up the networking process across the entire Federal Republic.

OPTIONS FOR THE FUTURE

As virgin legal entities, the five new *Länder* have better opportunities to establish an integrated communication order than did their West German counterparts in the early 1980s. One option, for instance, would be to set up a single regulatory authority for both public and private broadcasting, and to create separate legislation for radio and television, or to strengthen the role of the public broadcasters. Indeed, given their mandate for providing a basic service, the public broadcasters, more than ever, should assume an integrative function and smooth the traumatic transition towards democracy and the social market economy, as happened under Allied supervision after the Second World War in West Germany.

However, the political and technological imperatives of broadcasting in the eleven old *Länder* are also likely to determine the broadcasting order in the new *Länder*. The policy-making discretion of the five *Länder* has already been severely curtailed by the constitutional norms of the Federal Republic and the political domination by the West, which have tended to overrule the original East German socio-political regulatory ideals that were based on the principle of a civil society and the openness of its public sphere. Instead, principally because of the insecurity displayed by Eastern politicians in implementing the constitutional broadcasting norms of pluralism and independence from the state, their Western counterparts have already been able to impose their own more market-oriented structures. The opportunities for a new regulatory compromise that would arise from the dissolution of the GDR are now minimal. The new *Länder* will generally imitate the broadcasting legislation which has already been elaborated and tried in West Germany, including the regulatory arrangements for a dual system.

All sixteen *Länder* governments will have to sign a new Inter-*Land* Treaty in order to harmonise the regulation of nationally distributed channels. This, however, could preclude a new and potentially controversial round of negotiations on the articles of the Treaty, given the new political power constellation from 1991 of few conservative-led as against a majority of social democrat-led *Länder*, and Berlin with the CDU and SPD sharing in the government. In addition, detailed negotiations on the finances and organisation of the broadcasting system as a whole will be necessary when the new *Länder* join the ARD and accede to the ZDF Treaty and the licence fee treaty.

Last but not least, there is the EC Television Directive. Although this has been officially contested by the eleven *Länder* in the West (see Chapter 7), the Unification Treaty has changed the ground rules in the East: Article 10 (3) of the Unification Treaty unequivocally states that all EC legislative acts whose implementation or execution comes under *Länder* authority will have to be adhered to by the new *Länder*.

Editorial independence

Beyond the formal organisational questions of the allocation of frequencies, the economic viability and the organisation and supervisory control of the broadcasting institutions themselves lies the delicate question of editorial freedom. In West Germany the appointments of the directors-general of the public stations are made by the broadcasting councils. They have built on the broadly liberal tradition of appointing non-Nazi senior editorial staff, instituted by the Western Allied Powers after the Second World War, but they moderated it by distributing senior editorial appointments equally between supporters of the major West German political parties.

In the new *Länder*, however, the situation is distinctly different. In the GDR, senior editorial staff in the broadcasting institutions were nearly all members of the ruling Socialist Unity Party. Their training and ideological formation was specifically linked to serving the political agitational and propagandist needs of the party. Although the heads of the GDR's radio and television stations have now been sacked, virtually all former senior broadcasting personnel in the GDR were part of the party's propaganda elite. But since the new broadcasting institutions now have a decisively different role to play in the enlarged FRG, it is questionable how far the broadcasting personnel of the GDR institutions can adapt themselves to serve new political and social functions.

For the authorities, however, the supervision of these changes in key editorial personnel is a delicate matter. On the one hand, both the radio and television organisations of the GDR were overstaffed compared with those in West Germany, and therefore many people who were considered to be ideologically unsuitable could simply be made redundant on the grounds that their jobs are no longer necessary in a more streamlined capitalist structure. On the other hand, however, the authorities could not afford to institute a wholesale replacement of East German personnel with those trained in the West. This would smack too much of colonisation, rather than unification. In order to deliver the pluralist programming demanded by the Basic Law and the Federal Constitutional Court, it has become necessary for the authorities to 're-educate' senior editorial staff in the new broadcasting institutions in the East and to steer a fine line between the depoliticisation and the victimisation of those senior editorial staff who were originally trained and educated in the ways of the Socialist Unity Party.

TOWARDS INTEGRATION

The key decisions which must be taken in the early years of the 1990s on the allocation of broadcasting licences, on the balances between public broadcasting institutions and private broadcasters, on the size and dispersal of the new institutions which replace the old centralised GDR broadcasting system, and on the re-education and redeployment of senior editorial staff, will all help to shape a new broadcasting order linking the eleven *Länder* in the West of the Federal Republic to the five in the East of the country. It is likely that for several years there will be a substantial disparity in living standards and in social conditions between the two halves of the country. In addition, there may well continue to be substantially different political attitudes, once the euphoria of unification has ebbed away. The manner and the sensitivity with which the broadcasters, both public and private, report and interpret these differences are likely to play a key role in ensuring the future harmony of the new and enlarged Federal Republic.

Chapter 9

Conclusion: Beyond balanced pluralism

During the 1980s, German broadcasting went through a period of turbulent regulatory change. In 1961, the constitutional foundations of the ARD system were confirmed by the Federal Constitutional Court and ZDF was established the following year. But by the end of the 1970s the then CDU Minister-Presidents of Schleswig-Holstein and Lower Saxony were leading the struggle to break the public broadcasting duopoly of the ARD and ZDF, by attempting to dismantle the Hamburg-based NDR. Their initiative was stymied, however, by the Federal Administrative Court.

By the early 1980s, the new distribution technologies of cable and satellite seemed to offer new opportunities to German industrialists to expand the broadcasting business and create new export markets. When the Constitutional Court ruled in 1981 that private broadcasting *per se* was not illegal, the way ahead seemed clear. When the CDU came to power in the federal elections of 1982, it therefore adopted a new strategy to challenge the hegemony of the public broadcasters. Instead of trying to dismantle the ARD, it used its federal control of the DBP to open up new distribution channels to allow private, advertising-financed operators to compete with the public sector. This strategy was also motivated by industrial politics because it was intended to open up employment in the telecommunications sector, and create new investment opportunities, especially for small and medium-sized enterprises such as those involved in connecting cable systems and servicing MATV systems. It also pleased the advertisers, because it introduced price competition in the sale of airtime. And it pleased the party's ideologues, not only because it corresponded to their newly discovered liberal economic theory, but because it promised to bring editorial control of news and current affairs programmes in the new channels closer to the party's interests.

The 1986 decision of the Federal Constitutional Court was therefore as important as that in 1961. The Court accepted the new technological developments that seemed set to change the system, but it also guaranteed a role for the public service tradition. The challenge faced by the Court was how to structure and regulate a dual broadcasting order which had come into existence on the equivocal basis of the 1981 judgement. The problem was no longer centred simply on the acceptance of private commercial broadcasting. A basis was needed on which to shape the future structure of the whole broadcasting system, and the position within it of the public broadcasters. The court's solution was for the two public networks to continue to provide 'a basic service', but for the private sector to augment this as it saw fit, provided its programmes met certain minimum conditions.

PUBLIC/PRIVATE RELATIONS: THREE PARADIGMS

In spite, or possibly because, of this ruling, the broadcasting order in the Federal Republic appears far from settled. The root of the Court's, and therefore the FRG's, problem is the conceptual incompatibility between the constitutional principle of pluralism and the forces of a market-led economy. In order to preserve constitutional continuity and to ensure the effectiveness of the legal norms in the real world, the Court developed a hybrid regulatory concept. Private commercial organisations were to be regulated by systems derived from a public organisational model which were inspired by a social purpose. This triggered a tension between two different regulatory philosophies, which both aspire to underpin institutions in the Federal Republic. These are specific broadcasting regulation to guarantee the proper formation of public opinion and the development of citizenship; and economic regulation in the name of the free market. Emblematically, the broadcasting debate has opened up the contradictions inherent in the West German ideology of the 'social market economy'.

The tensions which the Court's decision created between the two modes of regulation became clearer as the *Länder* began to put the Court's judgement into practice. The 1987 Inter-*Land* Treaty tried to set up a dual order in which both public and private broadcasting were economically viable. Competition in the private television sector was restricted by allocating the new terrestrial frequencies to those companies which had already developed satellite and cable services; and by delaying the introduction of external pluralism in the private sector until there were at least three nation-wide private channels offering a diverse service, which could complement those of the public broadcasters. In addition, up to two per cent of the licence fee income could be used to finance the private regulatory authorities and to subsidise private sector transmission costs. For the public broadcasters, however, increased competition in the sale of airtime meant a cutback in advertising revenues and a decline in their programme budgets.

At the federal level, the Federal Cartel Office, supported and spurred on by the neo-liberal theorists on the Monopolies Commission, gave even stronger support to the private sector. It took the view that the size and strength of the public corporations needed to be cut back in order to allow the private sector to compete effectively with the public broadcasters. Cross-ownership was acceptable in the private sector since it had virtually no impact on the sale of advertising by either broadcasting or the press; and anyway it was justified because the publishers were providing the necessary economic stimulus for the private broadcasting market to compete with the public broadcasters on equal terms. The Federal Cartel Office has even tolerated the growth of networking and the pooling of advertising and programmes; and it has acquiesced in the common sale of airtime by the three main publisher-dominated private radio stations in Hamburg, Lower Saxony and Schleswig-Holstein.

Instead the Federal Cartel Office harried the public broadcasters. In particular, it banned WDR from participating in Radio NRW, the sustaining service for local radio stations set up by the regulatory authority in Northrhine-Westfalia; and it banned the four-year contract which ARD and ZDF had concluded with the German Sports Federation to broadcast a number of less popular sports. Both decisions may well be appealed to the Federal Constitutional Court.

There are therefore three different paradigms which are being used to shape the relations between public and private sector broadcasting. The Federal Constitutional Court based its decisions on pluralism in programmes, and saw the public broadcasters offering a basic service which the private broadcasters could augment. The *Länder*, however, were concerned to set up a dual system which afforded enough concessions and subsidies to the private broadcasters to enable them to survive, even though these might eat into the financial revenues of the public broadcasters, thus threatening their ability to continue to provide a basic service. The Federal Cartel Office uses yet a third paradigm. It is only interested in stimulating growth in the private sector until it is as large as the public corporations.

Although theoretically the Federal Constitutional Court is the senior court in the FRG, it has shown a marked reluctance to involve itself in economic regulation. So even though it put up a 'heroic fight' to maintain the public-service role of all broadcasting,[1] it also opened the way for broadcasting to be regulated by the market. At the root of the current tensions lie the technological pragmatism and the concessions the Court made to the dominant political majority in the FRG to create favourable economic conditions for private broadcasters, although the federal government still criticised the Court's judgements as too traditionalist.[2]

The Court overlooked the heavy dependence of ARD and ZDF on advertising finance and other commercial revenues. Competition between the public and private halves of the broadcasting order in the distribution, advertising and programme markets is already intense. In its future broadcasting decisions, the Court will almost certainly have to address the impact of the 'economics of the real world' on the new broadcasting order and consider a framework for regulating economic competition. This task will be even more difficult because whatever solution the Court devises, it will have to be put into practice by the Federal Cartel Office and by sixteen different *Länder*.

Although it will be amended to include the new *Länder*, the 1987 Inter-*Land* Treaty will probably continue to be the basis for any future harmonisation of *Länder* regulation. Although it has a number of grey areas, it remains the major political and legal embodiment of the criteria laid down by the Constitutional Court in earlier decisions.

Even so, the implementation of the Treaty by individual *Land* regulation leaves the regulatory authorities substantial discretion in interpreting its provisions. Until now, the authorities have often felt powerless and unsure of their legal position, because of their political ties with the *Länder* governments, and their cumbersome decision-making processes.

It is doubtful whether any policies for shaping the rapidly developing economic and technological complexities of the broadcasting market can be worked out by the *Länder* from first principles. In view of economic uncertainties, it is likely the authorities will continue to acquiesce in the private broadcasters' practices of self-regulation rather than enforce any formal regulatory procedures, thus increasing the danger of regulatory capture by those whom they were appointed to regulate.

The speedy unification of the FRG and the GDR in 1990, and the need to assimilate five new *Länder* into the FRG's federal structure, has added a new dimension to the German broadcasting scene. The comparative poverty of the new *Länder* in the East and the need to decentralise the GDR's old broadcasting system means that one of the authorities' prime concerns will be to ensure the economic viability of the newly enlarged system. This, in turn, will reinforce tendencies already apparent among the Western *Länder* of regulatory pragmatism, of accepting self-regulation by private broadcasters, and ultimately of regulatory capture by the private broadcasters.

It has already become clear that, in television at least, the ideal of external pluralism will have to be sacrificed to market conditions, mainly because commercially attractive distribution channels have only slowly become available. Instead, the *Länder* have increasingly had to include elements of internal pluralism in their regulatory practice in order to ensure the survival of a regulated private market. This has often meant sacrificing potential diversity both in the means of distribution and in editorial output. The television sector is thus characterised by national homogeneity and powerful multi-media interests. In radio, however, the lower costs and narrower bandwidths meant the *Länder* were more free to implement their individual broadcasting policies. But here too they had to accept that only consolidated enterprises, broadcasting to as wide an audience as possible, under conditions of minimum competition, would be able to survive. The elements of internal pluralism, necessary to balance this situation, are currently difficult to enforce, however. But the situation could change and the authorities become more proactive, since seven of the eleven *Länder* are now governed by social democrats, either alone or in coalition.

Despite the provisions of the Inter-*Land* Treaty, there is insufficient advertising to support the anticipated broadcasting revolution of the 'new media'. The federal CDU is already discussing directions for future change. In particular, it is proposing to review the public-service concepts underpinning public broadcasting and the regulatory authorities for private broadcasting. Changes to the licence fee system and a single federal regulatory authority are on its agenda.[3] Whether this will deepen the split between the policy makers in the *Bund* and the *Länder* remains to be seen.

It may be appropriate here to recall that, among other things, the Constitutional Court saw the public responsibility of all broadcasting in shaping the formation of opinion as vital to the democratic process. However, the regulators have to control private television, and to a large extent radio, under a contradiction which hampers their effectiveness. Their remit is one of public responsibility, while in reality the commercial broadcasters primarily fashion their programmes not to fulfil this goal, but to deliver audiences to their advertisers.

PROGRAMMING CHANGES

As yet, the size and quality of the editorial output from private broadcasting in the Western *Länder* is almost as unclear as the pattern of regulation. Although only a few content studies of private programme services have been carried out, some general tendencies may be worth noting.[4] As in other countries, the hopes of some politicians of being able to influence the editorial policies of private commercial broadcasters more easily than those of the public broadcasting corporations have not been borne out. Fears of political bias have not been substantiated. The national television stations and the large commercial radios cannot afford to alienate half their audience by adopting a partisan particular political stance. To date, the regulators have ensured that politically motivated local radio stations are limited in number, and the audience reach of the open channels is so small that they are unlikely to have a significant political impact anyway.

In radio in particular, political information programmes have shown their independence and a preference for investigative journalism which has not spared party-political allegiances, especially when a political scandal attracts audiences. Topical reports are frequently more subjective and stimulating than those on the public stations, where reticence and balance can create unattractive consensus reporting. Since audiences are highly appreciative of news programmes on the public channels, the private television channels also have been trying to improve the journalistic quality of their news output. But they find them expensive to produce. Light entertainment remains the big audience puller.

Unorthodox leftist views, which found it difficult to gain access to mainstream public and private radio, now have a small chance of getting their own, often non-profitmaking, stations. Three of these have been licensed, in Freiburg, Nuremberg and West Berlin, although none of them has a large market share and they have all had financial problems. On all three stations, minorities are given ample airtime; and there are also many programmes produced by women.

The real innovation of private broadcasting is local radio. Local news and information clearly meet a need. Although radio competes with local newspapers, it is faster. Different teams of radio and newspaper journalists often compete with one another, even if they are frequently employed by the same publisher. But there have been reports of local radios simply using newspaper items without even mentioning the source; and much local news is often little more than announcements of forthcoming events.

It is mainstream pop and rock that is the staple fare of the commercial radio stations. In addition there are a few specialist services, such as jazz stations. But in general expansion has produced more of the same and little diversity in available progamming. Ironically, in order to compete with the private sector for the same audience, the popular radio channels on the public stations, which sell the most airtime, have restyled their news output, and relegated nearly all background information and serious reporting to specialist channels.

The changes in private television have been similar. Apart from a few business programmes, the huge increase in programme hours has given audiences more music videos, light entertainment and talk shows; and more of the same old films and series. In line with its young modern image, RTL plus pulls its audiences with light-hearted sexual advice and erotic programmes; while SAT 1 projects an image of a dignified family channel.

The majority of private radio and television broadcasts provide hardly any socio-political background information. According to a former SAT 1 news editor:

> We want to produce a programme service which clearly shows
> the people that everyday life is worth living, and that it is
> worthwhile to be active. We want to present the world as it
> is. [That is] primarily positive, that is not to say that we keep
> problems under wraps . . . but we do not want to send people
> to bed . . . with the feeling that the next day they'll have to face
> a vale of tears [sic].[5]

News programmes, which are normally very short, are mainly
'rip and read' programmes, relying to a large extent on news
agency feeds. Outside broadcasts and foreign correspondents
are expensive to maintain, especially for television. On radio,
telephone interviews predominate; and on television, talking heads
and innumerable self-styled experts have replaced well-researched
in-house background material. Topical information programmes
emphasise the human interest touch; and the verbal style is
deliberately casual and easy-going, non-confrontational and apo-
litical. Although the audience-friendly, non-educational approach
of the presenters is appreciated, audiences also feel that they lack
the professionalism to which they have become accustomed from
the reporting standards of the public broadcasters. The private
stations' fare partly meets audience demand, but it is still not
profitable.

Meanwhile, the public broadcasting corporations are increasingly strapped for cash. So far, they have only managed to get a
limited increase in the licence fee. They are facing competition in
the sale of airtime, especially in radio. And there is a huge increase
in the costs of television programme material and programme
rights. All this can be felt in their programming policies. Instead
of increasing pluralism, economic competition is eating away at
the edges of the constitutional cornerstone of the West German
broadcasting system.

The ARD radio channels have been streamlined, and thus have
jettisoned the traditional public service ideal of mixed channels.
The aim of the exercise is to build listener loyalty to one radio
channel, by creating a predictable and firm programme structure,
and establishing channels with identifiably distinct outputs of music
and news, like those in BBC radio. Less money is available for
cultural specials, such as experimental music programmes or radio
plays. Money spent sponsoring cultural events will also be cut back
unless legislation, as in Hessen, earmarks additional funds for this

purpose. This is especially regrettable as cultural broadcasts, such as radio drama, are few and far between on private stations.

On public television, there are more repeats of expensive films and series; more co-productions and less material produced by the smaller independent German producers. Minority interest programmes and political magazines have already been rescheduled from prime time to late evening slots to make way for entertainment programmes; and the third programme channels, which do not take advertising, and which were a traditional outlet for education and advisory programmes, in-depth discussion and special movies, have been popularised.[6] If the corporations succeed with their request to spread the available advertising beyond the 8pm threshold, this will probably reinforce the tendency to schedule commercially competitive entertainment during prime time.

POLITICAL RESPONSES

Are the media politicians satisfied with the new broadcasting system they created? For different political motives, politicians of both the main parties are increasingly critical of public broadcasting's practice of cutting back in cultural programming and competing in the commercial marketplace. Ironically, many conservative politicians, especially those who fought to introduce private commercial broadcasting and to defeat the alleged socialist bias in the public broadcasting corporations, are disappointed with the poor quality of the commercial radio and television stations. They are particularly dismayed by what they deem to be the virtual disappearance of the cultural, folkloric and educational broadcasts. CSU members are quoted as calling the new programming 'boring drabness'.[7] And the popularised public radio stations, designed for mass appeal, have also occasioned numerous complaints.[8] Their situation now may be compared to that of the proverbial sorcerer's apprentice.

Conservative media politicians have started to appreciate afresh the value of the public-service corporations, not only as upholders of traditional conservative values, but also as a platform for their policies; and SPD politicans have always valued public broadcasting as a platform to spread their ideological message of social responsibility. It is doubtful, however, whether political interference in programme content will continue to be so easy in future. The need to face up to commercial competition may well force the public corporations to assert their political independence.

At first glance, compared with developments in other Western countries, it seems that the regulation of West German broadcasting has secured the constitutionally required, minimum standards of pluralism in private broadcasting and limited the free play of the market forces.[9] The varying decisions by the regulatory authorities on the organisation of the private broadcasting market have certainly created a complex, but economically precarious, federal structure which on the one hand has somewhat restrained the broadcasters and subjected them to the regulatory regime, at least during the licensing stage. On the other hand, it has created a regulatory differential which does not secure an effective regulatory framework at the national level.

Liberal economists close to federal government circles are criticising this regulatory framework for being bureaucratic and offering only 'loopholes', but not a liberalised broadcasting market. In particular, it is argued that the broadcasting market is distorted because of the public-interest obligations of the private broadcasters, and the licence fee supported public sector.[10]

At a second glance, the licensing decisions of the authorities have narrowed organisational diversity as they have restricted market entry, especially as at the end of a long licence period the broadcasters will probably have their licences renewed. Market choice is being narrowed beyond the politically desired level by strong concentration tendencies. The ideal of a pluralist federal broadcasting landscape, which had inspired so much of the original broadcasting legislation, is falling away before increasingly pragmatic regulation.

Many of the attempts by the legislators and regulatory authorities to enforce positive, enabling regulation and a diversity of programme output, as demanded by the Constitutional Court, have failed precisely because editorial pluralism cannot be created simply through a structure based on arbitrary criteria of organisational diversity. Not only has the ideal of external pluralism been contained, but editorial pluralism, which lies at the very heart of the public service, is being restricted in the process.[11]

To audiences, the German broadcasting system will soon look like that in the USA, Italy or France. Although these countries all have different regulatory approaches, they are only superficial compared with the developing structure of the international marketplace to which all broadcasters, both public and private, are increasingly exposed.[12]

Hans Bausch, the former head of the ARD network, who resigned over the issue of state control over broadcasting, summed up the situation of broadcasting regulation in the Federal Republic with some bitterness: 'It would be presumptuous to discover in this labyrinthine confusion a concept that befitted the idea of a liberal and pluralist political culture in the Federal Republic.'[13]

TOWARDS REGULATORY UNIFICATION?

The discrepancies between the rationale for West German regulation and its practices are likely to intensify. The present system of inter-*Länder* and *Länder/Bund* negotiations and informal procedures leaves too great a scope for technological determinism, legal black holes and party-political bickering to be able to fathom the internationalising communications market. Once the licences for the still limited national means of distribution have been awarded and the licensees have established themselves, what will justify the existence, let alone the subsidy from the licence fee, of eleven separate bureaucracies? The workloads will be routine and could be handled by administrative officers. The renewed emphasis of technology upon broadcasting regulation may then tend, in the longer term, to steer the developments in the Federal Republic back towards a unitary regulatory model, like those in in Canada, France and the USA. The standing conference of the *Länder* regulatory authorities might pragmatically develop into a permanent body, on the model of the Federal Communications Commission in the USA.

An official inter-*Land* body would, however, have to be accountable to both the *Bund* and the *Länder* in formal institutional and procedural arrangements, since a unitary regulation of the broadcast infrastructure would impinge on questions of broadcasting as well as telecommunications policy, and therefore both *Bund* and *Länder* jurisdictions. In the longer term, one might thus envisage a new body, a communications commission, made up of *Länder* and Telecommunications Ministry representatives, to co-ordinate the allocation of distribution facilities according to *Länder* imperatives, but to take account also of overall national communication needs. At the same time, this commission could either operate the distribution facilities itself, or, given the range of interests that are already involved in providing the broadcast infrastructure, it could authorise public utility organisations to operate the distribution facilities as a regional technological monopoly. In line with German pluralist practices, these utilities could have boards of directors from all interested parties, such as the public and private broadcasters, satellite operators, cable marketing companies, the local authorities and DBP Telekom. Any net profits could then be spent by the communications commission to facilitate network access to alternative broadcasters.

The *Länder* parliaments and regulatory authorities would remain responsible for setting regulatory priorities, awarding licences and supervising the programming obligations of the licensees. However, it is hard to imagine that the *Länder* would voluntarily cede any of their individual powers to a unitary body, under attack as they are at the moment at the federal and European levels. Moreover, bureaucracies like the regulatory authorities have an innate tendency to persevere once established.

TOWARDS REGULATORY FRAGMENTATION?

If changes in the technological infrastructure imply the need for a unitary regulatory body, then the fall-out from the EC TV Directive, and the manner of its implementation, could cause regulatory fragmentation, producing even wider divisions between the *Bund* and the *Länder*.

Although at first most *Länder* welcomed the technological and economic benefits of private broadcasting, their insistence that broadcasting is a cultural activity has been largely politically motivated. The appeal by Bavaria to the Federal Constitutional Court, supported by an array of SPD- and CDU-led *Länder*, against the federal government's approval of the TV Directive, has not yet been decided. The case is not primarily a protest against specific provisions in the Directive, but seeks to prove that *Länder* autonomy in broadcasting matters has been wrongly appropriated by the *Bund*. While the *Länder* deny the European Community the right to regulate cultural matters, they have felt that in EC policy matters, the *Bund* has already negotiated away much of their competences since the Single European Act was passed.

The appeal means that the transfer of the Directive's provisions into *Land* law will be not be smooth. If the *Länder* do not implement the Directive, the CEC could take the *Bund* to the

European Court of Justice, although ironically the *Bund* has no authority to force the *Länder* to implement EC legislation. Meanwhile, those *Länder* not involved in the court case may go ahead and modify their legislation individually. Broadcasting regulation in the Federal Republic could thus be threatened with renewed fragmentation. The liberal-conservative newspaper *Frankfurter Allgemeine Zeitung* has questioned whether private television would be able to survive at all under such conditions.[14]

Although the Inter-*Land* Treaty was only agreed in 1987, it is already cracking at the seams. Political disputes about its 'ideological' directions have surfaced around its lacunae. Its one achievement, which was to reassert *Länder* authority over broadcasting, even in the new technological environment, has been put into jeopardy by the EC's TV Directive. The problem is that, despite its often detailed rules, the Treaty does not articulate a coherent regulatory philosophy. It is marked by the absence of a clear regulatory framework for information and communication policy in the Federal Republic. The *Länder* need a wider 'communications constitution'[15] which could address the relationships between socio-cultural and economic regulation, which are precisely the functions which the information and broadcast media have to reconcile in modern society.

PROPOSALS FOR CHANGE

Between the twin drives towards a unitary regulatory structure and increasing fragmentation for broadcasting regulation in the FRG, a number of specific proposals have been put forward by different interest groups.

In a working paper on media policy, the federal CDU has outlined its proposals for change. In particular, it has proposed,

* a review of the public-sevice concepts underlying the work of the broadcasting corporations and a cost-benefit analysis of the regulatory authorities for private broadcasting;
* a single common regulatory body for both public-sector and private broadcasters;
* since in its present form, the licence fee distorts the entry conditions into the broadcasting market, to restrict the public broadcasting corporations to licence fee funding, and to give a share of the licence fee to private broadcasters to provide public-

interest programmes; or to abolish the licence fee altogether, although it doubts whether the advertising market could pay for all the existing channels; and

* all broadcasters to participate in activities to promote German and European films.[16]

Yet this approach has been challenged even within the conservative camp itself, particularly when it threatens the cultural autonomy of the *Länder*. In the medium term, public broadcasting has a role to play since it will provide both economic and programming competition for private broadcasting.[17] For the same reasons, the major brand advertisers are also interested in keeping the public broadcasting system. Former private broadcasting ideologues among the politicians have come to recognise not only the economic but also the cultural importance of the corporations, whether it is their contribution to German film production or their role as promoters of satellite channels and European culture. And they still offer the best platform for party politicians, the dissemination of party policy and the spread of certain values, designed to stabilise the social system.

But another view, coming from jurists, regulators and politicians alike, is more critical. The public-service legitimation for private broadcasting is a sham. It is not really intended to regulate for pluralism but to provide a constitutional alibi and to open up the broadcasting sector to market forces. Would it not therefore be more ethical to abolish altogether the present regulatory authorities, with their precarious funding from the public licence fee; leave the private broadcasting market to economic regulation under the anti-trust authorities; and to hand over the supervision of youth protection, which is not specific to broadcasting, to the general decency laws and a voluntary watchdog consisting of knowledgeable legal experts, administrators, broadcasters, and representatives of the audience? The accountability of the public broadcasting corporations could then be improved through public discussion and social awareness of their functions. Their output could be strengthened through adequate funding; and the possibilities for citizens' channels could be more fully examined, using the resources of the public sector and a levy on private broadcasters.[18]

The common element in these proposals is a move to disentangle the two major sources of broadcasting finance in the FRG, the licence fee and the sale of advertising. While the notion of a properly funded and regulated public sector, financed by the licence fee, and possibly a tax on private broadcasting, and matched by an advertising-funded private sector, has a certain logic, it ignores the mixed nature of most broadcasting services. It ignores, too, the need for a competitive approach of the public broadcasters to survive in a free market economy, be it that of the FRG or the EC. As the market in broadcasting becomes increasingly international, the simple division of powers between the *Bund* and the *Länder* will be difficult to maintain. The forthcoming decision of the Federal Constitutional Court over the approval of the EC TV Directive by the federal government will throw this question into even sharper relief. If it finds for the federal government, the traditional constitutional logic based on the need in a democracy to form public opinion in a rational, balanced and considered manner will be rendered secondary to the supranational economic needs of the international market in broadcast advertisements and sponsored programmes. If it finds for the *Länder*, then there will be a slim chance that broadcasting regulation in the FRG can still seek to ensure that pluralism in broadcast programmes, which are designed to improve the democratic process, can take precedence over pluralism between organisations, whose only economic role is to deliver audiences to advertisers and potential programme sponsors.

TOWARDS A NEW EUROPEAN ORDER

Beyond purely national concerns lies the FRG's vision of the EC and its role in EC politics. The recent CEC proposals for a future EC audiovisual policy imply that broadcasting regulation must be made even more subservient to economic regulation by the marketplace. The new free market would not only be international in scope, but would also extend to all forms of audiovisual distribution. To facilitate the economic development of new distribution systems, established broadcasters could face further restrictions on their ability to acquire programme rights; while to promote independent audiovisual production, they could be expected to subsidise a secondary programme market.

The CEC's vision of a free market in audiovisual distribution could even call into question the very existence of the public broadcasters, since theoretically the licence fee could be deemed to be a form of state aid, which is prohibited under the terms of the

EEC Treaty. As in the UK, the individual household has to pay the licence fee to receive all broadcasts. The revenue collected is then given to ARD and ZDF, and to the *Länder* regulatory authorities. In the FRG, domestic private broadcasters only benefit indirectly from the licence fee, while in other EC countries private broadcasters do not benefit at all.

Legal theory will be subsumed to political dealing, however. In the coming few years, broadcasting policy, not simply in the FRG but throughout the whole of the EC, will be but one facet of a wider European realignment. Already the federal government, together with the French government, has proposed a new European political union for 1993 which will go beyond the terms of the EEC Treaty, and aims to integrate a unified Germany with all its socio-political and economic uncertainties into the 'European house'. One of the key questions which the planners of the new order will have to address is the manner in which public opinion will be formed in the new wider Europe, and the role that will be assigned to broadcasting in a new European multi-media order.

In a very real sense, the principles of pluralism which underpin the regulation of German broadcasting date from the Allied vision of a new Germany to replace that of the Third Reich. The formation of public opinion was too important to be left either to the politicians or to the free market. Whether the federal government will insist on retaining these principles in the new European order remains to be seen. At the moment, the supranational economic framework of the EC is a weight which tips the scales further from content-based to market-based regulation of broadcasting in the Federal Republic.

The German Länder

Population [million]

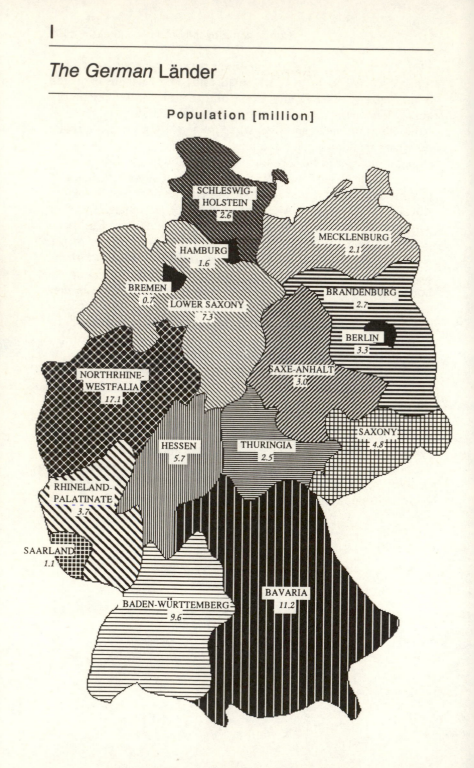

The public broadcasting corporations

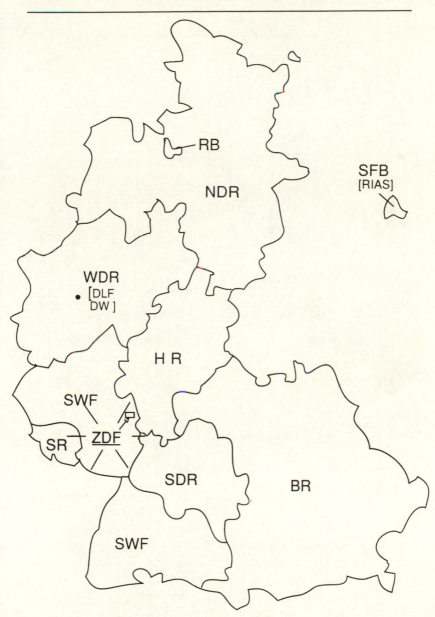

Areas of Bund *influence on broadcasting regulation*

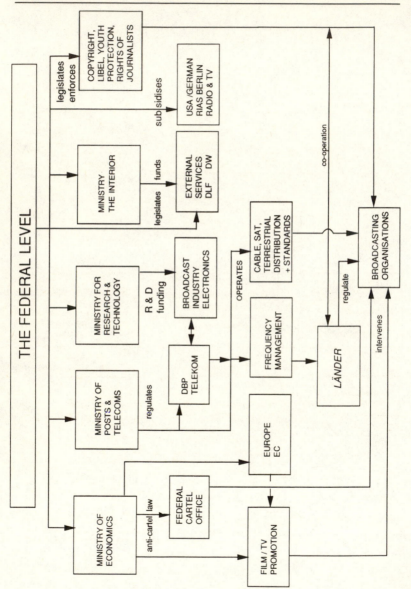

Broadcasting control structures

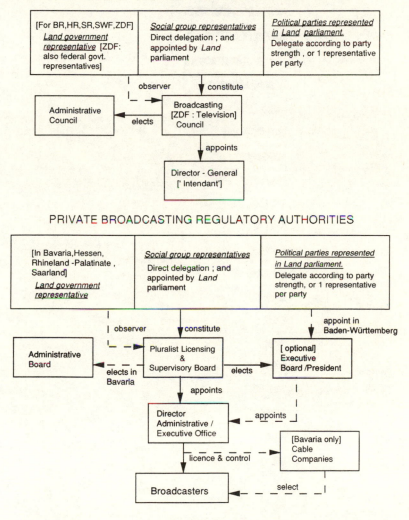

PUBLIC BROADCASTING CORPORATIONS

[For BR,HR,SR,SWF,ZDF] *Land government representative* [ZDF: also federal govt. representatives]	*Social group representatives* Direct delegation ; and appointed by *Land* parliament	*Political parties represented in Land parliament.* Delegate according to party strength , or 1 representative per party

observer — constitute

Administrative Council ← elects — Broadcasting [ZDF : Television] Council

↓ appoints

Director - General [' Intendant']

PRIVATE BROADCASTING REGULATORY AUTHORITIES

[In Bavaria,Hessen, Rhineland -Palatinate , Saarland] *Land government representative*	*Social group representatives* Direct delegation ; and appointed by *Land* parliament	*Political parties represented in Land parliament.* Delegate according to party strength, or 1 representative per party

appoint in Baden-Württemberg

observer — constitute

Administrative Board ← elects in Bavaria — Pluralist Licensing & Supervisory Board — elects → [optional] Executive Board /President

↓ appoints

Director Administrative / Executive Office — appoints ─┘

licence & control — — [Bavaria only] Cable Companies

Broadcasters ← — select — ┘

V

Pluralist structure of the broadcasting control boards

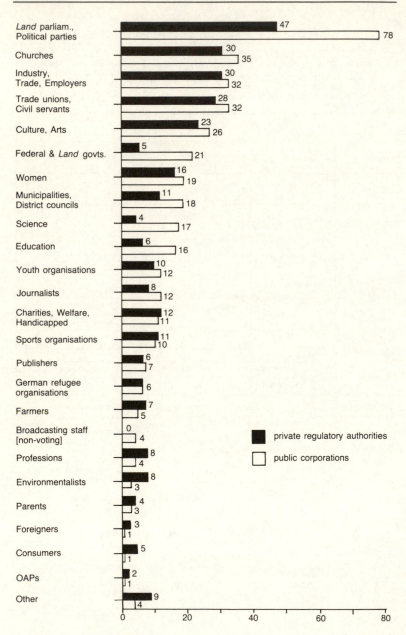

| | private regulatory authorities |
| | public corporations |

Budgets of the private regulatory authorities

LAND	BUDGET £ million	– of which % INFRASTRUCTURE SUBSIDIES	% OPEN CHANNEL FINANCE	% MEDIA RESEARCH
Baden - Württemberg	4.9	68	—	0.7
Bavaria	6.0	15	11	9.0
Berlin	1.4	0.7	47	—
Bremen	0.6	—	up to 75 planned	—
Hamburg	1.2	—	31	3.0
Hessen	1.5	85	—	—
Lower Saxony	3.6	90	—	—
Northrhine - Westfalia	7.7	8	40 reduced from 1990 surplus to WDR	6.0
Rhineland - Palatinate	1.9	36	10	—
Saarland .	0.7	—	39	—
Schleswig - Holstein	1.5	65 {	from 1990, promotion of open channels and media research instead	

[Figures 1989 Source: Wöste / Media Perspektiven; private regulatory authorities' information]

TV and radio reception 1989

Cable capacity	present 300 MHz system	expanded 450 MHz system
TV channels	24	35
VHF radio channels	27	30
Digital radio channels	16	16

[Source : DBP statistics]

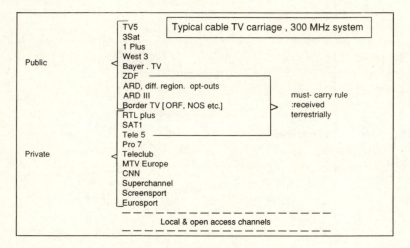

Typical cable TV carriage , 300 MHz system

Public
- TV5
- 3Sat
- 1 Plus
- West 3
- Bayer . TV
- ZDF
- ARD, diff. region. opt-outs
- ARD III
- Border TV [ORF, NOS etc.]

Private
- RTL plus
- SAT1
- Tele 5
- Pro 7
- Teleclub
- MTV Europe
- CNN
- Superchannel
- Screensport
- Eurosport

must- carry rule :received terrestrially

Local & open access channels

Major TV services		
Name	Status	Description
ARD 1	public	general interest
ZDF	public	general interest
Eins plus	public	cultural interest
3Sat	public	cultural interest
ARD III	public	cultural and education interest
RTL plus	private	general interest, erotic evenings
SAT 1	private	general interest, family viewing
Tele 5	private	general interest, young audience
Pro 7	private	general interest, some information

joint morning & lunchtime programming

TV and radio reception 1989

W. Germany

Population [incl. W.Berlin]	61 m
TV licences	24 m
Radio licences	27 m

Technical reach [national average]

ARD / ZDF	98% of homes
RTL plus	57% of homes
SAT 1	52% of homes
Tele 5	3% of homes

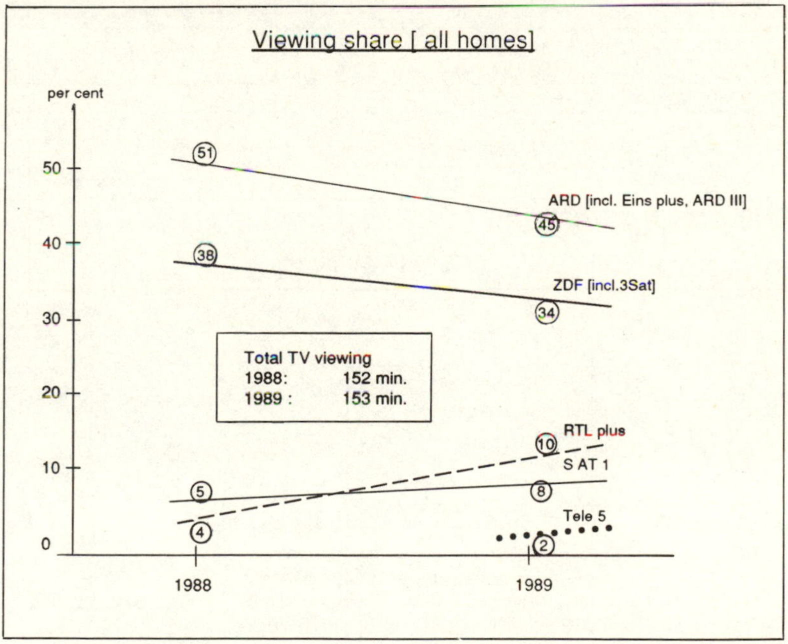
Viewing share [all homes]
per cent
50
40
30
20
10
0
(51)
ARD [incl. Eins plus, ARD III]
(45)
(38)
ZDF [incl.3Sat]
(34)
Total TV viewing
1988: 152 min.
1989 : 153 min.
RTL plus
(10)
S AT 1
(5)
(8)
Tele 5
(4)
(2)
1988
1989

[Source : Media Perspektiven ; Nowotny ; DBP statistics ; GFK ; own calculations]

TV and radio reception 1989

		THE RADIO STRUCTURE		
BROAD-CASTERS	PUBLIC No. OF SERVICES		PRIVATE No. OF SERVICES	
LÄNDER	*LAND* WIDE	LOCAL opt-outs	*LAND* WIDE	LOCAL
BADEN-WÜRTTEMBERG	SDR 4 SWF 3	3	—	> 55
BAVARIA	BR 4	—	1	50/60
BERLIN	SFB 4 [RIAS 2]	—	2	—
BREMEN	RB 4	—	—	—
HAMBURG	NDR 4 [1 specifically for Hamburg]		3	—
HESSEN	HR 4	3	1	—
LOWER SAXONY	NDR 4 [1 specifically for Lower Saxony]	4	1 [another licensed]	
NORTHRHINE-WESTFALIA	WDR 4	9	2 *Land* - wide programme suppliers:	45
RHINELAND-PALATINATE	SWF 3	3	1	opt - outs
SAARLAND	SR 4	—	1 [with particpation of SR]	
SCHLESWIG-HOLSTEIN	NDR 4 [1 specifically for Schleswig - Holstein]		1 [another licensed]	—
NATIONAL	DLF		1 [satellite & cable]	

[*Source*: Regulatory authorities; own research]

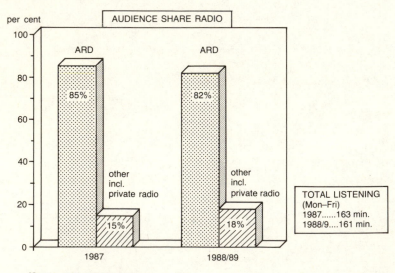

[*Source:* GFK; ARD Jahrbuch]

Broadcasting market

TOTAL MARKET VALUE 1989 £2.86 bn

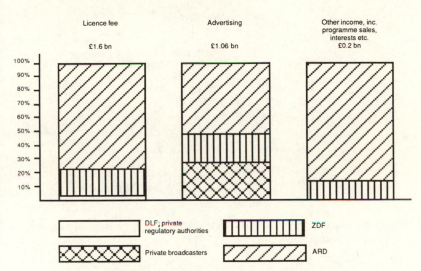

Licence fee	Advertising	Other income, inc. programme sales, interests etc.
£1.6 bn	£1.06 bn	£0.2 bn

Legend:
- DLF; private regulatory authorities
- Private broadcasters
- ZDF
- ARD

[Source : Media Perspektiven; ARD Jahrbuch; ZDF Jahrbuch; own calculations]

PERCENTAGES OF COMMERCIAL AIRTIME OF TOTAL BROADCAST OUTPUT [1989]		
	RADIO	TV
PUBLIC SECTOR	ARD 1.6*	ARD 2.8 ZDF 3.0
PRIVATE SECTOR	up to 10	SAT 1 8.4 RTL plus 6.2 Tele 5 4.9

* 1988

[Source : Krüger / Media Perspectiven;ARD Jahrbuch'89; information from regulatory authorities]

XI

Cross-connections in the television market

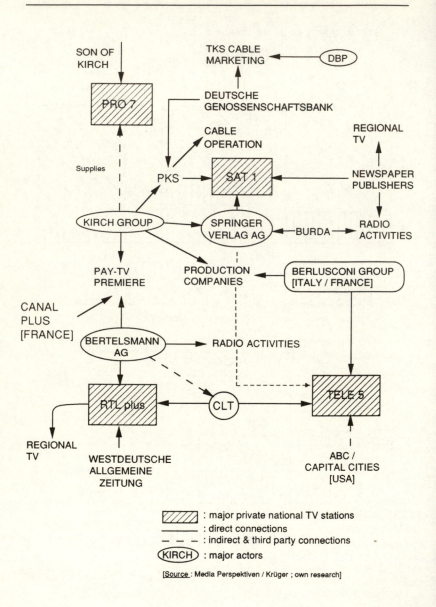

Notes

1 THE PHILOSOPHIES OF BROADCASTING PLURALISM

1. Exchange rate used: £1 = DM 3.
2. R. Breitling, 'The concept of pluralism', in *Three Faces of Pluralism*, ed. S. Ehrlich and G. Wootton, Westmead, Gower, 1980, p. 16.
3. For an analysis of German pluralism, cf. K. v. Beyme, 'The politics of limited pluralism? The case of West Germany', in Ehrlich and Wootton, op. cit., pp. 80–102; and K. v. Beyme, *The Political System of the Federal Republic of Germany*, Aldershot, Gower, 1983.
4. The Federal Republic of Germany, as its name indicates, is a federation, consisting of the Federal Republic as such (*Bund*) and eleven individual states (*Länder*, sing. *Land*) in West Germany prior to German unification in October 1990: Baden-Württemberg, Bavaria, Bremen, Hamburg, Hessen, Lower Saxony, Northrhine-Westfalia, Rhineland-Palatinate, Saarland, and Schleswig-Holstein. Up to October 1990, West Berlin had a special status as legally it came under Allied control instead of *Bund* control. Although West Berlin was a state divorced from the legislature of the Federal Republic, for all practical purposes, in particular in broadcasting regulation, it corresponded to the other *Länder*, and will therefore be referred to as a *Land*. In October 1990, five new *Länder* in the Eastern half of Germany were added: Brandenburg, Mecklenburg-Vorpommern, Saxe-Anhalt, Saxony, Thuringia. East Berlin merged with West Berlin into the *Land* Berlin, from which Allied control was now withdrawn.
5. Quoted in *Kommentar zum Grundgesetz für die Bundesrepublik Deutschland*, vol. I, Neuwied/ Darmstadt, Luchterhand, 1984, pp. 1275f. (All translations by the authors unless otherwise stated.)
6. ibid.
7. K. Hesse, *Grundzüge des Verfassungsrechts der BRD*, Karlsruhe, Müller, 1968, p. 60.
8. Beyme, *The Political System of the Federal Republic of Germany*, op. cit., pp. 90ff.
9. Hesse, op. cit., p. 65.

10. ibid., p. 200.
11. Cf. CDU, *Grundmaterial zum Medienkonzept der CDU*, 1972–1982 (CDU information, mimeo).
12. Cf. FDP, *Beschluss der Bundesparteitage der F.D.P.*, May and November 1986 (FDP information).
13. Cf. SPD, *Beschlüsse des Essener Parteitages der SPD zur Medienpolitik*, 1984 (SPD information).
14. Cf. Die Grünen, *Vorschlag für ein medienpolitisches Programm der Grünen*, Bundesversammlung, December 1985 (Die Grünen information).
15. W. Hoffmann-Riem, 'Rundfunkrecht und Wirtschaftsrecht – ein Paradigmawechsel in der Rundfunkverfassung', *Media Perspektiven*, no. 2 1988, p. 58.
16. Cf. A. Grosser, *Geschichte Deutschlands nach 1945*, Munich, dtv, 1974, pp. 136ff.
17. Cf. for instance W. Hoffmann-Riem, 'Verfassungsrechtliche und medienpolitische Konsequenzen des Urteils vom 4.11.86', *medium*, nos 1–3 1987, p. 19.
18. Cf. M. Stock, 'Das vierte Rundfunkurteil des Bundesverfassungsgerichts: Kontinuität oder Wende?', *Neue Juristische Wochenschrift*, vol. 40 (5) 1987, p. 217.
19. For an extended analysis, cf. S. Hasselbach and V. Porter, 'The re-regulation of West German broadcasting – some recent decisions of the Federal Constitutional Court', *Politics and Society in Germany, Austria and Switzerland*, vol. 1 (2) 1988, pp. 48–65.
20. *Grundgesetz für die Bundesrepublik Deutschland, The Basic Law for the Federal Republic of Germany*, ed. Press and Information Office of the Federal Government, Bonn, 1986 (official translation).
21. ibid.; for example, libel and defamation would come under this provision.
22. Cf. *Rundfunk in Deutschland*, vol. III, ed. H. Bausch, Munich, dtv, 1980, p. 429.
23. Cf. A. Williams, 'West German broadcasting in the eighties – plus ça change . . .', *ASGP Journal*, Spring 1984, p. 3.
24. Cf. C.D. Kleber, *Privater Rundfunk – Gestaltungsmöglichkeiten im Verfassungsrahmen*, Diss. Tübingen University, 1986, p. 95; for a different opinion, K. Stern, 'Neue Medien – Neue Aufgaben des Rechts?', *Deutsches Verwaltungsblatt*, vol. 97 (23) 1982, pp. 1114f.
25. Bavarian Constitutional Court, judgement of 27 September 1985; Divisional Court Berlin, judgement of 27 June 1986, both discussed in A. Hesse, 'Ausgewählte Rechtsprechung mit grundsätzlicher Bedeutung für die Rundfunkordnung in der Bundesrepublik Deutschland', *Rundfunk und Fernsehen*, vol. 35 (2) 1987, pp. 215f.
26. All *Länder* have press acts which regulate ethics rather than structure but there is no general act regulating pluralism of the press.
27. Cf. W. Hoffmann-Riem, in *Kommentar zum Grundgesetz für die Bundesrepublik Deutschland*, Neuwied/Darmstadt, Luchterhand, 1984, pp. 471ff.
28. Decision of 28 February 1961, printed in *Entscheidungen des Bundes-*

verfassungsgerichts, vol. 12, Tübingen, Mohr, 1961, p. 259; excerpts in Federal Government, *Medienpolitik*, ed. Press and Information Office, Bonn, 1985, pp. 72ff.

29. Cf. *inter alia* M. Bullinger, 'Satellitenrundfunk im Bundesstaat, *Archiv für Presserecht*, vol. 16 (1) 1985, pp. 1–14; H. Schneider, in *Rundfunk und Fernsehen im Lichte der Entwicklung des nationalen und internationalen Rechts*, ed. J. Schwarze, Baden-Baden, Nomos, 1986 (Europäisches Recht, Politik und Wirtschaft 123), pp. 13–27.

30. Decision of 4 November 1986, printed in *Media Perspektiven Dokumentation*, no. IV 1986, p. 244.

31. Cf. Federal Government, *Medienpolitik*, op. cit., pp. 72f.

32. ibid., p. 77.

33. Decision of 5 February 1991, cases no. *1 BvF 1/85* and *1 BvF 1/88* (mimeo).

34. Decision of 4 November 1986, op. cit., p. 227.

35. Cf. *Rundfunk in Deutschland*, op. cit., pp. 439ff; excerpts in A. Williams, *Broadcasting and Democracy in West Germany*, Bradford, Bradford University Press, 1976, p. 271; and in Federal Government, *Medienpolitik*, op. cit., p. 83.

36. Decision of 16 March 1981, printed in *Media Perspektiven*, no. 6 1981, pp. 421ff.

37. H.W. Klein and W. Lauff, 'Neue Medientechnik – neues Rundfunkrecht', *Aus Politik und Zeitgeschichte* (supplement to *Das Parlament*), 19 December 1981, p. 12.

38. Decision of 4 November 1986, op. cit.

39. Decision of 24 March 1987, printed in *Media Perspektiven Dokumentation*, no. III 1987, pp. 145ff; decision of 5 February 1991, op. cit.

40. Decision of 4 November 1986, op. cit.

41. Ibid., pp. 234ff.; Decision of 24 March 1987, op. cit., p. 160.

42. Decision of 4 November 1986, op. cit.

43. Cf. Bundesverband Kabel und Satellit, *Presseerklärung*, Bonn, 5 March 1986.

44. Inter-*Land* Treaty 1987, 'Staatsvertrag zur Neuordnung des Rundfunkwesens 1/3 April 1987', printed in *DLM Jahrbuch 88*, ed. Direktorenkonferenz der Landesmedienanstalten, Munich, 1988, pp. 307–15; English translation printed as 'Germany-Interprovincial Broadcasting Treaty 1987 [sic]', *Commercial Laws of Europe*, no. 1 1989, pp. 96–111. Where possible the authors quote from the translation.

45. *Ministerpräsidenten*, heads of the *Länder* governments; they represent their *Land* in dealings with other *Länder* and the *Bund*.

46. 'Beschluss der Ministerpräsidenten betr. Konzept der Länder zur Neuordnung des Rundfunkwesens, 18 Oct. 1984', printed in *Deutsches Presse- und Rundfunkrecht*, ed. W.D. Ring, Munich, Verlag für Verwaltungspraxis F. Rehm, 1977–87, pp. F-I 1.2.

47. Cf. R. Kopp, 'Der Dissens der Ministerpräsidenten', in *Das Ringen um den Medienstaatsvertrag der Länder*, ed. P. Glotz and R. Kopp, Berlin, Spiess, 1987, pp. 57ff.

48. For the CDU and SPD positions, cf. 'Ministerpräsidenten zerstritten

– das Ende der ARD', *Neue Medien Newsletter*, no. 12 March 1986, pp. 1f.

49. Printed in *Media Perspektiven Dokumentation*, no. III 1988, pp. 186ff.
50. Cf. Kopp, op. cit., p. 64; 'Stellungnahmen der Länder zum Scheitern des Medienstaatsvertrages', *Funk Korrespondenz*, no. 44 1985, p. 1.
51. The federal government expected yearly rentals of £8.3–10 m per channel, cf. decision of the federal government of 13 March 1985, printed in *Medienpolitik*, op. cit., p. 24.
52. Cf. Federal Government, *Programm zur Verbesserung der Rahmenbedingungen des privaten Rundfunkmarktes*, Bonn, Press and Information Office, 25 June 1986; Baden-Württemberg, Landtag, 'Begründung zum Staatsvertrag über die gemeinsame Nutzung eines Fernseh- und eines Hörfunkkanals auf Rundfunksatelliten', *Drucksachen*, no. 9/301 1986, p. 11; the private broadcasters' lobby group, Bundesverband Kabel und Satellit, *Presseerklärung*, 5 March 1986, expressly welcomed the decision.
53. Cf. Schneider, op. cit., p. 26.
54. Both treaties printed in *Media Perspektiven Dokumentation*, no. I 1986, pp. 43–86.
55. Saarland, Landtag, 'Begründung zum Staatsvertrag zur Neuordnung des Rundfunkwesens', *Drucksachen*, no. 9/1205 1987, p. 1. Translation by the authors; for the provisions of the actual Treaty, we use where possible its English translation, cf. 'Interprovincial Broadcasting Treaty', op. cit.
56. Cf. F. Müller-Römer, 'Die Entwicklung der Satellitentechnik', *Media Perspektiven*, no. 7 1989, p. 416.

2 THE REGULATION OF SIGNAL DISTRIBUTION

1. Cf. W. Hoffmann-Riem on the interpretation of Article 5 of the Basic Law, in *Handbuch des Verfassungsrechts der BRD*, ed. Benda, Maihofer and Vogel, Berlin/New York, Gruyter, 1983, p. 440.
2. Cf. statement by Deutsche Post on occasion of the drafting of the Basic Law, K.-B. v. Dremming, R. W. Füsslein and W. Matz, 'Entstehungsgeschichte der Artikel des Grundgesetzes', *Jahrbuch des öffentlichen Rechts der Gegenwart*, vol. 1, Tübingen, Mohr, 1951, fn 76.
3. Order by the Military Governor of the US Army, 22 November 1947, quoted in *Rundfunk in Deutschland*, vol. III, ed. H. Bausch, Munich, dtv, 1980, pp. 33f.
4. So Bredow, former Reichspost secretary, who initiated the development of radio in the Weimar Republic; cited in *Rundfunk in Deutschland*, op. cit., vol. III p. 30.
5. US draft for a declaration on the freedom of broadcasting in Germany, May 1946, printed in ibid., pp. 72f.
6. Announcement by the British Zone Military Government, printed in ibid., p. 56.
7. Cf. ibid., p. 309.

8. H. Bausch, 'Medienpolitisches Missvergnügen', in *ARD Jahrbuch 1988*, Frankfurt a.M., ARD, 1988, p. 18.
9. Cf. *Entscheidungen des Bundesverfassungsgerichts*, vol. 12, Tübingen, Mohr, 1961, pp. 205ff.
10. ibid.
11. ibid.
12. ibid., p. 238.
13. ibid.
14. Cf. *Rundfunk in Deutschland*, op. cit., vol. IV, pp. 859ff.
15. Cf. pro DBP, W. Berndt and H.-W. Hefekäuser, '"Media" and Telecommunications', in *Prospects of Telecommunications Policy*, Bonn, Bundesministerium für das Post- und Fernmeldewesen (English pre-print from Jahrbuch der Deutschen Bundespost 1985); pro *Länder*, J. Scherer, *Telekommunikationsrecht und Telekommunikationspolitik*, Baden-Baden, Nomos, 1985 (Materialien zur interdisziplinären Medienforschung vol. 16).
16. Cf. W. Hoffmann-Riem in *Handbuch des Verfassungsrechts der BRD*, op. cit., pp. 441f.
17. R. Woldt, 'Mythos Kabel', *Media Perspektiven*, no. 10 1989, p. 593.
18. Own estimates and *Screen Digest*, November 1990, p. 242; cf. also B. Nowotny, 'Germany: The slow march of cable', in *The European Experience*, ed. G. Nowell Smith, London, British Film Institute, 1989, p. 46.
19. Cf. Woldt, op. cit., p. 592; and DBP quarterly press releases on cable connections.
20. Kommission für den Ausbau des technischen Kommunikationssystems, *Telekommunikationsbericht*, Bonn, Bundesministerium für das Post- und Fernmeldewesen, 1976.
21. For a summary of the arguments, cf. S. Hiegemann, *Kabel- und Satellitenfernsehen*, Bonn, Bundeszentrale für politische Bildung, 1988, pp. 33f.
22. 'Beschluss der Ministerpräsidentenkonferenz vom 12. bis 14. November 1980', printed in L. Späth, *Das Kabel – Anschluss und die Zukunft*, Stuttgart, Bonn aktuell, 1981, pp. 111–14.
23. Germany, Bundestag, 'Zwischenbericht der Enquete-Kommission "Neue Informations- und Kommunikationstechniken"', *Drucksachen*, no. 9/2442 1983, pp. 37ff.
24. ibid. p. 37, pp. 190f, p. 233.
25. ibid pp. 190f, p. 233.
26. Bavarian Constitutional Court, decision of 27 September 1985, reviewed in A. Hesse, 'Ausgewählte Rechtsprechung mit grundsätzlicher Bedeutung für die Rundfunkordnung in der Bundesrepublik Deutschland', *Rundfunk und Fernsehen*, vol. 35 (2) 1987, p. 215.
27. Cf. M. Bullinger, *Kommunikationsfreiheit im Strukturwandel der Telekommunikation*, Baden-Baden, Nomos, 1980, p. 20.
28. Cf. 'Antwort der Bundesregierung auf die grosse Anfrage der CDU/CSU, 22 Feb. 1980', printed in *Deutsches Presse- und Rundfunkrecht*, ed. W.-D. Ring, Munich, Verlag für Verwaltungspraxis F. Rehm, 1977–87, pp. F–I 2.2ff.

29. H. Krath, 'Kabel- und Satellitenversorgung', *Fernmeldejournal*, no. 13 1985, pp. 3f (special print).
30. Cf. *Rundfunk in Deutschland*, op. cit., vol. IV, p. 989.
31. 'Medienpolitische Beschlüsse der Bundesregierung, 13 May und 25 June 1981', printed in Späth, op. cit., pp. 143–6.
32. 'Bericht der Rundfunkkommission der Ministerpräsidenten, 7 Feb. 1980', printed in *Deutsches Presse- und Rundfunkrecht*, op. cit., pp. F–I 1.1ff.
33. Cf. Federal Government, 'Vorstellungen des Bundes für eine Medienordnung der Zukunft', printed in *Medienpolitik*, ed. Press and Information Office, Bonn 1985, pp. 12ff.
34. D. Goodhart and H. Dixon, 'Fortress Rhine lowers the drawbridge', *Financial Times*, 30 June 1989, p. 22.
35. Cf. Federal Government, 'Vorstellungen des Bundes . . .', op. cit., pp. 12ff, emphasis added.
36. Cited in H. Blüthmann, 'Zauberer im Kabelzirkus', *Die Zeit*, 29 June 1984, p. 21.
37. Quoted in M. Snow, 'Telecommunications and media policy in West Germany: Recent developments', *Journal of Communications*, Summer 1982, p. 27 (translated by Snow).
38. Cf. Germany, Bundestag, 'Antwort der Bundesregierung', *Drucksachen*, no. 10/499 1983.
39. Cf. 'Antwort der Bundesregierung auf die kleine Anfrage der Fraktionen der SPD and FDP betr. Rundfunksatelliten-Projekt, 7 Sept. 1981', printed in *Deutsches Presse- und Rundfunkrecht*, op. cit., pp. F–I 4ff.
40. Cf. T. Schnöring, *FuE-Förderung des Bundesministeriums für Forschung und Technologie im Telekommunikationsbereich*, Bad Honnef, Wissenschaftliches Institut für Kommunikationsdienste, 1989 (Diskussionsbeiträge zur Telekommunikationsforschung 51), p. 76.
41. Cf. 'Bericht der Rundfunkkommission der Ministerpräsidenten, 2 Jan. 1980', printed in *Deutsches Presse- und Rundfunkrecht*, op. cit., p. 9.
42. The Eutelsat and Intelsat satellites are classified by the ITU as telecommunications satellites. Because of the required dish size and costs, they are not generally intended for direct-to-home reception. Instead, the signals are redistributed in cable systems and SMATVs.
43. Cf. J. Prott, *Die zerstörte Öffentlichkeit*, Göttingen, Steidl, 1986, p. 38.
44. Cf. F.-W. v. Sell, 'Privater Satellitenrundfunk vorbei am geltenden Verfassungsrecht?', *Rundfunk und Fernsehen*, vol. 32 (2) 1984, pp. 185ff; F. Müller-Römer, 'Fernmeldesatelliten. Zuführung von Rundfunkprogrammen zu Kabelinseln mittels Fernmeldesatelliten', *Media Perspektiven*, no. 7 1985, pp. 540ff.
45. G.M. Hellstern, W. Hoffmann-Riem, J. Reese and M. P. Ziethen *Rundfunkaufsicht in der Bundesrepublik Deutschland I*, ed. Press and Information Office of the *Land* government Northrhine-Westfalia, Düsseldorf, 1989, p. 143.
46. Cf. R. Gross, 'Zum Stand der Diskussion über den Satellitenrundfunk', *Media Perspektiven*, no. 1 1984, pp. 45ff.

47. Cf. for the position of the CDU *Land* government, Baden-Württemberg, Landtag, *Drucksachen*, no. 9/1385 1985.

48. Cf. exemplarily, §31, 'Hessisches Privatrundfunkgesetz', *Gesetz- und Verordnungsblatt für das Land Hessen, I*, 8 December 1988, p. 395.

49. For example, Lower Saxony only grants licences for some thirty per cent of the spare cable capacity, the remainder being reserved for relayed programming.

50. Cf. 'Bundespost versetzt Eins plus und 3Sat', *Funk Korrespondenz*, no. 37 1986, p. 1.

51. Cf. 'Verwaltungsanweisung zu §75 (TKO)', *Amtsblatt des Bundesministers für das Post- und Fernmeldewesen*, no. 40 1988, p. 633.

52. Cf. Hesse, op. cit., pp. 213f; J. Scherer, *Frequenzverwaltung zwischen Bund und Ländern*, Frankfurt a.M./Berlin, A. Metzner, 1987 (Beiträge zum Rundfunkrecht 39); W. Löwer, *Fernmeldekompetenz und Funkwellenzuteilung im Bundesstaat*, Erlangen, Verlag für Wissenschaft und Leben Georg Heidecker, 1989 (preprint from *Jahrbuch der Deutschen Bundespost* 1989).

53. Cf. Hellstern *et al.*, op. cit., pp. 46f, 225f, 408ff.

54. Cf. Article 6, 1987 Inter-*Land* Treaty and statement of reasons (*Begründung*), Saarland, Landtag, *Drucksachen*, no. 9/1205 1987.

55. *ARD Jahrbuch 1990*, Frankfurt a.M., ARD, 1990; *ZDF Jahrbuch 1989*, Mainz, ZDF, 1990.

56. Cf. 'Bundespost senkte die Satellitenpreise', *Frankfurter Rundschau*, 22 February 1989; M.-L. Hauch-Fleck, 'Flug ins Nichts', *Die Zeit*, 18 August 1989, p. 15.

57. Cf. Germany, Bundestag, 'Entwurf eines Gesetzes zur Neustrukturierung des Post- und Fernmeldewesens und der Deutschen Bundespost (Poststrukturgesetz - PostStruktG), mit Beschlussempfehlung und Bericht des Ausschusses für das Post- und Fernmeldewesen (15. Ausschuss)', *Drucksachen*, no. 11/4316 1989; passed by the federal parliament in June 1989.

58. ibid., §22.

59. 'Comparison of the version of the Telecommunication Installations Act applicable today with the draft amendments in the form of a synopsis', printed in Ministerium für das Post- und Fernmeldewesen, *Reform of the Postal and Telecommunications System in the Federal Republic of Germany*, Heidelberg, R.v.Decker's/G. Schenk, 1988 (appendix).

60. For a summary of the latest arguments, see SPD Bundestagsfraktion, *Milliardendefizite bei der Breitbandverkabelung*, SPD document 1764, Bonn, 21 July 1989.

61. Cf. 'Projektgesellschaft Kabelkommunikation übernimmt Postgeschäfte', *epd Kirche und Rundfunk*, no. 16 1989, p. 10; 'PKK will jetzt eigene Kabelnetze bauen', *Frankfurter Rundschau*, 9 February 1989.

62. ibid.

3 THE REGULATORY STRUCTURES FOR PUBLIC AND PRIVATE BROADCASTING

1. For further details, cf. R. Collins and V. Porter, 'West German Television: the crisis of public service broadcasting', *Sight and Sound*, vol. 49 (3) 1980, pp. 172–7.
2. ZDF, which does not broadcast radio programmes, has a television council.
3. E. Etzioni-Halevy, *National Broadcasting under Siege*, London, Macmillan, 1987, pp. 93ff.
4. Cf. N. Grunenberg, 'Kopfnicken und Katzbuckeln', *Die Zeit*, 11 December 1987.
5. Cf. 'Versandet Rundfunk-Volksbegehren der FDP in Bayern?', *epd Kirche und Rundfunk*, no. 15 1989.
6. Decision of 14 February 1971, *Entscheidungen des Bundesverfassungsgerichts*, vol. 47 1971, Tübingen, Mohr, pp. 198ff.
7. 'Staatsvertrag zur Neuordnung des Rundfunkwesens in der Bundesrepublik Deutschland, 1/3 April 1987', printed in *DLM Jahrbuch 88*, ed. Direktorenkonferenz der Landesmedienanstalten, Munich, 1988, pp. 310f; all translations by the authors unless otherwise stated.
8. All legislation is printed in *DLM Jahrbuch 88*, op. cit., pp. 307–611; with the exception of the Hessen act, printed in *Media Perspektiven Dokumentation*, no. II 1988, pp. 106–29; and the Bremen act, printed in *epd Kirche und Rundfunk*, no. 14 1989, pp. 2–9.
9. With the exception of Saarland and Bavaria.
10. So far, there is no female director.
11. The same practice applies to the public broadcasting councils.
12. Cf. Bavarian Constitutional Court, decision of 21 November 1986, printed in *Deutsches Presse- und Rundfunkrecht*, ed. W.-D. Ring, Munich, Verlag für Verwaltungspraxis F. Rehm, 1977–87; ibid., decision of 27 May 1987, case no. *Vf.7-VI-87, Vf.11-VI-87* (mimeo).
13. Cf. its decisions of 2 October 1985, printed in *Die öffentliche Verwaltung* August 1986, pp. 659ff; and of 18 August 1987, no. *25 CE 86.03578* (mimeo).
14. Cf. *inter alia* 'Nicht ganz preussisch', *Der Spiegel*, no. 11 1989, pp. 17f.
15. Cf. 'Verordnung, 2 July 1988', *Niedersächsisches Gesetz- und Verordnungsblatt*, no. 23 1988, pp. 131f.
16. M. Wöste, 'Nur knapp die Hälfte für Lizensierung und Kontrolle', *Media Perspektiven* no. 5 1990, pp. 289–93; and authorities' information.
17. Cf. §14 of the 1961 ZDF inter-*Land* treaty, printed in *Medienrecht. Rechtsgrundlagen für das ZDF*, Mainz, ZDF July 1987 (5th edn) (ZDF Schriftenreihe 17) or §39 of the 1988 Hessen private broadcasting act, op. cit.
18. *Grundsätze für die Zusammenarbeit im ARD-Gemeinschaftsprogramm 'Deutsches Fernsehen'*, Frankfurt a.M., ARD, December 1982 (mimeo).

19. Cf. ZDF, *German Television*, ed. ZDF Information and Press/PR department, Mainz, 1985, p. 12.
20. Printed in *ARD Jahrbuch 1988*, Frankfurt a.M., ARD, 1988, p. 216 (emphasis added).
21. For example WDR act 1985, NDR treaty 1981, Radio Bremen act 1979; excerpts in *ARD Jahrbuch 1988*, op. cit., pp. 212–52.
22. *ARD Jahrbuch 1988*, op. cit., p. 204.
23. The FRG with West Berlin, the GDR, Austria, Switzerland, Liechtenstein, parts of Northern Italy, Belgium and Luxembourg.
24. Cf. *DLM Jahrbuch 88*, op. cit., p. 418, pp. 480f., pp. 539ff. (in Northrhine-Westfalia only for television channels).
25. Cf. 'Private TV-Veranstalter beteiligen sich an Filmförderung', *epd Kirche und Rundfunk*, no. 16 1989.
26. Cf. '5. Film/Fernseh-Abkommen', printed in *Media Perspektiven Dokumentation*, no. I 1989, pp. 38–49.
27. Cf. *DLM Jahrbuch 88*, op. cit.
28. Cf. 'ZDF bewertet Filme jetzt selbst nach Jugendschutzbestimmungen', *epd Kirche und Rundfunk*, no. 22/23 1989.
29. Cf. S. Ory, 'Gesetzliche Regelungen des Jugendschutzes beim Rundfunk', *Neue Juristische Wochenschrift*, no. 47 1987, pp. 2967–74.
30. Cf. *Strafgesetzbuch* (criminal code) §131, §184; *Gesetz über die Verbreitung jugendgefährdender Schriften in der Öffentlichkeit; Gesetz zur Neuregelung des Jugendschutzes in der Öffentlichkeit vom 25. Februar 1985*; explained in Federal Government, *Medienbericht '85*, ed. Press and Information Office, Bonn, 1986, pp. 103ff.
31. Cf. Ory, op. cit.; *Bericht des Rundfunkausschusses Nordrhein-Westfalen über seine Tätigkeit 1985–1987*, Düsseldorf, June 1987, pp. 144ff (mimeo).
32. Cf. Bundesverband Kabel und Satellit, *Praktische Anwendungsgrundsätze für den Jugendschutz*, Bonn/Mainz, 25 August 1987.
33. Cf. T. Kleist, 'Jugendmedienschutz', in *DLM Jahrbuch 88*, op. cit., p. 91.

4 FROM LEGISLATIVE THEORY TO REGULATORY PRACTICE

1. Decision reviewed in A. Hesse, 'Ausgewählte Rechtsprechung mit grundsätzlicher Bedeutung für die Rundfunkordnung in der Bundesrepublik Deutschland', *Rundfunk und Fernsehen*, vol. 36 (3) 1988, p. 391.
2. Cf. Hessen, Landtag, *Drucksachen*, no. 12/2478 1988, p. 53.
3. §18, amendment in Baden-Württemberg, Landtag, *Drucksachen*, no. 9/5076 1987, p. 15.
4. Cf. broadcasting act printed in *DLM Jahrbuch 88*, ed. Direktorenkonferenz der Landesmedienanstalten, Munich, 1988, p. 360.
5. Cf. *epd Kirche und Rundfunk*, no. 19 1989, pp. 14f.
6. The Japanese advertising agency Dentsu with film maker Alexander Kluge, producing cultural programmes.

7. An association of mainly newspaper publishers, producing regional TV magazines.
8. *epd Kirche und Rundfunk*, no. 17 1989, p. 10; no. 20 1989, pp. 14f.
9. Decision of 27 May 1987, case no. *Vf.7-VI-87*, *Vf. II-VI-87*, pp. 25ff (mimeo).
10. Bavarian Administrative Court, decision of 18 August 1987, no. *25 CE 86.03578*, p. 10 (mimeo).
11. J. Schmitz, 'Privatradios: Beispiel Nürnberg', *epd Kirche und Rundfunk*, no. 17 1989, pp. 3ff.
12. Cf. 'Eklat im Medienrat', *Funk Korrespondenz*, no. 11 1988, pp. 2f.
13. Cf. NDR 3, *Medienreport (12): Medien '89 – Zwischenbilanzen*, ed. M. W. Thomas, Hamburg, NDR Öffentlichkeitsarbeit, 1989, p. 28.
14. Quoted in *Der Spiegel*, no. 13 1989, p. 239.
15. Cf. U. M. Krüger, 'Programmanalyse 1989', *Media Perspektiven*, no. 12 1989, pp. 776ff.
16. ibid., 'Programmanalyse 1988', *Media Perspektiven*, no. 10 1988, pp. 637ff.; and ibid., 'Programmanalyse 1989', op. cit., pp. 776ff.
17. ibid.
18. Cf. Hessen broadcasting act, printed in *Media Perspektiven Dokumentation*, no. II 1988, p. 173; Lower Saxony act printed in *DLM Jahrbuch 88*, op. cit., p. 452.
19. *Ministerialblatt für Nordrhein-Westfalen*, no. 11 1988, p. 163.
20. §11, Bremen act, printed in *epd Kirche und Rundfunk*, no. 14 1989, p. 4.
21. Cf. Hessen, Landtag, *Plenarprotokolle*, no. 11/101 1987, pp. 5871ff.
22. Cf. NDR 3, *Medienreport (11): Medienindustrie und Medienmärkte*, ed. M. W. Thomas, Hamburg, NDR Öffentlichkeitsarbeit, 1988, pp. 992ff.
23. §61, Berlin cable trial act, printed in *DLM Jahrbuch 88*, op. cit., p. 406.
24. Cf. 'Berlins Finanzsenator: Im Medienbereich nichts "übers Knie brechen"', *epd Kirche und Rundfunk*, no. 21 1989, p. 11.
25. Cf. B. Schulz and G. Harzheim, 'Lokales Fernsehen in Berlin – Erfahrungen aus dem Kabelpilotprojekt', *Media Perspektiven*, no. 5 1988, pp. 265ff.
26. Cf. 'Radio Hühnerstall dreht auf', *Neue Medien*, no. 11 1987, pp. 58ff; 'Wenn Vielfalt durch Vielzahl garantiert werden soll', *Funk Korrespondenz*, no. 41 1987, pp. 1ff.
27. Interview with the authors, March 1989.
28. §31, printed in *DLM Jahrbuch 88*, op. cit., pp. 473ff.
29. Information from the Northrhine-Westfalian regulatory authority.
30. Cf. 'Die Einführung der Buchhaltung im Journalismus', *Süddeutsche Zeitung*, 20 March 1989, p. 24.
31. Northrhine-Westfalia, *2. Rundfunkänderungsgesetz*, Düsseldorf, 16 Feburary 1990 (mimeo).
32. Cf. 'Privatradios mit gravierendem Defizit im Programm', *epd Kirche und Rundfunk*, no. 19 1989.
33. Cf. 'Nachrichten, Musik und sonst noch was?', *Frankfurter Rundschau*, 16 February 1989.

34. Cf. Bavarian Administrative Court, decision of 26 May 1988, no. *M5S88.1516* (mimeo).
35. Cf. J. Engler, 'Das Rundfunksystem der Bundesrepublik Deutschland', in *Internationales Handbuch für Rundfunk und Fernsehen 1988/89*, Baden-Baden, Nomos, 1988, pp. B110ff; W. Thaenert, 'Kontrolle privater Rundfunkveranstalter', in *DLM Jahrbuch 88*, op. cit., pp. 44ff.
36. A staff member of the Hamburg regulatory authority, quoted in G.-M. Hellstern, W. Hoffmann-Riem, J. Reese, *et al.*, *Rundfunkaufsicht I*, ed. Press and Information Office of the *Land* Northrhine-Westfalia government, 1989, p. 260.
37. An SPD member of the Berlin regulatory board, quoted in Schulz and Harzheim, op cit., pp. 266f.

5 ALTERNATIVE FORMS OF BROADCASTING IN THE FRG

1. Cf. 'The Radio as an Apparatus of Communication', in *Brecht on Theatre*, ed. J. Willett, London, Methuen, 1961, pp. 51–3.
2. Cf. H. H. Fabris, 'Medienjournalismus und Bürgerkommunikation', *Rundfunk und Fernsehen*, vol. 29 (2–3) 1981, pp. 200ff.
3. Cf. H.-J. Schulte, *Untersuchung und Analyse der Nutzerstruktur des Offenen Kanals Berlin*, Abschlussbericht, Berlin, 31 January 1989 (mimeo), pp. 18ff.
4. The late Dortmund open channel director C. Longolius, quoted in J. Gerth and P. Widlok, 'Lokaler Rundfunk und Offener Kanal', in *DLM Jahrbuch 88*, ed. Direktorenkonferenz der Landesmedienanstalten, Munich, 1988, p. 72; all translations by the authors unless otherwise stated.
5. Cf. Report on the cable trial 1986, Berlin, Abgeordnetenhaus, *Drucksachen*, no. 10/1479 1987, p. 14.
6. Cf. amendmendment to WDR act, '2. Rundfunkänderungsgesetz, 7 March 1990', printed in *ARD Jahrbuch 1990*, Frankfurt a.M. 1990, pp. 438–9.

6 THE REGULATION OF THE MARKET

1. Inter-*Land* Treaty 1987, 'Staatsvertrag zur Neuordnung des Rundfunkwesers 1/3 April 1987', printed in *DLM Jahrbuch 88*, ed. Direktorenkonferenz der Landesmedienanstalten, Munich 1988, preamble, translated as 'Germany – Interprovincial Broadcasting Treaty 1987', *Commercial Laws of Europe*, no. 1 1989, p. 96. Where possible the authors quote from the translation.
2. Federal Constitutional Court, decision of 16 March 1981, printed in *Media Perspektiven*, no. 6 1981, p. 437, emphasis added; decision of 4 November 1986, printed in *Media Perspektiven Dokumentation*, no. IV 1986, p. 242.
3. K. v. Trotha, 'Neue Chancen für eine freiheitliche Gesellschaft. Neue Medien aus der Sicht der CDU', *Das Parlament*, 30 August 1986.
4. Federal Ministry for Economics Affairs, *Wettbewerbspolitik in der sozialen Marktwirtschaft*, Bonn-Duisdorf, n.d., p. 31.

5. DBP Telekom, *Pressemitteilung*, Bonn, 23 January 1990.
6. Cf. E. Witte, *Neue Fernsehnetze im Medienmarkt*, Heidelberg, R.v. Decker's/Schenck, 1984 (net-Buch Telekommunikation).
7. Saarland, Landtag, 'Begründung zum Rundfunkstaatsvertrag 1987', *Drucksachen*, no. 9/1205 1987, p. 2.
8. Figures by Gesellschaft für Kommunikationsforschung, printed in *ARD Jahrbuch 1990*, Frankfurt a.M., 1990, pp. 190–1.
9. Cf. GfK data in 'Fernsehnutzung 1989', *Media Perspektiven*, no. 1 1990.
10. Information from Bundesverband Kabel und Satellit, Bonn, January 1990.
11. Western Satellite Treaty, 'Staatsvertrag über die Veranstaltung von Fernsehen über Satellit 29 June and 29 July 1989', Hessen, Landtag, *Drucksachen*, no. 12/5115 1989; also printed in *Media Perspektiven Dokumentation*, no. II 1989, pp. 73–8.
12. Art. 2, 'Germany-Interprovincial Broadcasting Treaty 1987', op. cit., p. 99, emphasis added.
13. ibid., p. 103
14. Cf. *epd Kirche und Rundfunk*, no. 22/23 1989, p. 7.
15. Art. 3, 'Germany-Interprovincial Broadcasting Treaty 1987', op. cit., p. 4.
16. Cf. J. Steinbach, 'Werbemarkt 1989', *Media Perspektiven*, no. 4 1989, p. 205.
17. Cf. H. Bühringer, 'Gründe für ein neues Verfahren zur Festsetzung der Rundfunkgebühren', *Media Perspektiven*, no. 1 1985, pp. 1–4.
18. K. Berg, 'The Inter-*Land* Treaty on the Reform of the Broadcasting System in the FRG', *EBU Review Programmes, Administration, Law*, vol. 93 (2) 1988, p. 43.
19. 'State governments agree on licence fee', *Media Bulletin*, vol. 5 (4) 1988.
20. Cf. 'Beschluss des Bayerischen Verwaltungsgerichtshofs vom 6. Juli 1988', printed in *Media Perspektiven Dokumentation*, no. II 1988, pp. 89–105.
21. Inter-*Land* Treaty 1987, op. cit., Art. 3(3) and Art. 7(6).
22. Cf. the rules of the German Advertising Council of January 1974, printed in *DLM Jahrbuch 88*, ed. Direktorenkonferenz der Landesmedienanstalten, Munich, 1988, pp. 618f; ZDF Inter-*Land* Treaty and the decision of the Minister-Presidents of 8 November 1963, in *ZDF Informationen zur Fernsehwerbung*, Mainz, ZDF, 1985/86.
23. Cf. Saarland, Landtag, op. cit., pp. 11f.
24. Cf. 'Richtlinien für die Werbesendungen des Zweiten Deutschen Fernsehens, 17 March 1989', printed in *Media Perspektiven Dokumentation*, no. I 1989, p. 51; *ARD-Richtlinien über die Trennung von Werbung und Programm, 23 March 1988*, Frankfurt a.M., ARD, 1988; 'Gemeinsame Richtlinien der Landesmedienanstalten', printed in *DLM Jahrbuch 88*, op. cit., pp. 615ff.
25. Cf. 'Stellungnahme von ARD und ZDF zu dem beim Bundesverfassungsgericht anhängigen Verfahren der Bayerischen Staatsregierung gegen die Bundesregierung zur EG-Rundfunkrichtlinie, 14/15

June 1989', printed in *Media Perspektiven*, no. 11 1989, p. 726.
26. Cf. 'ARD und ZDF erhöhen Werbefernseh-Preise', *Frankfurter Rundschau*, 18 August 1988, p. 9; 'Competition forces ARD to cut rates', *Broadcast*, 15 September 1989.
27. Cf. S. Hasselbach and V. Porter, 'The Re-regulation of West German broadcasting', *Politics and Society in Germany, Austria and Switzerland*, vol. 1 (2) 1988, pp. 54f.
28. Cf. Art. 9(5) of the 1987 Inter-*Land* Treaty, op. cit.; 'Umstrittene Werbung zwischen Windeln', *Süddeutsche Zeitung*, 5 June 1989, p. 25; 'SAT 1 lehnt kostenlose Werbung für Parteien ab', *Frankfurter Rundschau*, 20 July 1989, p. 21.
29. G.-M. Hellstern, W. Hoffmann-Riem, J. Reese, and M. P. Ziethen, *Rundfunkaufsicht III*, ed. Press and Information Office of the *Land* Government Northrhine-Westfalia, Düsseldorf, 1989, p. 49, p. 197.
30. Cf. P. Turi, 'Heftig abmahnfähig. Schleichwerbung im privaten Hörfunk', *medium*, no. 4 1988, pp. 41–3.
31. Direktorenkonferenz der Landesmedienanstalten, *Pressemitteilung*, Düsseldorf, 6 November 1989.
32. Cf. 'Richtlinien für die . . . des ZDF', op. cit.; *ARD-Richtlinien . . ., 23 March 1988*, op. cit.; 'Gemeinsame Richtlinien der Landesmedienanstalten . . .', op. cit.
33. Art. 7, Inter-*Land* Treaty, op. cit.
34. Cf. A. Hesse, 'Ausgewählte Rechtsprechung mit grundsätzlicher Bedeutung für die Rundfunkordnung in der Bundesrepublik Deutschland', *Rundfunk und Fernsehen*, vol. 36 (3) 1988, pp. 382ff.
35. Cf. K. Berg, 'Report from Germany', *EBU Review Programmes, Administration, Law*, vol. 40 (3) 1989, p. 32.
36. The practice by which the supplier of a programme, which often is an advertising agency, retains advertising time within the programme instead of selling it for cash to the broadcaster; cf. *Der Spiegel*, no. 40 1988, pp. 149f. for the situation in the FRG.
37. '"Die einzige Einflussmöglichkeit ist die Festsetzung der Gebühren"', *Frankfurter Rundschau*, 13 July 1988, p. 14.
38. Bundesverband Kabel und Satellit, *Presseerklärung*, Bonn, 13 March 1987.
39. Cf. Art. 8, 1987 Inter-*Land* Treaty, op. cit.
40. Cf. B.-P. Lange, 'Die Werbemärkte der Zukunft', *Media Perspektiven*, no. 3 1989, pp. 117ff.; W. Seufert, *Struktur und Entwicklung des Rundfunk-Werbemarktes*, ed. Press and Information Office of the *Land* Government Northrhine-Westfalia, Düsseldorf, 1988 (Begleitforschung des Landes Nordrhein-Westfalen zum Kabelpilotprojekt Dortmund vol. 11).
41. 'Aktiengesetz 1965', printed in *Bundesgesetzblatt* part I 1965, p. 1089; translated as *German Stock Corporation Act*, Chicago, Ill., Commerce Clearing House Inc. (Common Market Reports 1967).
42. 'Related enterprises are legally independent enterprises which, in relation to each other, are majority-owned and majority-owning enterprises, controlled and controlling enterprises, members of an affiliated group of companies, interlocking enterprises, or parties to

an enterprise agreement.', *German Stock Corporation Act*, op. cit., p. 37.

43. For a criticism of the *Aktiengesetz*, cf. Germany, Monopolies Commission (Monopolkommission), *Die Wettbewerbsordnung erweitern: Hauptgutachten 1986/87*, Baden-Baden, Nomos, 1988, pp. 343f.
44. Cf. H. Röper, 'Formationen deutscher Medienmultis 1989', *Media Perspektiven*, no. 12 1989, p. 746; ibid., 'Stand der Verflechtung von privatem Rundfunk und Presse 1989', *Media Perspektiven*, no. 9 1989, pp. 542ff.
45. Quoted in *Broadcast*, 14 October 1988, p. 56.
46. Cf. H. Röper, 'Stand der Verflechtung . . .', op. cit., p. 746; press statistics compiled by W. Schütz, 'Deutsche Tagespresse 1989', *Media Perspektiven*, no. 12 1989, pp. 748–75.
47. Cf. 1986 decision, printed in *Media Perspektiven Dokumentation*, no. IV 1986, p. 235.
48. H. Röper, 'Daten zur Konzentration der Tagespresse in der Bundesrepublik Deutschland im 1. Quartal 1987', in *Daten zur Mediensituation in der Bundesrepublik 1987*, Frankfurt a.M., Media Perspektiven, 1988, pp. 38ff.
49. Cf. H. Meyn, 'Die Medienlandschaft in der Bundesrepublik Deutschland', in *Medienpolitik*, ed. Landeszentrale für politische Bildung Baden-Württemberg, Stuttgart, Kohlhammer, 1987, pp. 38ff.
50. Cf. H. Diederichs, 'Daten zur Konzentration der Publikumszeitschriften in der Bundesrepublik Deutschland im 4. Quartal', *Media Perspektiven*, no. 8 1987.
51. Normally, mergers are only controlled if the combined turnover is £1.7 million (DM 500 m).
52. H. Klatt, 'Medienpolitik in einer sich wandelnden Medienlandschaft', in *Medienpolitik*, op. cit., pp. 14ff.
53. Cf. B.-P. Lange, op. cit., p. 130; the German Monopolies Commission is more concerned, cf. *Die Wettbewerbsordnung erweitern. . .*, op. cit., p. 224; for an illustration of the publishers' arguments, cf. R. Niemann, 'Rechtlich-organisatorische Gestaltungsformen aus der Sicht der privaten Programmanbieter', in *Neue Medien*, Melle, Knoth, 1984, p. 219.
54. Cf. Seufert, op. cit., pp. 217, 252ff.
55. Cited in *Broadcast*, 14 October 1988, p. 56.
56. Cf. §15(1)(3) Hessen private broadcasting act, printed in *Media Perspektiven Dokumentation*, no. II 1988, pp. 106–29.
57. Cf. *Zwischenbericht des Kabelrats*, Berlin, Anstalt für Kabelkommunikation, November 1989.
58. Cf. H. Röper, 'Stand der Verflechtung . . .', op. cit., pp. 538f.
59. Cf. Federal Constitutional Court, decision of 4 November 1986, op. cit., pp. 242f.
60. Statement by the Hamburg government on its broadcasting act, Hamburg, Bürgerschaft, *Drucksachen*, no. 11/3769 1985, p. 23.
61. Funk & Fernsehen Nordwestdeutschland GmbH & Co. KG, application for a radio licence, printed in *Media Perspektiven*, no. 5 1987, pp. 317, 319.

62. This refers to those acquisitions involving two partners (i.e. the majority of them) and all relationships based on a legal agreement, not merely transfers of capital; cf. Germany, Bundestag, 'Bericht des Bundeskartellamtes über seine Tätigkeit 1985/86', *Drucksachen*, no. 11/554 1987, pp. 110ff.

63. J. Hughes, A. Mierzwa and C. Morgan, *Strategic Partnerships as a Way Forward in European Broadcasting*, London, Booz-Allen & Hamilton, 1989.

64. Cf. H. Röper, 'Formationen deutscher Medienmultis . . .', op. cit., pp. 739ff.

65. Cf. C. Jens, 'Privater Hörfunk – eine Verlegerdomaine', *Media Perspektiven*, no. 1 1989, pp. 35f.; for example, Verlagsgesellschaft Madsack GmbH & Co. KG. in Hanover, which counts among the 200 largest media concerns of the world with a turnover of over £320 million in 1988, is such a regional publishing group; others include the WAZ Group in Northrhine-Westfalia, the second largest newspaper publishing group in West Germany after Springer Verlag; the Rheinpfalz Group in Rhineland-Palatinate and the Süddeutscher Verlag in Bavaria.

66. Cf. Germany, Bundestag, 'Bericht des Bundeskartellamtes über seine Tätigkeit . . .', op. cit., pp. 110ff.

67. Cf. M. Wöste, 'Networkbildung durch die Hintertür?', *Media Perspektiven*, no. 1 1989, pp. 9ff.

68. Cf. the various arguments in *Rundfunk im Wettbewerbsrecht*, ed. W. Hoffmann-Riem, Baden-Baden, Nomos, 1988 (Materialien zur interdisziplinären Medienforschung vol. 20), pp. 13ff.

69. The Monopolies Commission in Cologne is an independent body of five experts who are appointed by the federal president upon suggestion of the federal government. It reports biennially on concentration tendencies and the work of the Federal Cartel Office.

70. This philosophy is clearly expressed in its *Programm zur Verbesserung der Rahmenbedingungen des privaten Rundfunkmarktes*, *Bulletin*, no. 77 1986 Bonn, Press and Information Office of the Federal Government, 25 June 1986.

71. Cf. *Rundfunk im Wettbewerbsrecht*, op. cit., pp. 23f.

72. Cf. Monopolies Commission, op. cit., p. 72.

73. Federal Constitutional Court, decision of 4 November 1986, op. cit., p. 236.

74. In Bavaria, the SPD brought forth a motion for such an amendment, but the CSU government majority in the *Land* parliament squashed it.

75. Cf. Germany, Bundesrat, 'Stellungnahme zum 7. Hauptgutachten 1986/87 der Monopolkommission', *Drucksachen*, no. 343/89 1989.

76. Germany, Bundestag, 'Siebtes Hauptgutachten der Monopolkommission 1986/87. Stellungnahme der Bundesregierung', *Drucksachen*, no. 11/4804 1989.

77. Cf. Monopolies Commission, op. cit., p. 231.

78. Quoted in 'Und schwupp, da ist der Zusammenschluss', *Neue Medien*, no. 10 1987, pp. 22–5.

79. Monopolies Commission (Monopolkommission), *Hauptgutachten 1984/85*, Baden-Baden, Nomos, 1986, p. 453.
80. Cf. ibid., *Die Wettbewerbsordnung erweitern* . . ., op. cit., pp. 223ff.
81. ibid.
82. Cf. Markenverband e.V., *Proceedings of the conference organised by Arbeitskreis Werbefernsehen der deutschen Wirtschaft*, Hamburg, 17/18 November 1988.
83. Cf. *Programm zur Verbesserung* . . ., op. cit.
84. Cf. *Rundfunk im Wettbewerbsrecht*, op. cit., pp. 84ff.
85. Cf. for example §34 of the NDR Treaty, *NDR Staatsvertrag*, Hamburg, Norddeutscher Rundfunk, 1980:
    (1) The NDR must not, either directly or indirectly, participate in an enterprise that conducts business for a commercial or other economic purpose. Excluded are press agencies and enterprises
    1) to which NDR entrusts . . . the operation of broadcast advertising
    2) which are directly or indirectly financed only by the NDR or other public-service corporations.
    (2) In specific cases, to satisfy the demands of economic efficiency and the legal duties of the NDR, other exemptions from para. (1) are permissible upon agreement of the administrative council.
86. Cf. 'Gemeinsame Stellungnahme von ARD und ZDF zum 7. Hauptgutachten 1986/87 der Monopolkommission und Stellungnahme der Bundesregierung', printed in *Media Perspektiven Dokumentation*, no. II 1989, pp. 141ff.; M. Wittig-Terhardt, 'Rundfunk und Kartellrecht', *Archiv für Presserecht*, vol. 17 (4) 1986, pp. 298ff.
87. Cf. Wittig-Terhardt, op. cit., p. 299.
88. Saarland, Landtag, 'Protokollerklärungen [declaration of intent] der Regierungschefs der Länder zum Staatsvertrag zur Neuordnung des Rundfunkwesens', *Drucksachen*, no. 9/1205 1987.
89. Cf. 'Private übernehmen NDR-Werbesendung', *Frankfurter Rundschau*, 2 October 1989, p. 17.
90. Cf. 'SR-Beteiligung an Radio Salü entspricht dem Auftrag', *epd Kirche und Rundfunk*, no. 22/23 1989, p. 13.
91. Federal Cartel Office (Bundeskartellamt), decision no. *B6-743100-U-71/88*, Berlin, 18 July 1989 (mimeo).
92. Cf. *inter alia*, Northrhine-Westfalia, Landesanstalt für Rundfunk, *Pressemitteilung*, December 1988, p. 9.
93. Printed in *Media Perspektiven Dokumentation*, no. III 1987, pp. 189ff.
94. Cf. statement by ARD/ZDF and the German Sports Federation, printed in *Media Perspektiven Dokumentation*, no. III 1987, pp. 199f.
95. Cf. 'Black-out in der ersten Reihe', *Der Spiegel*, no. 29 1989, pp. 144f.; 'SPD-Politiker wünscht Kampf um Senderechte', *Frankfurter Rundschau*, 29 June 1989, p. 21; D. Marsh, 'Germans beaten by Wimbledon TV deal', *Financial Times*, 12 July 1989.
96. U.M. Krüger, 'Programmanalyse 1989', *Media Perspektiven*, no. 12 1989, p. 721.
97. Cf. E. W. Fuhr, 'The broadcaster's right to the free reporting of public events', *EBU Review Programmes, Administration, Law*, vol. 39 (6) 1988, p. 41.

98. 'Entwurf: 1. Staatsvertrag zur Änderung des Rundfunkstaatsvertrages vom 1./3. April 1987 (Staatsvertrag zur Fernsehkurzberichterstattung) Stand: 21. Dezember 1989', printed in *Media Perspektiven Dokumentation*, no. II 1989, pp. 130ff.
99. Cf. J. Kruse, 'Sport-Kurzberichte im Fernsehen und wirtschaftliche Interessen', *Media Perspektiven*, no. 1 1990, pp. 1ff.

7 THE EUROPEAN DIMENSION

1. TV Directive (89/552/EEC), printed in *Official Journal of the European Communities*, no. L 298 1989, pp. 23–30.
2. With the passing of the Single European Act, the former veto power of each member state in the Council has been replaced by the requirement for a qualified majority for all decisions concerning the establishment of the common internal market, cf. Art. 100 and 100a of the EEC Treaty as amended by the Single European Act 1987; printed in *Treaties establishing the European Communities. Treaties amending these Treaties. Single European Act*, Luxembourg, Office for Official Publications of the European Communities, 1987 (vol. I), pp. 207–609, 1005–84.
3. Art. 59 to 66, EEC Treaty, printed in ibid.; Art. 60 stipulates that services are provided for remuneration.
4. CEC, *Television without Frontiers* (Com (84) 300 final), Brussels, 14 June 1984.
5. Decision of 26 April 1988, case no. 352/85, *Proceedings for the European Court of Justice of the European Communities*, no. 10 1988, Luxembourg, European Court of Justice.
6. European Parliament, *Session Documents*, 8 December 1987.
7. Cf. the declaration by the Federal Minister of the Interior, Conference of Ministers, Vienna, 9/10 December 1986.
8. Cf. Federal Constitutional Court, 'Verfahren über den Antrag festzustellen, dass die Bundesregierung durch den Kabinettsbeschluss vom 8. März 1989 dahingehend, der von der Kommission der Europäischen Gemeinschaften dem Rat vorgeschlagenen "Richtlinie des Rates zur Koordinierung bestimmter Rechts- und Verwaltungsvorschriften der Mitgliedstaaten über die Ausübung der Rundfunktätigkeit" (EG-Rundfunkrichtlinie) grundsätzlich zuzustimmen, den Freistaat Bayern in seinen Rechten aus Art. 30 GG verletzt hat', case no. *2 BvG 1/89*, reported in *Common Market Law Reports*, Part I 1990, p. 649; Germany, Bundesrat, *Drucksachen*, no. 462/89 1989; 'Stellungnahme von ARD und ZDF zu dem beim Bundesverfassungsgericht anhängigen Verfahren der Bayerischen Staatsregierung gegen die Bundesregierung zur EG-Rundfunkrichtlinie', printed in *Media Perspektiven*, no. 11 1989, pp. 724ff.
9. For an analysis of the relationship between the *Länder*, the *Bund* and the EC, cf. S. Bulmer and W. Paterson, *The Federal Republic of Germany and the European Community*, London, Allen & Unwin, 1987.

10. Cf. *inter alia* C. Starck, *Überholt Europa die Rundfunkkompetenz der Länder?* University of Göttingen, 29 August 1988 (mimeo); M. Bullinger, 'Rundfunkordnung im Bundesstaat und in der Europäischen Gemeinschaft', *Archiv für Presserecht*, vol. 16 (4) 1985, pp. 262ff.

11. Cf. *inter alia* I. Schwartz, 'Broadcasting Without Frontiers in the European Community', *Journal of Media Law and Practice*, vol. 6 (1) 1985, pp. 26–46.

12. Cf. J. Delbrück, *Die Rundfunkhoheit der deutschen Bundesländer im Spannungsfeld zwischen Regelungsanspruch der EG und nationalem Verfassungsrecht*, Frankfurt a.M./Berlin, A. Metzner, 1986 (Beiträge zum Rundfunkrecht 37).

13. Cf. Germany, Bundesrat, op. cit., p. 8; emphasis supplied. All translations by the authors unless otherwise indicated.

14. Cf. *Entscheidungen des Bundesverfassungsgerichts*, vol. 31, Tübingen, Mohr, 1971, p. 329.

15. Cf. 'Stellungnahme von ARD und ZDF . . .', op. cit., pp. 725f.; interview with NDR legal adviser Prof. Berg, *ARD Magazin*, no. 3 1989, p. 4.

16. Cf. *Entscheidungen des Bundesverfassungsgerichts*, op. cit., vol. 37, pp. 271ff.; vol. 73, pp. 339ff.; vol. 75, pp. 223ff.

17. Appeal by Prof. Lerche, Munich, on behalf of the Bavarian government to the Federal Constitutional Court, 6 April 1989, p. 19 (mimeo).

18. Council of Europe, *European Convention on Transfrontier Television*, Strasbourg, December 1989 (European Treaty Series 132).

19. ibid., Art. 27(1).

20. TV Directive, op. cit. (89/552/EEC), Art. 2(2).

21. Cf. Federal Constitutional Court, case no. *2 BvG 1/89*, op. cit., p.7.

22. Cf. TV Directive, op. cit. (89/552/EEC), Arts. 3, 19.

23. ibid., Art. 22.

24. ibid., Art. 18.

25. Bundesverband Kabel und Satellit, *Stellungnahme zum Entwurf einer Richtlinie des Rates der Europäischen Gemeinschaften über die Ausübung der Rundfunktätigkeit vom 27. März 1988 sowie zum Entwurf einer Europäischen Konvention über grenzüberschreitendes Fernsehen vom 22. Juni 1988*, Bonn, n.d., p. 28.

26. Cf. 'Stellungnahme von ARD und ZDF . . .', loc. cit., pp. 726f.

27. TV Directive, op. cit. (89/552/EEC), Arts 7 to 9; Council of Europe, *European Convention*, op. cit. Arts 11–16

28. Cf. TV Directive, op. cit., Art. 6, for the definition of 'European works' which provides for the inclusion of 'works from German territories where the Basic Law does not apply'.

29. Cf. U. M. Krüger, 'Programmanalyse 1989', *Media Perspektiven*, no. 12 1989, pp. 798ff.

30. TV Directive, op. cit., (89/552/EEC) Art. 4(1); Council of Europe, *European Convention*, op. cit., Art. 10(1), emphasis by the authors.

31. TV Directive, op. cit. (89/552/EEC) Art. 4(2).

32. Cf. the political declaration of intent attached to the TV Directive, point 16.

33. Cf. 'Stellungnahme von ARD und ZDF . . .', op. cit.; Bundesverband Kabel und Satellit, op. cit., pp. 11ff.
34. Cf. D. Kirk, 'Inside the Golden Triangle', *Broadcast*, 10 February 1989.
35. TV Directive, op. cit. (89/552/EEC) Art. 16; Council of Europe, *European Convention*, op. cit. Art. 8.
36. Council of Europe, *European Convention*, op. cit., Art 9.
37. ibid.; emphasis added.
38. Case no. *62/79*, printed in *European Court Reports*, 1980, p. 881.
39. CEC (COM(88) 172 final), *Green Paper on Copyright and the Challenge of Technology – Copyright Issues Requiring Immediate Action*, Brussels, 7 June 1988.
40. CEC (COM(88) 232 final), *Seventeenth Report on Competition Policy*, Luxembourg Office for Official Publications of the EEC, 1988, p. 17.
41. Cf. European Court of Justice, *Wood Pulp*, 28 September 1988, reported in *Financial Times*, 29 September 1988.
42. I. VanBael and J.-F. Bellis, *Competition Law of the EEC*, Bicester, CCH Editions, 1987, p. 14; W. Elland, 'Merger Control by the EEC Commission', *European Competition Law Review*, vol. 8 1987, p. 167.
43. European Court of Justice, *Verband der Sachversicherer*, 27 January 1987.
44. Cf. G. Lockley, *TV Broadcasting in Europe and the New Technologies*, Brussels/Luxembourg, CEC, 1988, pp. 278ff.
45. CEC (COM(88) 232 final), *Seventeenth Report on Competition Policy*, op. cit., pp. 64ff.
46. S.B. Hornsby, 'Competition policy in the 80's: More policy less competition?', *European Law Review*, vol. 12 1987, p. 99.
47. Cf. 'Commission decision of 15 September 1989 relating to a proceeding under Article 85 of the EEC Treaty' (89/536/EEC), printed in *Official Journal of the EC*, no L 284 1989, pp. 36ff.
48. Cf. 'Letzte Runde im Film-Poker', *Neue Medien*, no. 7 1988, pp. 44f.
49. Cf. the statement by former commissioner P. Sutherland to the European Parliament, 17 December 1987, quoted in *Common Market Law Reports*, antitrust supplement part 9 1988, p. 652.
50. (89/536/EEC), 'Commission decision of 15 September 1989 . . .', op. cit., p. 40.
51. CEC (COM(90) 78 final), *Communication from the Commission to the Council and Parliament on Audiovisual Policy*, Brussels, 21 February 1990.
52. ibid., p. 3.
53. ibid., p. 17.
54. ibid., p. 18.
55. ibid.
56. ibid., p.19; emphasis added.
57. '5. Film/Fernseh-Abkommen, 19 July 1989 printed in *Media Perspektiven Dokumentation*, no. I 1989, pp. 38–49.
58. CEC (COM(90) 78 final), loc. cit., pp. 19ff.

59. ibid.
60. ibid.
61. ibid.
62. ibid.
63. EEC Treaty, printed in *Treaties establishing the European Communities . . .*, op. cit.
64. CEC (COM(90) 78 final), op. cit., p. 20.
65. ibid.
66. TV Directive (89/552/EEC), loc. cit., p. 24; cf. also CEC, *Amended Proposal for a Council Directive* (COM(88) 154 final – SYN 52), Brussels, 21 March 1988, p. 20.
67. The CEC commissioned two reports on the connections between cross-border concentration and diversity in media of the member states: *TV Broadcasting in Europe and the New Technologies*, by G. Locksley (1989), and *Impact des nouvelles technologies sur la concurrence dans l'industrie de la télévision en Europe*, by G. Vienne and J.P. Jeandon (1989).
68. European Parliament, op. cit., explanatory statement, p. 41.
69. Cf. CEC, *Eighteenth Report on Competition Policy*, Brussels/Luxembourg, 1989, pp. 257ff.
70. CEC, *Seventeenth Report on Competition Policy*. Brussels, Luxembourg, 1988, pp. 297ff.
71. ibid., pp. 248ff.
72. *Council Regulation (EEC) on the Control of Concentrations between Undertakings*, Brussels, 21 December 1989 (mimeo).
73. CEC (COM(90) 78 final), op. cit., p. 21.
74. ibid.
75. ibid.
76. M. Stock, 'Europäisches Medienrecht im Werden – Probleme und Chancen', *Rundfunk und Fernsehen*, vol. 37 (2–3) 1989, pp. 181ff.

8 BROADCASTING REGULATION IN THE FIVE NEW *LÄNDER*

1. 'Vertrag zwischen der Bundesrepublik Deutschland und der Deutschen Demokratischen Republik über die Herstellung der Einheit Deutschlands', printed in *Bulletin*, September no. 104, 6.1990, Bonn, Press and Information Office of the Federal Government, pp. 877– 1120; English translation from *Treaty between the Federal Republic of Germany and the German Democratic Republic on the Establishment of German Unity*, internal document by the German Foreign Office.
2. ibid.
3. 'Beschluss der Volkskammer über die Gewährleistung der Meinungs-, Informations- und Medienfreiheit', 5 February 1990, printed in *Rundfunk und Fernsehen* no. 1 1990, pp. 78–80.
4. 'Überleitungsgesetz zu Hörfunk und Fernsehen (Rundfunk) der Deutschen Demokratischen Republik', printed in *Rundfunk und*

Fernsehen, vol. 38 (3) 1990, pp. 435–45; see also H. Odermann, 'Der Umbruch und die Mediengesetzgebung in der DDR', ibid., pp. 377–84.

5. Odermann, op. cit., p. 383.
6. 'Eckwerte für die Medienordnung in einem vereinigten Deutschland, 30 May 1990', printed in *Rundfunk und Fernsehen*, vol. 38 (3) 1990, pp. 455–8.
7. *Treaty, between the Federal Republic of Germany and the German Democratic Republic . . .*, op. cit., Art. 27.
8. P. Hoff, 'Das Fernsehsystem der Deutschen Demokratischen Republik', *Internationales Handbuch für Rundfunk und Fernsehen 1988/89*, Baden-Baden, Nomos, 1988, p. B 120.
9. C. Wild, 'Fernseh- und Hörfunknutzung in der DDR im Frühjahr 1990', *Media Perspektiven*, no. 9 1990, p. 566; W. Kleinwächter *et al.*, 'Zur Entwicklung von Telekommunikation und Rundfunk in den ostdeutschen Landern', Paper written for Komtech GmbH, Frankfurt, on occasion of a seminar on *The Convergence of Broadcasting and Telecommunications in the European Community: A Comparative Study*, London, Centre for Communication and Information Studies, March 1991.
10. Cf. *Screen Digest*, November 1990, p. 242; and authors' own estimate.
11. Cf. 'Gesamtdeutsche Rundfunkordnung: eine Zwischenbilanz', *Post-Politische Information*, no. 2 September 1990, pp. 4ff.
12. Wild, op. cit., p. 564.
13. Cf. 'Germans fight for spoils', *Television Business International*, April 1990, pp. 5–6; 'ARD pays the penalty for German unification', *Television Business International*, October 1990, p. 12.
14. Cf. J.C. Busch, 'Broadcasting in Berlin. Federal Regulation and German Unification', *CCIS Occasional Paper* no. 1 June 1990.

9 CONCLUSION: BEYOND BALANCED PLURALISM

1. W. Hoffmann-Riem, 'Rundfunkrecht und Wirtschaftsrecht – ein Paradigmawechsel in der Rundfunkverfassung', *Media Perspektiven*, no. 2 1988, p. 62.
2. Cf. 'Privater Rundfunk hat es schwer', *Frankfurter Allgemeine Zeitung*, 16 February 1988.
3. Excerpts from a federal CDU discussion paper on strategies for the media market of the 1990s, printed in 'Finden sich ARD/ZDF und private Sender unter einem Dach wieder?', *Frankfurter Rundschau*, 1 July 1988, p. 10.
4. Cf. U. M. Krüger, 'Programmanalyse 1988', *Media Perspektiven*, no. 10 1988, pp. 637ff; ibid., 'Programmanalyse 1989', *Media Perspektiven*, no. 12 1989, pp.776ff; the Hans-Bredow-Institut, Hamburg, and the Institute for Communication Science at the University of Göttingen both analysed the Northern German radio output in 1989.
5. Quoted in NDR 3, *Medienreport (12): Medien '89 – Zwischenbilanzen*, Hamburg, NDR Öffentlichkeitsarbeit, 1989, p. 52.

6. Cf. 'Unter der Planierraupe des Konkurrenzkampfes', *Frankfurter Rundschau*, 16 September 1988, p. 18.
7. Cf. 'Neues Mediengesetz in Baden-Württemberg', *Frankfurter Allgemeine Zeitung*, 12 December 1987; 'Stabhochsprung mit der Salzstange', *Der Spiegel*, no. 13 1989, p. 243.
8. Cf. 'Gegen die Durchhörbarkeit', *Süddeutsche Zeitung*, 16 February 1989, p. 47.
9. Cf. J. Engler, 'Das Rundfunksystem der Bundesrepublik Deutschland', in *Internationales Jahrbuch für Rundfunk und Fernsehen*, Baden-Baden, Nomos, 1988/89, B 113.
10. Cf. 'Wirtschaftsexperten: Mehr Markt im Rundfunk', *Frankfurter Rundschau*, 12 December 1989, p. 16.
11. Cf. W. Hoffmann-Riem, *The Philosophy of Broadcasting (Re-)regulation: The West German Approach*, Paper delivered at the CCIS/Goethe-Institut Conference 'Whither Pluralism', Goethe-Institut, London, November 1989.
12. ibid.; for the broadcasting systems in these *Länder*, cf. G.-M. Hellstern, W. Hoffmann-Riem, J. Reese, and M. P. Ziethen, *Rundfunkpolitik II*, ed. Press and Information Office of the *Land* Government of Northrhine-Westfalia; and short overviews in *Internationales Handbuch für Rundfunk und Fernsehen*, op. cit.
13. H. Bausch, 'Zur Entwicklung des Rundfunks seit 1945', in P. Glotz and R. Kopp, *Das Ringen um den Medienstaatsvertrag der Länder*, Berlin, Spiess, 1987, p. 31; translation by the authors.
14. L. Weber, 'Ohne Grenzen, aber mit Schranken', *Frankfurter Allgemeine Zeitung*, 11 April 1989, p. 12.
15. M. Stock, 'Funktionsgarantie als Verfassungsverstoss?', *Rundfunk und Fernsehen*, vol. 37 (1) 1989, p. 121.
16. Federal CDU discussion paper on strategies for the media market of the 1990s, op. cit., p. 10.
17. E. Stoiber (CSU) in a letter to H.-E. Schleyer, author of the CDU discussion paper on the media, printed in *Frankfurter Rundschau*, 27 July 1988, p. 14.
18. Cf. for similar suggestions M. Bullinger, 'Freiheit und Gleichheit in den Medien', *Juristische Zeitung*, vol. 62 (6) 1987, pp. 257 ff.

Select bibliography

OFFICIAL DOCUMENTS ON BROADCASTING REGULATION

Baden-Württemberg private broadcasting act, 'Landesmediengesetz Baden-Württemberg 16 December 1985, amended 14 December 1987', printed in *DLM Jahrbuch 88*, ed. Direktorenkonferenz der Landesmedienanstalten, Munich, 1988, pp. 327–54.

Bavaria private broadcasting act, 'Medienerprobungs- und -entwicklungsgesetz 22 November 1984, amended 8 December 1987', printed in *DLM Jahrbuch 88*, op.cit., pp. 357–70 (valid until December 1992).

Berlin cable trial act, 'Kabelpilotprojektgesetz 27 July 1984, amended 18 December 1987', printed in *DLM Jahrbuch 88*, op.cit., pp. 389–407 (valid until June 1990).

Bremen private broadcasting act, 'Bremisches Landesmediengesetz', *Gesetzblatt der Freien Hansestadt Bremen*, no. 6 1989, pp. 77–93, printed in *epd Kirche und Rundfunk*, no. 14 1989.

Council of Europe, *European Convention on Transfrontier Television*, 5 May 1989, Strasbourg, December 1989 (European Treaty Series no. 132).

Deutsches Presse- und Rundfunkrecht, ed. W.-D. Ring, Munich, Verlag für Verwaltungspraxis F. Rehm, 1977 with updates.

European Communities, CEC, 'Commission decision of 15 September 1989', *Official Journal of the European Communities*, no. L 284, 3 October 1989, pp. 36–44.

—— CEC, *Communication from the Commission to the Council and Parliament on audiovisual policy*, Brussels, 21 February 1990 (COM(90) 78 final).

—— TV Directive, 'Council Directive of 3 October 1989 (89/552/EEC)', *Official Journal of the European Communities*, no. L 298, 17 October 1989, pp. 23–30; political declaration of intent by the Council printed in *Media Perspektiven Dokumentation*, no. II 1989, pp. 115–26.

Federal Cartel Office, 'Bericht des Bundeskartellamtes über seine Tätigkeit in den Jahren 1985/1986', Bundestag, *Drucksachen*, no. 11/554 25 June 1987.

—— Beschluss vom 27. August 1987 (Globalvertrag), Berlin, printed in *Media Perspektiven Dokumentation*, no. III 1987, pp. 189–98; Beschluss des Bundesgerichtshofs vom 14. März 1990 (Globalvertrag), printed in ibid., no. II 1990, pp. 45–64.

—— Beschluss vom 18. Juli 1989 (Radio NRW), decision no. *B6-743100-U-71/88*, Berlin, Bundeskartellamt (mimeo).

Federal Constitutional Court, decision of 28 February 1961, *Entscheidungen des Bundesverfassungsgerichts* (*BVerfGE*), vol. 12, Tübingen, Mohr, 1961, pp. 205ff.; excerpts in *Medienpolitik*, ed. Press and Information Office of the Federal Government, Bonn, 1985.

—— decision of 27 July 1971, *BVerfGE*, vol. 31, Tübingen, Mohr, 1971, pp. 314ff.; excerpts in *Medienpolitik*, ed. Press and Information Office of the Federal Government, Bonn, 1985.

—— decision of 16 March 1981, *BVerfGE*, vol. 57, Tübingen, Mohr, 1981, pp. 295ff.; printed in *Media Perspektiven*, no. 6 1981, pp. 421–43.

—— decision of 4 November 1986, *BVerfGE*, vol. 73, Tübingen, Mohr 1986, pp. 118ff.; printed in *Media Perspektiven Dokumentation*, no. IV 1986, pp. 213–47.

—— decision of 24 March 1987, *BVerfGE* vol. 74, Tübingen, Mohr, 1987, pp. 297ff.; printed in *Media Perspektiven Dokumentation*. III 1987 pp. 145–68.

—— decision of 5 February 1991; Federal Constitutional Court, case no. 1 BvF 1/85 and 1 BvF 1/88 (mimeo).

Federal Government, *Medienbericht '85*, Bonn, Press and Information Office, 1987.

—— *Medienpolitik*, Bonn, Press and Information Office, 1985. (Collection of official documents and statements by the federal government since 1982).

Federal Minister of Posts and Telecommunications, *Reform of the Postal and Telecommunications System in the Federal Republic of Germany*, Heidelberg, R.v.Decker's/Schenk, 1988.

—— 'Bekanntmachung der Neufassung der Telekommunikationsordnung 16 July 1987 (TKO)', *Amtsblatt des Bundesministers für das Post- und Fernmeldewesen*, no. 91 1987, pp. 1393–802.

Hamburg private broadcasting act, 'Hamburgisches Mediengesetz 3 December 1985, amended 12 November 1987', printed in *DLM Jahrbuch 88*, op.cit., pp. 413–34.

Hessen private broadcasting act, 'Hessisches Privatrundfunkgesetz 30 November 1988', *Gesetz- und Verordnungsblatt für das Land Hessen, I*, no. 28 1988, pp. 385–401; draft as adopted printed in *Media Perspektiven Dokumentation*, no. II 1988, pp. 106–29.

Inter-*Land* Treaty on the reorganisation of broadcasting in the Federal Republic, 'Staatsvertrag zur Neuordnung des Rundfunkwesens in der Bundesrepublik Deutschland 1/3 April 1987', printed in *DLM Jahrbuch 88*, op.cit., pp. 307–15 (as 'Interprovincial Broadcasting Treaty 1987 (Germany)' printed in *Commercial Laws of Europe*, no. 1 1989, pp. 96–111). Explanatory statement: Saarland, Landtag, *Drucksachen*, no. 9/1205 1987.

—— on the right of access for the purpose of brief reports (final draft),

'Entwurf: 1. Staatsvertrag zur Änderung des Rundfunkstaatsvertrages vom 1./3. April 1987 (Staatsvertrag zur Fernsehkurzberichterstattung) 21 December 1989', printed in *Media Perspektiven Dokumentation*, no II 1989, pp. 130–41.

—— on the level of the licence fee and the financial equalisation between the broadcasting corporations, 'Staatsvertrag über die Höhe der Rundfunkgebühr und zur Änderung des Staatsvertrages über einen Finanzausgleich zwischen den Rundfunkanstalten (Rundfunkfinanzierungsstaatsvertrag) 23 September 1988', printed in *Media Perspektiven Dokumentation*, no. III 1988, pp. 186–9.

—— on renewing the NDR, 'Staatsvertrag über den Norddeutschen Rundfunk 20 August 1980' and explanatory statement, Schleswig-Holstein, Landtag, *Drucksachen*, no. 9/677 1980.

Lower Saxony private broadcasting act, 'Niedersächsisches Landesrundfunkgesetz 23 May 1984, as amended 9 February 1987 and 28 October 1987', printed in *DLM Jahrbuch 88*, op.cit., pp. 449–70.

Monopolies Commission, *Die Wettbewerbsordnung erweitern: Hauptgutachten 1986/87*, Baden-Baden, Nomos, 1988 (Hauptgutachten der Monopolkommission 7).

Northern Satellite Treaty, 'Staatsvertrag über die Veranstaltung von Fernsehen über Rundfunksatellit, 20 March 1986', printed in *DLM Jahrbuch 88*, op.cit., pp. 321–5.

Northrhine-Westfalia, WDR act, revised in connection with the introduction of private broadcasting, 'WDR-Gesetz 19 March 1985', revised and newly published 11 January 1988, printed in *Media Perspektiven Dokumentation*, no. II 1988, pp. 157–68; private broadcasting act, 'Rundfunkgesetz für das Land Nordrhein-Westfalen 19 January 1987', revised and newly published 11 January 1988, printed in *DLM Jahrbuch 88*, op.cit., pp. 473–506; private broadcasting and WDR acts amended, '2. Rundfunkänderungsgesetz 16 February 1990', Düsseldorf, Landtag (mimeo).

Rhineland-Palatinate private broadcasting act, 'Landesrundfunkgesetz Rheinland-Pfalz 24 June 1986, as amended 5 July 1988', printed in *DLM Jahrbuch 88*, op.cit., pp. 519–33.

Saarland public and private broadcasting act, 'Landesrundfunkgesetz 11 August 1987', printed in *DLM Jahrbuch 88*, op.cit., pp. 539–65.

Schleswig-Holstein private broadcasting acts, 'Landesrundfunkgesetz 27 November 1984', printed in *DLM Jahrbuch 88*, op.cit., pp. 575–98; completely revised 'Landesrundfunkgesetz 18 December 1989', *Gesetz- und Verordnungsblatt für Schleswig-Holstein*, no. 21 1989, pp. 225–45.

Southern Satellite Treaty, 'Staatsvertrag über die gemeinsame Nutzung eines Fernseh- und eines Hörfunkkanals auf Rundfunksatelliten', 12 May 1986, printed in *DLM Jahrbuch 88*, op.cit., pp. 307–20.

Treaties establishing the European Communities. Treaties amending these Treaties. Single European Act, Luxembourg, Office for Official Publications of the European Communities, 1987 (vol. I).

Unification Treaty, 'Vertrag zwischen der Bundesrepublik Deutschland und der Deutschen Demokratischen Republik über die Herstellung der Einheit Deutschlands', *Bulletin*, no. 104, 6 September 1990, Bonn, Press and Information Office of the Federal Government, pp. 877–1120 (English translation as 'Treaty between the Federal Republic of Germany and the German Democratic Republic on the Establishment of German Unity', German Foreign Office).

Western Satellite Treaty, 'Staatsvertrag über die Veranstaltung von Fernsehen über Satellit 29 June and 29 July 1989', Hessen, Landtag, *Drucksachen*, no. 12/5115 1989; also printed in *Media Perspektiven Dokumentation*, no. II 1989, pp. 73–8.

OTHER USEFUL LITERATURE

ARD Jahrbuch, Frankfurt a.M., ARD. (Statistical yearbook on the activities and accounts of the ARD public broadcasting corporations, their statutes, agreements concerning the public broadcasters, and policy statements of the corporations.)

Bundestags- and *Bundesrats-Drucksachen*. ('Hansard'-type records of the debates in the federal parliament including bills and government reports; a computerised index of specified areas can be obtained from Deutscher Bundestag, Referat Sach- und Sprechregister, Bundesrat-Drucksachenstelle, D-5300 Bonn; copies can be purchased from Verlag Dr Hans Heger, Postfach 200821, D-5300 Bonn 2.)

Daten zur Mediensituation in der Bundesrepublik, Frankfurt a.M., Media Perspektiven. (Biennial collection of data on press, broadcasting and film in the FRG; last issue 1989.)

DLM Jahrbuch 88, ed. Direktorenkonferenz der Landesmedienanstalten, Munich, Bayerische Landeszentrale für Neue Medien 1988. (Handbook containing the relevant private broadcasting legislation, information on the private broadcasting regulatory authorities, a list of all the private broadcasters in the *Länder*, a comprehensive statistics section and articles by the regulators; next edition to be published in 1990.)

Hellstern, G.-M., Hoffmann-Riem, W., Reese, J. *et al.*, *Rundfunkaufsicht I-III*, ed. Press and Information Office of the *Land* Government Northrhine-Westfalia, Düsseldorf 1989 (Begleitforschung des Landes Nordrhein-Westfalen zum Kabelpilotprojekt Dortmund vol. 16). (I: Empirical study of the regulatory organisation, practices and effectiveness by *Länder*; II: analysis of the regulation of broadcasting in the UK, USA and France; III: comparative analysis of the regulatory developments in the FRG.)

Internationales Handbuch für Rundfunk und Fernsehen, ed. Hans-Bredow-Institut, Universität Hamburg, Baden-Baden, Nomos (editions 1986/87 and 1988/89). (Comprehensive handbook containing information on the broadcasting politicians, regulators and public and private broadcasters, advertisers and research organisations; bibliography on mass communications, historical overview, statistics on advertising, and articles on the development of German and international broadcasting.)

Landtags-Drucksachen and *Gesetz- und Verordnungsblätter*. (Each *Land* parliament documentary office issues the *Drucksachen* as its own

'Hansard'; each *Land* government publishes legislation and statutory orders in *Gesetz- und Verordnungsblätter*.)

Media Perspektiven, Frankfurt a.M. (monthly). (Magazine of the association of the ARD advertising subsidiaries, containing articles and data on the German and international media; and special issues *Media Perspektiven Dokumentation*, containing all relevant broadcasting legislation and decisions by the courts of law and the Federal Cartel Office.)

Rundfunk in Deutschland I-IV, ed. H. Bausch, Munich, dtv, 1980. (The classic of German broadcasting literature; very detailed account of the history and development of German broadcasting up to 1980 including documents and photographs.)

ZDF Jahrbuch, Mainz, ZDF. (Statistical yearbook of the second television public broadcasting corporation.)

Suggestions for further reading – English-language literature

BOOKS

Political system

Beyme, K. v., *The Political System of the Federal Republic of Germany*, Aldershot, Gower, 1983.

Blair, P.M., *Federalism and Judicial Review in West Germany*, New York, Oxford University Press, 1981.

Basic Law for the Federal Republic of Germany, Bonn, Press and Information Office of the Federal Government, 1986.

Broadcasting

Dyson, K. and Humphreys, P., *Broadcasting and New Media Policies in Western Europe*, London, Routledge, 1988.

Etzioni-Halevy, E., *National Broadcasting under Siege: A Comparative Study of Australia, Britain, Israel and West Germany*, Basingstoke, Macmillan, 1987.

Humphreys, P. J., *Media and Media Policy in West Germany. The Press and Broadcasting since 1945*, New York/Oxford/Munich, Berg, 1990.

Kuhn, R., *Broadcasting and Politics in Western Europe*, London, Cass, 1985.

Sandford, J., *The Mass Media of the German-Speaking Countries*, London, Oswald Wolff, 1976.

Williams, A., *Broadcasting and Democracy in West Germany*, Bradford, Bradford University Press in association with Crosby Lockwood Staples, 1976.

ARTICLES AND ESSAYS

Berg, K., 'The "fourth broadcasting judgement" of the Federal Constitutional Court', *EBU Review Programmes, Administration, Law*, vol. 38 (3) 1987, pp. 37–43.

—— 'The Inter-*Land* Treaty on the reform of the broadcasting system in the Federal Republic of Germany, and the fifth decision of the Constitutional Court', *EBU Review Programmes, Administration, Law*, vol. 39 (2) 1988, pp. 40–9.

Collins, R. and Porter, V., 'West German television. The crisis of public-service broadcasting', *Sight & Sound*, Summer 1980, pp. 172–7.

Fuhr, E. W., 'The broadcaster's right to the free reporting of public events', *EBU Review Programmes, Administration, Law*, vol. 39 (6) 1988, pp. 39–41.

—— 'Report from Germany', *EBU Review Programmes, Administration, Law*, vol. 40 (3) 1989, pp. 30–5.

Hardt, H., 'The accommodation of power and the quest for enlightenment, West Germany's press after 1945', *Media Culture and Society*, vol. 10 (2) 1988, pp. 135–62.

Hasselbach, S., 'Access and alternative radio in the Federal Republic of Germany', *On Air Off Air*, January 1990, pp. 16–17.

Hasselbach, S. and Porter, V., 'The re-regulation of West German broadcasting. Major broadcasting decisions of the Federal Constitutional Court', *Politics and Society in Germany, Austria and Switzerland*, vol. 1 (2) 1988, pp. 48–65.

—— 'The 1987 Inter-*Land* Treaty: West German broadcasting re-regulation between politics and the market place', *Politics and Society in Germany, Austria and Switzerland*, vol. 3(2) 1990, pp. 9–46.

Head, D., 'Advertising and the media in West Germany', *Contemporary German Studies. Occasional Papers*, no. 5 1988 (University of Strathclyde), pp. 41–56.

Hoffmann-Riem, W., 'Law, politics and the new media. Trends in broadcasting regulation', *West European Politics*, vol. 9 (4) 1986, pp. 125–46.

—— 'Federal Republic of Germany', in *International Handbook of Broadcasting Systems*, ed. P. T. Rosen, New York/Westport/London, Greenwood Press, 1988, pp. 91–104.

Kleinsteuber, H. J., 'Federal Republic of Germany (FRG)', in *Electronic Media and Politics in Western Europe*, ed. H. J. Kleinsteuber, D. McQuail and K. Siune, Frankfurt/New York, Campus, 1986 (Euromedia Research Group handbook of national systems), pp. 44–68.

Nowotny, B., 'Germany: The slow march of cable', in *The European Experience*, ed. G. Nowell-Smith, London, British Film Institute, 1989, pp. 37–49.

Porter, V., 'The re-regulation of television, pluralism, constitutionality and the free market in the USA, West Germany, France and the UK', *Media Culture and Society*, vol. 11 1989, pp. 5–27.

Porter, V., Barbrook, R. and Hasselbach, S., 'Pluralism before profit? The re-regulation of radio broadcasting in France and the FRG', *Radio*, no. 2 1990, pp. 12–13 (part two: The Federal Republic of Germany).

Sandford, J., 'What are the media for? Philosophies of the media in the FRG and GDR', *Contemporary German Studies. Occasional Papers*, no. 5 1988 (University of Strathclyde), pp. 5–24.

Snow, M. S., 'Telecommunications and media policy in West Germany:

Recent developments', *Journal of Communication*, Summer 1982, pp. 10–32.

Williams, A., 'West German broadcasting in the eighties – plus ça change . . .?', *ASGP Journal*, Spring (7) 1984, pp. 3–35.

—— 'Pluralism in the West German media: The press, broadcasting and cable', *West European Politics*, vol. 8 (2) 1985, pp. 84–103.

—— 'The impact of the new technologies on the West German media', *Contemporary German Studies. Occasional Papers*, no. 5 1988 (University of Strathclyde), pp. 25–40.

Index